AMERICAN CAPITALISM

TWO VISIONS

AMERICAN CAPITALISM

TWO VISIONS

RAYMOND S. FRANKLIN

Queens College—The City University of New York

RANDOM HOUSE NEW YORK

THIS BOOK IS DEDICATED
TO MY FATHER, JOSEPH FRANKLIN
AND MY TEACHER, GEORGE WOODARD

First Edition
1 3 5 7 9 8 6 4 2
Copyright © 1977 by Random House, Inc.

Library of Congress Cataloging in Publication Data

Franklin, Raymond S
    American capitalism.

    Includes bibliographical references.
    1. Economics—History—United States.
    2. United States—Economic conditions.
    3. Radicalism—United States.   I. Title
    HB119.A2F7   330.1   76-39851
    ISBN 0-394-31261-9

Acknowledgment is gratefully made to the following publishers:
    The New York Times—John K. Galbraith, "On History, Foolishness and Vietnam," July 12, 1975, © 1975 by The New York Times Company; John K. Galbraith, "Eleanor and Franklin Revisited," March 19, 1972, © 1972 by The New York Times Company; Paul Samuelson, "Taking Stock of War," March 14, 1973, and W. Leontief, "Sails and Rudders, Ships of State," March 16, 1973, © 1973 by The New York Times Company. Reprinted by permission.
    Praeger Publishers, Inc.—E. J. Mishan, excerpts from The Costs of Economic Growth, © 1967 by E. J. Mishan. Reprinted by permission.

Manufactured in the United States of America
Text designed by Rodelinde Albrecht

PREFACE

This book is about radical economics. It provides a discussion of the central radical paradigm and answers some questions that are frequently asked: What is radical economics? How does it differ from mainstream economics? Because answering these questions involves a critique of mainstream economics, it has been necessary first to define the mainstream position and its mode of analysis. We have tried to do this as accurately as possible. Our hope is that a confrontation between the two opposing theoretical frameworks will facilitate deeper understanding of the real American economy.

The book is divided into four parts. In Part One, consisting of a single chapter, we deal with ideology (encompassing value judgments, ethics, and modes of reasoning) in relation to economic analysis. We define ideology and explore the way in which mainstream economists seek unsuccessfully to avoid its clutches. Radical economists, in contrast, view ideology as inherent in economic analysis and tend to make it an explicit part of their reasoning.

Part Two consists of a description of the basic contours of mainstream economic thinking. We deal with the way in which the classical theory of perfect competition and Keynesian wisdom have been combined to explain and justify the noncompetitive realities of contemporary American capitalism. The assimilation of Keynesian thought in the United States in the post–World War II period receives special attention.

In Part Three we explore the origin and nature of contemporary radical economics: its underlying assumptions and view of history, society, and the economy, particularly as they are related to aspects of public policy. We investigate the Marxian and neo-Marxian framework within which contemporary radicals develop their theories. Such individual topics as corporate power, the work process, growth, inflation, and imperialism are analyzed within this unified framework.

In the concluding chapter (Part Four) we deal with the question of whether we are at the brink of another worldwide depression comparable to that of the 1930s. Although this discussion is necessarily speculative, it is not simply crystal ball gazing. The speculations arise from an analytical framework that relates long-run business cycles and class conflict to changes in the social order.

One final word: The radical paradigm has not yet evolved into a completely formulated and consistent body of thought. Naturally, this book represents my own version of it. I have tried to emphasize central portions of the radical argument, with some modifications and reformulations, which constitute a reasonably consistent theoretical system. My own modest contribution involves a suggestion of how aspects of Marxian reasoning and new currents in radical thinking about state finance can be wedded to Joseph Schumpeter's theory of business cycles and innovations.

ACKNOWLEDGMENTS

A number of people have kindly commented on early drafts or portions of this book. I want to thank Keith Aufhauser, Michael Edelstein, Peter Eilbott, Albert Fried, Nora Gonzales, Fanny Greber, William Hamovitch, Richard Morganstern, Ralph Nelson, William K. Tabb, Lloyd Raines, Solomon Resnik, Mark Rosenblum, Richard Sutch, and Frank Warren.

Chapter 8 is a rewritten and elaborated version of "The Challenge of Radical Political Economics," which appeared in the *Journal of Economic Issues*. Chapter 10 contains portions of a review of *Monopoly Capital*, which appeared in *Canadian Dimension*. I thank both these journals.

Four persons have been especially helpful in the book's final stages. I owe particular appreciation to Barbara Kaplan, Robert Lekachman, Carl Riskin, and Lynn Turgeon.

I would, also, like to thank my editor, Edward Friedman, and the entire Random House staff for their assistance.

Econ 110a : Chs 1,2,5, 6, 8, 10, 11, 12, 13, 14, 15

CONTENTS

II

III

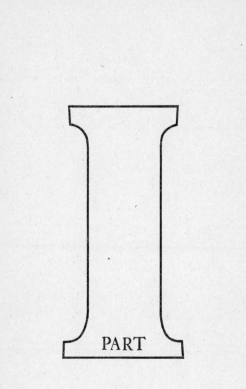

PART I

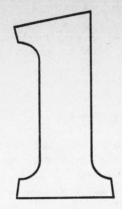

IDEOLOGY
IN ECONOMIC THINKING

Contemporary economists can be divided into two opposing groups: mainstream and radical thinkers. Mainstream economists accept the basic tenets of the capitalist system. They believe in the virtues of the market, where decisions about production and consumption are made by private owners of wealth and income to enhance individual gain. Under the market system, goods are supplied by businesses, which organize resources, capital, and labor to meet the requirements of production. The costs of labor services are viewed as income to the workers, who, as private consumers, spend this earned income on goods and services. This interaction between producers, who determine supply, and consumers, who determine demand, leads to the distribution of income, the nationwide division of goods and services among individuals, families, and other groups. Overall, the emphasis is on the way in which producers and consumers follow the dictates of their own self-interest while operating independently of one another. "If I do not look out for myself, who will?" is the sentiment believed to strike the most responsive chord in individuals within the system.

Although the private sector is viewed as paramount, it does require the aid of supportive governmental policies. Mainstream economists believe that only a private market, or capitalist, system buttressed by government policies can ensure a proper balance between freedom, on the one hand, and the provision of security and material well-being on the other.[1]

In contrast, radical economists reject the basic principles of the capitalist system. They believe that its inherent contradictions are so profound that it can provide neither sustained employment at reasonably high levels nor a humane lifestyle for the majority of its citizens. They also believe that the specific dynamics of the development of present-day capitalism will ultimately produce the emergence of conflict between the government, which operates as a guardian of the business system, and the general population. Because they view the business system as the primary source of society's malaise and the government as the guardian of this system's overall interests, radicals expect the government increasingly to become part of the problem, rather than part of the solution. As a result, radicals do not foresee a future that promises, as mainstream economists believe, the continuation of the existing delicate balance between freedom and security. On the contrary, radicals assume a necessary decline in both freedom and security as the unsolved problems inherent in the capitalist system accumulate.

In the radical view, the solution to the problems emanating from the capitalist breakdown includes public ownership of society's wealth, planning of production by public authorities, control of production by those who do the work, and elimination of income inequalities. Such changes require the cultivation of patterns of collective, rather than private, consumption and the nurturing of group, rather than individual, incentives. Radical economists believe that only collectively owned enterprises, democratic work places, and government planning involving large-scale participation of the governed can bring about socially desirable results.

The basic differences between mainstream and radical economists run deep. They involve different views of human nature, human potential, and humanity's relation to the environment. As a result, they have different views of history and the evolution of economic systems, which account for the differences in their ideologies and their analytical analysis methods. It is for this reason that our initial concern in this book is with the role of ideology in economic thinking.

THE STUDY OF ECONOMICS AND ECONOMISTS

What is economics? This sounds like a simple question, but it is more difficult to answer than we might at first assume. Economics has been defined in a variety of ways. Here are two of the definitions common among mainstream economists:

1. "Economics specializes in the study of that part of the total social system which is organized through exchange and deals with exchangeables."[2]
2. "The study of how people . . . end up choosing, with or without money, to employ scarce productive resources that could have alternative uses, to produce various commodities and distribute them for consumption."[3]

On the radical side of the ledger, economics is considered to be

3. The study of the "generation and absorption of the surplus" . . . and its "modes of utilization."[4]
4. "The study of the social laws governing the production and distribution of the material means of satisfying human needs."[5]

The first definition emphasizes trade and transactions related to goods and services that have already been produced and are already owned. The work process that creates wealth is ignored. The second definition emphasizes a particular condition—scarcity—that guides the choices that people make in the processes of production and consumption. The third definition is concerned with the portion of the whole product above some minimum requirement—surplus—and how it is used. The final definition centers on the ways in which classes of people are interrelated in the production, distribution, and consumption of goods and services.

Differences among economists, however, transcend such definitions. Any survey of economists would reveal divergent opinions on matters of public policy, the importance of power, the uses of mathematical models, the role of consumers, and the nature of the empirical foundations on which economics is based.[6] The multiplicity of opinions among economists has been humorously summarized in the suggestion that, if all the economists in the world were laid end to end, no two would reach the same conclusion. It was not without reason that one eminent mainstream economist, Jacob Viner, was driven to suggest some years ago that economics is what economists do. This suggestion is not inconsistent with the cynical admonition of the radical British economist Joan Robinson, who stated that the "purpose of studying economics is not to acquire a set of ready-made answers to economic questions, but to learn how to avoid being deceived by economists."[7] The primary implication of these quips, intended or not, is that the subject matter of economics is the study of economists, as well as of the economy. A further implication is that economists' formulations may, at times, be divorced from an understanding of the actual economy.

REALITY AND THE WAY ECONOMISTS THINK

Given the possibility that economists do not always understand with certainty the economy that they study, we might be tempted to ask, Why not bypass the deliberations of professional economists and simply look at the hard facts? How do people go about earning their livings and making ends meet? How do business leaders make decisions? How do the government and its network of agencies respond to the problems of the economy? But, as "stubborn" as facts may be, they do not speak for themselves. No individual's economic experience is sufficiently varied to produce a general understanding of the economy of a nation as large as the United States. The experience of the ordinary consumer, who receives income for services rendered and buys goods to meet his or her needs, is different from that of a stockbroker who watches a ticker tape all day. The experience of assembly-line workers, whose jobs are so repetitious that they spend most of their working time engaged in fantasy, is far removed from that of gentlemen of leisure whose incomes are derived from clipping coupons each month. Individual experiences cannot be readily collected, added up, and extrapolated to produce meaningful generalizations about how the economy functions, how it has evolved, and how it is expected to develop in the future—at least not without a method of inquiry, or style of reasoning, that transcends concrete experience. An adequate method involves such steps as developing a priori hypotheses that can be validated by data, finding experiences to serve as prototypes for those of whole classes of individuals or individual organizations, and breaking down information so that it can be measured and related to other sets of data.

Economists establish analytical categories that focus on very small portions of reality; vast portions of reality are ignored because they are deemed irrelevant to understanding the economy. Categories like wealth, income, consumption, human capital, surplus, productive and unproductive labor, and waste all reflect some degree of arbitrariness in both their *content* and *use*, in the information contained within the boundaries of each category, and in the way in which these categories are related to each other in the explanation of the system's performance. This arbitrariness has prompted one mainstream economist to note, all too briefly, that "questions [economists] ask, and from what perspective . . . [they] . . . photograph the 'objective' reality—these are themselves at bottom subjective in nature."[8]

In essence, the process of understanding the actual economy is a process of theorizing, of abstracting from the concrete ways in which people experience it. This process involves building models, or maps, of the real economy. But a map is not, of course, to be confused with the terrain itself. To paraphrase Kenneth Boulding, a well-respected maverick in the economics profession: A student who wants to study how real people experience the real economy had probably better leave economics and the social sciences and try literature or read biographies. Most of the economist's work, even that which is empirical, involves a great deal of abstracting and theorizing. This advice does not imply disapproval of abstracting or theorizing, both of which are essential; it is a warning against confusing theory with reality. "We would be foolish to try to go for a walk across a map, but a map may be very helpful if we are going for a real walk."[9]

Two warnings are in order here: First, if we are to put trust in maps that cannot be readily and pragmatically tested on real trips (as most theories in the social sciences cannot), it is necessary at least to understand how the maps were constructed and for what purposes they were designed. Second, it is necessary, as we have suggested, to avoid confusing the abstractions inherent in maps with features of the real terrain.

Yet, despite occasional and brief admissions that economists do think subjectively and that their "maps" are very different from reality, most mainstream economists discuss economics as if it enjoyed the scientific certainty of the physical sciences. Accordingly, they often argue that economics is like physics or chemistry, except that economists cannot perform the controlled experiments typical of the more exact sciences.

In the radical view, mainstream economists are hesitant to examine the fact that "at bottom" their work is highly subjective. There are three reasons for this: First, such an examination would unmask the pretense that economics is a science. Second, it would reveal the extent to which mainstream economics is tied to the values of the capitalist system. And third, it would compel acceptance of the radical claim that much of mainstream economics is vibrant with ideology, a claim that the mainstream applies only to radical economics.

POSITIVE VERSUS NORMATIVE ECONOMICS

In order to cope with the realities underlying economic propositions and to satisfy a desire to classify them neatly under two distinct headings ("objective" and "subjective"), mainstream economists engage in a game that involves switching roles from "I as a scientist" to "I as a citizen." As scientists, mainstream economists like to think of their subject as value-free, that is, objective and unbiased. They claim that their approach is applicable "to any society, and that in principle it can be made to serve almost any political ends."[10] As citizens, they accept the need to make value judgments about economic policies and issues and, in the final analysis, about the system as a whole. These two supposedly distinct kinds of thinking are designated by the terms "positive economics" and "normative economics."

Positive economics is concerned with "the [objective] facts and the principles which govern the actual course of economic systems," without value judgments about the way that the systems function. Normative economics, in contrast, "goes on to make [subjective] judgments on whether one state of the system is better than another, and goes on from there to make prescriptions and gives advice in regard to policies to be followed."[11] Positive economics is concerned with what "is," normative economics with what "ought to be." This distinction is often buttressed by an analogy of the following sort: As a scientist, I believe that an increase in taxes, based upon my analysis of what "is," will bring about unemployment. As a citizen, I believe that unemployment is "bad" and therefore that taxes should not be increased. As a scientist, I believe that Mr. Jones's heart condition will bring about his death in three months. As a citizen, I do not wish his death and believe that his death will be untimely and bad for his family.

Although mainstream economists recognize that ideology does occasionally creep into "objective" economic statements, most would probably agree with Robert Solow's advice to his colleagues that they should "seek ways to make [economics] as nearly value-free as it is possible."[12] This advice rests on the underlying assumption that economists *can* make statements and do research that are in general free of ideological content, that is, without implicit values, ethical judgments, and normative assumptions.

This notion of "value-free" thinking arises from a sharp theoretical separation of means and ends. Furthermore, the ends—social goals, institutions, laws, and values—are simply taken as given, as permanent features not to be altered by the process of economic analysis. The content of such goals, laws, and values is said to be of no particular concern for economics as such, and economics is therefore considered neutral or value-free. It becomes pure technology, a box of tools, unrelated to the ends being served. The role of mainstream economists, once they have mastered the tools of the discipline, is simply to discover the most efficient, or technically feasible, means to realize given goals. By predicting the likely consequences of various alternative policies, they help to facilitate rational choices by the various "free floating" economic decision makers, who must juggle limited means in order to achieve maximum outcomes.

Mainstream economists, acting not as citizens but as professional economists, consider an economy that produces mainly comic books, popcorn, and alcoholic beverages just as valid as one that produces chamber-music concerts, homes, and libraries. As long as the goods and services are selected and produced under "proper" competitive conditions by consumers and producers respectively, the mainstream economist, as a professional, would be unable to make any value judgments about them. This sort of economist is like an engineer; from the engineer's point of view, the same suspension bridge can be designed for a fascist, communist, or democratic capitalist government. The design of a bridge is assumed to be independent of the type of system that commissioned it.[13] In this sense, the economist, with his or her value-free kit of economic tools, is, by definition, a value-free professional, a neutral person capable of serving a variety of ends.

Table 1.1

PERCEIVING ECONOMIC REALITY

Mainstream economics	Positive economics "What is"	Normative economics "What ought to be"

Radical economics	Analytic function	IDEOLOGY ⟷	Legitimizing function

---

Economists' perceptions of reality are determined by the delineations of their system of study. The normative-positive distinction is one such delineation in the system of mainstream economics. Ultimately, radical economists assert, mainstream economists do not abide by their normative-positive distinction, even though they claim its validity for analysis. For radical economists, ideology functions as the mediator between the analytic and legitimizing functions, categories that incorporate the mainstream's positive and normative economics.

Radicals deny the possibility of a value-free economics and therefore the usefulness of the distinction between positive and normative economics, as well as the complete separation of ends and means. The end or "goal" of a bridge, for example, is to support a flow of trucks, cars, or trains. The design and materials used will be closely related to, even dictated by, the ends for which it is being constructed. As in engineering, so in the economy: Basic goal changes in society will alter the economic means devised to achieve them.

The idea that a value-free economic position is possible arises partly from the absence among mainstream economists of values distinct from those of the system that they study and serve. Partly, they assume, as we have noted, that means are unrelated to specific ends and that the same means can be applied to any constellation of economic or social goals. In the radical view, this notion of a purely instrumental role is itself *part* of the value system that justifies the mainstream economist's accommodating role in the capitalist system.

Although in theory mainstream economists favor the separation of objective positions from value-laden ones, in fact, it is difficult to find many mainstream economists who practice their beliefs. In the words of Kenneth Boulding:

> Certainly the classical economists had no hesitation about making a strong case for free trade, or even against it. The Keynesian economists have . . . no qualms about prescribing remedies for depressions or inflations. The development economists, too, show little hesitation about offering good advice to poor countries who want to get rich quick.[14]

When there is a systematic and general failure to practice what is preached over long periods of time, there is, at the very least, prima facie evidence of a much deeper problem with the basic distinction between positive and normative economics than mainstream thinkers are willing to explore. In the radical view, the distinction is erroneous because it contradicts the way people learn to think about the world. And, as a practical matter, it obscures the extent to which ideology permeates mainstream economics.

THE NATURE OF IDEOLOGY

For radical political economists, the proper study of economics begins with ideology because no economy can exist "unless its members have common feelings about what is the proper way of conducting its affairs; and these common feelings are expressed in ideology."[15] Knowledge of how economists as a group are related to these common feelings is critical to understanding their ideological persuasions.

In the broadest sense, ideology refers to a "system of thought . . . [a] set of beliefs and ideas, which form a framework . . . for . . . particular notions, analyses, applications and conclusions."[16] More specifically, ideology involves values, moral judgments, and ethics used to justify some events and condemn others. It facilitates the adoption and ranking of individual and community goals. It designates the most practical or desirable means to achieve various possible ends. And it suggests the kinds of questions that economists ask, the ways in which they define problems, the categories they invent to organize "facts," and the relevant time horizon for evaluating the effectiveness of alternative policies. Ideology ultimately encompasses the basic elements that make up theories of human nature, society, and history.[17] Ideology, in sum, determines the economist's value judgments and the way that he or she reaches them, the assumptions on which they are based, and what is included or omitted in deliberations about the nature of the economy.

Ideology serves two main purposes. First, it facilitates analytical efforts that influence the ways in which we assemble and relate facts. Second, it provides a mode of justifying the functioning or malfunctioning of a social organization. The latter purpose of ideology is reflected in sentiments propagated by the dominant classes in order to maintain and continue the existing stratification of the social order. It has less to do with establishing truth (the first purpose of ideology) than with maintaining power.

The two purposes, which incorporate the simpler positive-normative distinction made by mainstream economists, frequently overlap. It is not always possible to separate the analytic and legitimizing functions. More generally, it is impossible to make serious observations of a "purely" scientific or objective nature that are not connected, at some level, with an ideological system. A few examples will perhaps suffice to illustrate how values and assumptions related to ideology become inextricably woven into economic statements and observations that appear "detached."

TRADE

There are important implications, for example, in the simple exchange of a bottle of wine and a loaf of bread between two individuals, W and B.[18] Why should mainstream economists be so interested in observing this seemingly trivial act? The fact is that mainstream economic theory ascribes a great deal of significance to such an exchange. It is assumed, in the absence of coercion to trade, that both W and B will be better off after the exchange than before. If not, there would be no satisfactory explanation of the exchange; it would have to be recorded as random behavior, of no interest to economists. It is further assumed by mainstream economists that society as a whole is better off after such an exchange: If the two participants are better off without anyone else becoming worse off, then the whole society must be better off. Exchange between W and B thus seems a "good thing."

Concealed in this simple scenario, however, are a number of assumptions arising from a general ideological system that determines the way in which mainstream economists view the act of trade. The assumption that there is no coercion, the view that the whole society is better off when two of its members are better off, and the failure to ask whether or not W and B legitimately own the commodities traded are all ideologically rooted propositions.

Let us examine the assumption that there is no coercion, or, in more affirmative terms, the assumption that trade involves voluntary actions by all parties concerned. Although individual freedom is generally valued as an end in itself, an economic goal that society should strive to achieve, mainstream economists view freedom as simply instrumental; that is, they view it only as a condition of the market necessary for trade to take place. When such a condition exists, then it can be said that the exchange improves the well-being of both parties and perhaps of the whole society as well.

But *is* society better off? This conclusion involves still another assumption—that each person is an independent entity with individual preferences that are not necessarily interrelated.[19] Let us suppose that a third party observes W and B and is terribly envious of the improvement in their respective positions. Is the society better off then? The answer could be yes if we chose, as mainstream economists are prone, to exclude the question of interpersonal feelings. Mainstream economists might say that envy is not a good, rational, or proper response and that it *ought* to be ignored in the examination of voluntary exchange relations. Perhaps. But such statements are not void of ethical content.

Another problem that emerges in the wine-bread exchange is whether the goods traded are legitimately owned by W and B. What if W traded a stolen bottle of wine? Would everyone still be better off? How does the true owner fit into the picture? This point raises an historical question about the origin of ownership of resources, which take the form, at any given moment, of the commodities flowing freely among individuals. Following the sentiment conveyed in the expression "possession is nine-tenths of the law," mainstream economists choose to ignore the origins of ownership. They *assume* that whatever is traded is legitimately owned. Legitimacy itself is defined in legal terms, implying enforcement by the existing power of the state. The existing system of ownership upon which trade depends is thus justified. Mainstream economists rarely think of asking, Is much of the western land that is continually traded by its current possessors legitimately owned? Did the Indians forgo their territorial rights under voluntary conditions similar to those that confer legitimacy on current trading of the same land?

AID TO THE POOR

Mainstream economists generally oppose giving welfare recipients payments in kind (for example, food stamps); they prefer instead payments in money income. Payment in kind is said to restrict choice, whereas payment in money enhances it. In this instance the mainstream belief is not based on empirical findings or objective evidence; it is based on the a priori assumption that the welfare recipient's knowledge of his or her needs is superior to that of an expert. It follows, therefore, that the welfare recipient *ought* to have freedom (a valued condition) if he or she is to receive maximum satisfaction from the aid.

Given the welfare recipient's environment of uncertainty and disorder, insufficient knowledge, and desperation, which frequently results in preoccupation with the immediate present at the expense of the future, an alternative mode of reasoning might be entertained. An expert might be in a better position to decide what constitutes the welfare recipient's needs in the long run. We might assume that freedom of choice has little relevance in some situations and that benefits can best be achieved if individuals are *not* given freedom to spend aid money according to their own preferences. This suggestion results from a different view of the real benefit of freedom as an instrument for achieving well-being, a view drawn from an alternative ideological framework.

DEFICIT SPENDING

Let us suppose that the consequences to consumers of decreasing taxes and not changing the level of government spending would be the same as if taxes were held constant and the level of government spending increased; let us suppose that both policies would stimulate increases in the Gross National Product (GNP). The choice of means to a larger GNP would then depend upon the relative strengths of at least two considerations. If the predominant concern were political expediency, the "decrease in taxes" would probably be chosen, for that is the one most preferred by business-people, whose political influence is considerable. As a matter of fact, those were precisely the considerations behind the Kennedy-Johnson tax cut of 1964, which was supported by most mainstream economists. The business community opposed the deficit caused by increased government spending, but it had no objection to a deficit derived from a decrease in taxes.[20] Expediency thus dictated endorsing the preferences of the business community, or dominant class, in choosing policies that would lead to more employment.

If, on the other hand, a deficit generated by increased government spending combined with holding the tax line were considered likely to cause less pollution, to benefit the long-term unemployed more, and to lead to a more desirable composition of output, then increasing government spending might be the preferred means to more employment. The choice would be based on the value-laden specification of goals. If the goals were defined in very narrow terms, without reference to other goals, then the particular means selected to alter employment would be affected in a particular way. As the way in which we choose to specify goals is not "objective," the means selected cannot be neutral.

LAND AND PRODUCTIVITY

We can examine the seemingly neutral statement that "land is productive." Mainstream economists do not usually question its validity or consider its possible ideological content. Yet the statement is neither apolitical nor value-free. Land requires tilling, fertilizing, weeding, and other operations if economically valuable crops are to grow. From a different perspective, it could then be argued that there would be no output without work; that it is work, not land, that is productive.[21] Once stated, the point is obvious: Land never grew corn by itself. We do not, of course, suggest that a worker could produce corn without land. The rewording of this simple statement ultimately leads us to question whether land ownership per se should entitle an individual to an income. What kind of ownership arrangements is preferable if we seek to achieve productive effort, social equality, or the nurturing of a meaningful work process? These and similar questions are all value-laden and connected to a broader ideological framework.

THE NATURAL STATE OF HUMANITY

Mainstream propositions and statements are based on assumptions, frequently unstated, about the basic nature of people or the basic forms that organizations must take. For example, it is often assumed that people are naturally acquisitive and selfish, that every system has a hierarchy or bureaucracy, and that it is "natural" for individuals to weigh their choices in terms of costs and benefits. The general theoretical edifice of mainstream economics requires the recognition of certain "immutable" attributes (for example, aggressive impulses) of the individual in society. In responding to critics, mainstream economists often *judge* it impractical to imagine individuals without these attributes. Such assumptions about human nature, history, and society, moreover, guide decisions about what kinds of institutions are best for controlling acquisitive or bureaucratic individuals. The assumption of acquisitiveness is often used to denigrate arrangements that might replace competitive ones.

These five examples illustrate the radical claim that the distinction between the positive and the normative made by mainstream economists cannot be observed in practice. It is impossible to devise economic categories and analytic modes that are value-free or devoid of moral content. The distinction, therefore, is not useful or worth pursuing.

BELONGING TO THE PROFESSIONAL CLUB

Another way in which ideology comes into the picture can be seen in the ways that economists function inside their own "professional club" (a loose conglomeration of associations that bring economists together for talk, fraternity, and business). The club, in turn, can be seen as an instrument used by the dominant powers in the economy as a source of knowledge, ideas, values, and modes of reasoning that help to maintain, support, or further acceptance of the existing system. The ways in which the club and powers cooperate do not necessarily imply a master plan or a clearly defined area within which control is exercised. What needs emphasis is that the economist cannot avoid involvement (explicit or not) in the political or economic status quo, for he or she is "morally imbedded" and "inextricably bound up with the objects of his scrutiny."[22] The economist, like social scientists in general, "is a member of a group, a class, a society, a nation, bringing with him feelings of animus or defensiveness to the phenomena he observes. In a word, his position in society—not only his material position but his moral position—[colors his or her analysis in a pervasive fashion]."[23]

As members of a professional club, which itself serves a larger social system that needs ideological justification, clarification, and even moderate criticism to improve its own performance, individual economists seek to meet the expectations of other club members in order to achieve or maintain status. There is always considerable peer pressure to adopt certain kinds of reasoning, to address particular questions and ignore others, to submit articles to the "right" publications, to choose the "right" assumptions and use the "proper" techniques so that tenure and promotion can be ensured. There is pressure to conform to the thinking that emanates from the most respected members of the profession. To the degree that the club itself has an ideological interest in analyzing and evaluating the economic problems of the existing system within a predetermined framework and to the degree that money for research is supplied by foundations or the government (both of which seek to perpetuate the prevailing social order), the typical economist learns how to choose "freely" his or her assumptions for analysis.[24] This pressure, in turn, determines how the economist will articulate the problem and which aspects of it he or she will emphasize or neglect. Economists quickly learn what falls outside the traditionally defined boundaries of the discipline. There is a strong centralizing tendency at work, and it is more comfortable to work with the tendency than against it.

CONCLUSION

Economics is the study of the economy, but it is also the study of what economists do. We cannot avoid examining the abstractions that emanate from the minds of economists if we are to understand the real economy, even though the relation between the two may seem dubious. When we ask, therefore, what is mainstream economics or what is radical political economy, we are asking how economists define economics, how they define the central economic problems on which they base their analyses. We are, in essence, asking about their ideological predispositions, the analytic and legitimizing propositions that they formulate and use to assist in the understanding (or misunderstanding) of the real economy. The critical weakness of mainstream economic thinking is its pretense of developing a value-free social science. This is an illusion and serves to obscure the extent to which mainstream economics is simply a rationalization of the status quo or the prevailing social order.

NOTES

1. There are, of course, differences among mainstream thinkers. Broadly speaking, there is a minority of economists who are strong advocates of permitting the market alone to determine the course of American society and oppose the expanding role of government that has occurred since the 1930s; they constitute the *conservative* wing of the economic profession. The majority of economists in the mainstream tradition, those in the broad middle range so to speak, accept in principle the role of government as it has developed since the 1930s; essentially, they seek to improve its functioning. Although the majority thus believes in the general efficacy of the private market, it also considers governmental intervention necessary and potentially salutary. It views the government as a *legitimate* partner, a counterweight, an instrument capable of correcting deficiencies in the private sector.

2. Kenneth E. Boulding, *Economics as a Science* (New York: McGraw-Hill, 1970), p. 123.

3. Paul A. Samuelson, *Economics*, 10th ed. (New York: McGraw-Hill, 1976), p. 3.

4. Paul A. Baran and Paul M. Sweezy, *Monopoly Capital* (New York: Monthly Review Press, 1966), p. 8. Copyright © 1966 by Paul M. Sweezy. Reprinted by permission of Monthly Review Press.

5. Oskar Lange, *Political Economy* (Oxford: Pergamon, 1963), p. 7.

6. See, for example, Walter W. Heller, "What's Right with Economics," *The American Economic Review* 45 (March 1975): 1–2.

7. Cited in J. K. Galbraith, *Economics and the Public Purpose* (Boston: Houghton Mifflin, 1973), p. 11.

8. Samuelson, *Economics*, footnote 2, p. 8.

9. Boulding, *Economics as a Science*, p. 75.

10. Benjamin Ward, *What's Wrong with Economics* (New York: Basic Books, 1972), p. 27.

11. Kenneth E. Boulding, *Economic Analysis*, 4th ed. (New York: Harper & Row, 1966), vol. 2, p. 251.

12. Robert M. Solow, "Science and Ideology in Economics" in *Readings in Economics, 1974/75* (Guilford, Conn.: Dushkin, 1974), p. 9.

13. This analogy has been borrowed from a mainstream colleague, Albert Levinson, who

mentioned it during a departmental seminar at Queens College in 1973.

14. Boulding, *Economic Analysis*, pp. 251–252.

15. Joan Robinson, *Economic Philosophy* (Chicago: Aldine, 1962), p. 4.

16. Maurice Dobb, *Theories of Value and Distribution Since Adam Smith* (Cambridge: Cambridge University Press, 1973), pp. 1–2.

17. For a discussion of some of the specific elements that enter into the construction of an ideology, see C. Wright Mills, *The Marxists* (New York: Dell, 1962), p. 13.

18. For a broad discussion of the implications of trade between individuals, see Murray N. Rothbard, "Value Implications of Economic Theory," *The American Economist* 43 (Spring 1973): 35–36.

19. See Kenneth Boulding, "Economics as a Moral Science," *The American Economic Review* 59 (March 1969): 1–12. Also see Chapter 2 of this book for a further discussion of the point.

20. See Herbert Stein, *The Fiscal Revolution in America* (Chicago: University of Chicago Press, 1969), Chapter 16.

21. Joan Robinson and John Eatwell, *An Introduction to Modern Economics* (London: McGraw-Hill, 1973), p. 9.

22. Robert L. Heilbroner, *An Inquiry into the Human Prospect* (New York: Norton, 1974), p. 23.

23. *Ibid.*

24. For an extended discussion of this problem, see Ward, *What's Wrong with Economics*, Chapter 1.

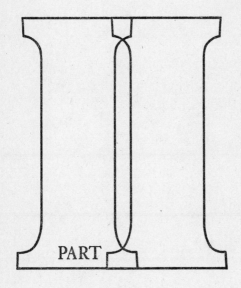

PART

THE CAPITALIST UTOPIA:
LOGIC, CONFLICT, AND HARMONY

At the core of mainstream economics—definitions, categories, views of human nature, the general organization of parts in relation to the whole—are the act of production, on the one hand, and the act of consumption, on the other. The theoretical propositions underlying these activities determine the ways in which mainstream economists collect, organize, and interpret data from the real economy. They operate even when mainstream economists criticize rather than justify the way that the economy functions.

MAINSTREAM ECONOMICS DEFINED

The definition of mainstream economics has changed little since Lionel Robbins first stated it in 1932: Economics is "the science which studies human behavior as a relationship between ends and scarce means which have alternative uses."[1] However arid such a definition may seem, it still has a respectable place in most elementary textbooks. The key part of Paul A. Samuelson's slightly elaborated definition in the latest edition of his textbook describes, economics as the "study of how people . . . end up choosing, with or without money, to employ scarce productive resources that could have alternative uses. . . ."[2]

This definition is the cornerstone of the mainstream explanation of how individual producing and consuming units make basic choices; how they arrange inputs or incomes in the most efficient way; how they interact to determine the relative values of peanuts and popcorn, for example; how resources are allocated among firms and industries throughout the market system by means of prices. The definition is the basis of *microeconomics*, which is concerned with the particular aspects of the economy that include relative values and trade-offs: the price of labor relative to that of machinery, the price of bread relative to that of wine, the burden (disutility) to the individual of more work relative to the value (utility) of more leisure, the value of present income relative to that of future income. Microeconomics views the twigs, branches, and individual trees of a forest from the ground level rather than the whole forest from an airplane.

Implicit in the definition of mainstream economics is a desire to ascribe to it a purely analytical and deductive character. As a discipline it seems to take on the character of geometry, with formal proofs derived from a few simple assumptions.

THE CENTRAL ECONOMIC PROBLEM

According to mainstream thinkers, the central economic problem is *scarcity*. Without this notion, there would be no mainstream economic theory as we know it (there may, however, be real economic patterns of considerable complexity that could be studied in an organized fashion on some other basis). Scarcity, it should be noted, is not an objective phenomenon; even from the vantage point of mainstream economics, it is closely related to the individual's perception of his or her condition. Resources (like land, labor, machinery, and minerals), whatever their absolute quantities, can in fact be quite inadequate *relative* to the demand for them. Because people's wants are assumed to generate a demand greater than the means available to satisfy them, *choice* becomes necessary. It is for this reason that mainstream economics has on occasion been defined as the science of choice. The situation seems in a sense parallel, at least in formal terms, to the relation between time, ticking away hour by hour, and life itself. If we assume that there are always more things that we wish to accomplish than time allows, then each life choice must be made at the expense of others. The "perfect" life is defined by the use of time in the most efficient possible way. Life goals must be maximized within the limits of available time. All economic decision makers, whether they are consumers, producers, demanders, or suppliers, must choose among a vast number and variety of ends to which their scarce means are to be applied.

As the idea of scarce resources and unlimited wants is assumed to approximate an elemental condition of the real world, it seems important to develop an economic arrangement that will eliminate waste, an arrangement that will enable producers to efficiently produce the constellation of goods and services that consumers want most. The arrangement of the economy that, in the view of mainstream economists, will best ensure productive efficiency and maximum consumer satisfaction is the perfectly competitive market. It is for this reason that they devote so much time and space to explicating the idea of perfect markets.

By *market* we mean a place where people can trade, a locus for buying and selling. Labor markets are places where laborers exchange (sell or supply) their services for money to buyers or demanders of such services. Product markets are places where goods are exchanged for money. The stock market is a place where various kinds of business shares are bought and sold. The word "place" should not be taken literally; a market does not have to be a location. The international bond market consists of innumerable telephone connections among buyers and sellers. Thus a market can also be a means or a way in which people can trade.

It is one thing to talk about markets, but another to talk about *perfect* markets. An ideal competitive market system requires many perfect markets. The essential properties of such markets are fundamental to the mainstream view of economic reality, politics, and the social system in general. They will be discussed here under five headings: large numbers, free entry and mobility, homogeneity, complete knowledge, and rational self-interest.

LARGE NUMBERS

Every perfect market consists of so large a number of buyers and sellers that no *one* buyer or seller can influence the commodity price by his or her individual action. The individual's input into the market, either as a buyer or as a seller, is an infinitesimal proportion of the total. For example, the amount of wheat that one farmer produces is a very small fraction of the total produced each year. If such markets existed, business firms, for example, would be very small in comparison with today's large corporations. In such markets the individual buyers and sellers would be price acceptors, rather than price setters. They would be comparable to the average individual consumer in a large department store who decides to buy or not to buy at the going market price; individual consumers do not believe that their decisions will send a ripple through the market or affect what others will do. In a perfect market, producers would have similar perceptions and would simply accept the going market price in the industry, deciding only how much to produce. The price would thus be determined by the sum of aggregate forces, and no one individual would be aware of his or her particular influence on it.

FREE ENTRY AND MOBILITY

New firms must be free to enter a profitable industry without incurring prohibitive costs or encountering obstacles from other firms or from the political arena. Over time, supply tends to increase through the formation of new firms within the more profitable industries. Labor too must be motivated and ready to move from one industry to another, from one region to another, in response to market forces that stimulate the pursuit of narrowly defined economic interests.

HOMOGENEITY

All commodities of a given industry or class are said to be homogeneous or interchangeable in the eyes of the consumer. This implies that all the commodities produced for sale in a given market are identical. The consumer is assumed to be indifferent to who produces the specific item. Trade names, packaging differences, and other minor differences have no impact. Producers in such markets therefore do not spend money on persuasive or combative advertising, which would simply mean added costs that would diminish profits. There is no point in spending money trying to influence a consumer to buy your corn rather than Joe's corn if it is assumed that the consumer knows that all corn is simply corn.

COMPLETE KNOWLEDGE

All buyers and sellers have complete knowledge of the market situation and of their alternatives. Here we have the notion that consumers, on the one hand, know about products, prices, and the available alternatives and that producers, on the other hand, know the costs and productivities of all the various input factors, as well as the nature of the demand for the products.

RATIONAL SELF-INTEREST

Basically, producers are thought to seek maximum returns (profits) from their productive efforts and consumers to seek maximum satisfaction from the use of their personal income. This emphasis on self-interest implies that each individual acts in the context of larger market forces without concern for the social consequences of his or her action; no one individual seeks to incorporate the plans of others into his or her own design. Individual choice and contemplation of gain are private, without deliberate accommodation to those of the group or the larger society.

Self-interest and the quest for privately accumulated riches have been recognized as possessing both positive and negative qualities. They seem positive because they nurture productive effort; individuals work hardest and most diligently when they do so for their own gain. But self-interest and acquisitiveness are also antisocial and must therefore be regulated. The function of competition in a market system is that of a *social regulator*. Although each person would like to obtain for himself or herself as much as possible at the expense of others, he or she is prevented from doing so because others in a competitive market will undersell or undercut. The result is material advantage for the majority interests, which are identified as consumers.

SELF-REGULATION AND FREEDOM

The notion of self-regulation is crucial to the way in which mainstream economists think about the economy.[3] Self-regulation involves automatic action that is independent of external influences or control. Economic processes are said to be self-regulating when they require no conscious planning or coordination.

The human body has many self-regulating mechanisms. Perhaps the best example of a self-regulating mechanism is the thermostat. A thermostat regulating building heat, once set, automatically controls room temperature at a specific level, turning on or off the heating system whenever the temperature goes below or above the specified level. The thermostat works automatically only after it has been set by someone outside the mechanism itself.

Although self-regulation of a market means that no outside noneconomic institution can be used to influence its functioning, the market system itself, and often specific markets as well, must be created by external social or political organizations. One such organization is the state, which can induce or sanction the emergence of market relations by granting individuals and businesses property rights and establishing the rules by which they can compete with one another. The state then supposedly steps aside to allow the market to function without further interference.

Self-regulation presupposes that all forms of income—wages, salaries, rents, interests, and profits—are created, maintained, or changed by the market forces of supply and demand. That is, self-regulation involves "the institutional separation of society into an economic and political sphere [in which] economic activity [becomes] isolated and imputed to a distinctive economic motive."[4] The mainstream conception of the economy is based on the idea that the real economy has been isolated from society as a whole and then set in motion following rules that are unrelated to and unaffected by noneconomic institutions, such as the state or other social organizations. To the extent that these noneconomic institutions prevent the economic engine from operating smoothly and efficiently, mainstream economists view them as frictions that interfere with the running of the economic engine; they must therefore be either removed or retained at the cost of some kind of economic deprivation or trade-off.[5] This sharp dichotomy, moreover, gives freedom a singularly economic dimension: It is generally claimed, at least among the more conservative mainstream economists, that the absence of free markets is equivalent to the absence of a free society; to be against the free market economy is ultimately to be an enemy of freedom in general. This point has been sharply stated by Milton Friedman, one of the nation's leading conservative economists: "Underlying most arguments against the free market is a lack of belief in freedom itself."[6] The virtue of a self-regulating market system, to continue Friedman's reasoning, is that it reduces "the range of issues that must be decided through political means, and thereby . . . minimize[s] the extent to which government need[s] to participate in the game."[7] In essence, the free competitive market, by removing politics and political motives in the broadest sense from the economic sphere, achieves not only economic freedom but also personal, social, and political freedom.

At the risk of redundancy, we point out that the notion of rational self-interest in the context of the competitive market requires the concept of "economic man," a kind of ideal figure solely motivated by the desire for profit or wealth. The motive for working, for constructing factories, for growing food and making shoes, for relocating capital, for investing time in improving one's skills, for deciding to introduce a new production technique, or for searching for new resources is assumed to be an outgrowth of the pursuit of material gain. The economic motive, in more concrete terms, is not mixed or muddled by religion, humanism, patriotism, attachment to neighborhood or community, or ethnic identity. Noneconomic institutions—for example, church, state, voluntary associations, political parties, and so on—are assumed to be *passive* in relation to the exigencies of the market.

INNOVATION AND ECONOMIC GROWTH

The long-run outcome of freeing the economic engine from social and political restraints is believed to be a continuous and dramatic rise in the material well-being of society. For this reason it is possible to assume that private vices, when properly harnessed under perfectly competitive conditions, will lead to social virtues.

Of course, the basis for all sustained material gains is technological progress, the *sine qua non* of a continually rising standard of living. In the competitive market, the profit motive *compels* individual producers to introduce technological innovations and cost-reducing methods as rapidly as they are profitable. When, for example, one producer is able to introduce a technological change that reduces his costs, his rate of return rises above that of other firms. This rise stimulates an expansion of his production that further enhances his profits. Other profit-seeking producers are *compelled*, if they wish to remain competitive, to imitate the original innovator and thus lower costs and expand. Finally, new firms, adopting the best technology presently available, shift from lower-profit industries in order to take advantage of more profitable opportunities. In the end, the supply of commodities increases, prices decrease, and the excessive profits that initially started the process of expansion are eliminated. The "benefits of progress are passed onto the community as a whole, not bottled up in the [firms or industries where they happened] to arise."[8]

THE NOTION OF OPTIMUM

When production and consumption are so efficiently arranged that it is impossible to improve the lot of either producers or consumers by any further changes, optimal conditions are said to have been achieved. Before elaborating on this oversimplified definition, we must digress briefly.

The mainstream notion of the *optimum* is peculiar in that it does not necessarily refer to a desirable arrangement, despite the usual implication of the term. The reason is simply that the whole production and consumption system can be optimally arranged for *any* set of relative prices and for *any* degree of inequality in the distribution of incomes. Relative prices and the distribution of income are considered in theory to be established by aggregate forces *before* the production and consumption adjustments that lead to the optimum condition.

As Kenneth Boulding pointed out a number of years ago: "[In looking at two societies], roughly comparable in per capita income and technology . . . one of which income is very highly concentrated in the hands of a small ruling class and . . . the other of which is widely distributed among an independent peasantry," we might well find the peasant society more livable. Yet, because of market imperfections and the like, such a society might be far from meeting optimal conditions as defined by economists. In contrast, an aristocratic society, however unequal its income distribution, could exhibit optimum conditions.[9] It was not fortuitous that Boulding concluded his discussion with the wry comment that the mainstream notion of the optimum in welfare economics does not "differentiate the top of a molehill from that of Mount Everest."[10] Although it makes a considerable difference whether optimum market conditions occur in a context of relative deprivation or relative affluence—or of relative social equality or inequality—most mainstream thinkers refuse to deal with the question of income distribution. Robert A. Gordon, former president of the American Economic Association (1976), noted that most of his colleagues with a theoretical bent "show little interest in the determinants of the personal distribution of income and wealth" and raised some embarrassing questions:

> From the point of view of human welfare—a concept that will not go away no matter how uncomfortable it makes the economic theorist—can we ignore the personal distribution of income? Which is more relevant: a rigorous demonstration as to how resources can be most efficiently allocated under ideal conditions that have never existed, or a much cruder exploration of how wealth and income came to be distributed as they in fact are and what might be done to affect the distribution of income in one way or another?[11]

Regardless of the answers to Gordon's questions, it is possible to say that, given a predetermined price and income distribution, the whole production system is most *efficient* when it is not possible, with the resources and technology available, to increase the value of production in any one part of the system without reducing it in another part. The whole consumption system is most *efficient* when it is impossible for any one consumer to be subjectively or psychologically better off without making someone else worse off.[12] In this way, production and consumption mesh. The resources that have to be used up in production of goods and services correspond to the subjective pains and pleasures of consumers as they contemplate their purchases.

The "ideal" situation is reached when scarce resources are used in the most productively efficient way in order to satisfy wants in the order that they have been ranked by consumers. When all consumers have maximized their satisfactions from the purchase of goods and services, when all suppliers of labor services have reached the point where extra income from longer time on the job brings no additional consumer satisfactions, and when all the producers have achieved the maximum possible profit at the existing level of resources, the system has achieved its optimum. It must be repeated that these conditions are possible with any set of relative prices and any degree of inequality in the distribution of income and wealth.

THE NEUTRALITY OF PRODUCERS

Under competitive productive conditions, producers do not determine the goals or ends of the system. Individual producers, in fact, are assumed to *have* no power or ability to affect such ends. They are viewed by mainstream economists simply as instruments, or cogs in the system, seeking their own survival; the general outcome of their efforts leads to fulfillment of the larger goals established by independent consumers. In this sense, producers are assumed in theory to be neutral with respect to the goals established by "sovereign" consumers, who determine *what* to consume on the basis of psychological or biological needs. Regardless of how consumers allegedly determine their wants, it is essential to the system that they should not be influenced by producers. Producers should make no value judgments about the constellation of goods and services that are demanded.

HUMAN NATURE

Among the many reasons why mainstream economists consider their professional approach value-free, as we have discussed in Chapter 1, their conception of the human being is critical. To some extent, the individual is also conceived as neutral or instrumental vis-à-vis the functioning of the larger system. "Mainstream economics assumes characteristics similar to rational mechanics. Neither the ends as such, nor the means as such . . . are of interest [to economists]. In particular, economics is indifferent as to the ends in the sense that it cannot pass judgment on [them.]"[13]

The use of mechanics as an analogy to understand mainstream economics requires a particular view of human nature and psychology. Mainstream economics, as Benjamin Ward has declared, is based on three principles of human behavior:

> *Hedonism* or the . . . pleasure-pain principle characterizes man in terms of . . . the satisfaction of the urgent demands of the body and mind; there is a clear corollary of natural indolence that follows fairly directly from the avoidance of pain. *Rationalism* is means-ends orientation, the use of deliberative choice among alternatives in seeking the satisfactions of drive-reduction. *Atomism* is the assertion of the essential separateness and autonomy of each man from every man, with the consequent stabilization of values by means of processes internal to the individual human organism.[14]

What Ward has described is a person who is self-centered in the narrowest terms, someone not concerned with the general consequences of his or her individual actions. Such persons are assumed to know themselves better than anyone else can know them, and they base their behavior on self-knowledge and private calculations about pursuing pleasure and avoiding pain. They are rational and therefore capable of acting as if they were making mathematical calculations of means in relation to ends. Moreover, both their self-centered motives and their calculations are not assumed to be derived from social relations in any meaningful way. Each person is assumed to be autonomous, an "island unto himself." Mainstream economics greatly underplays the social, developmental, and historical bases of human development and existence. Although its proponents, in their reflective moments, will admit that this view of human nature is an abstraction useful only for theoretical purposes, they can rarely be induced to consider alternative abstractions that might represent inconvenient human realities more closely. The apparent reason for such dogmatism is a vested ideological interest in the mechanical metaphor, the cornerstone of mainstream economic thought.

SOME FINAL CONSIDERATIONS

Five major points must be stressed if we are to understand the mainstream perspective.

First, in a competitive market the instruments of production (land, machinery, factory buildings, natural resources, and the like) are privately owned by many individuals.

Second, the competitive economic system has two independent and free decision-making groups: producers and consumers. Workers are assumed to be relatively passive, prepared to take orders from owners of the means of production, especially *within* each firm, where the businesspeople are assumed to be autonomous.

Third, each decision-making unit is said to pursue its own self-interest without concern for the social consequences of its actions. Businesspeople maximize profits; consumers (which includes everyone) maximize satisfactions by the way that they spend their income for commodities. Workers balance the burden of more work against the utility of more income. Savers deny themselves present gratification in order to achieve future pleasure. The social good that allegedly results from individual vices is unintended and even unplanned or unconscious.

Fourth, the means to a good life are defined quantitatively: More goods are preferred to fewer goods, more profit to less, expansion to stagnation. Markets must be nurtured and enlarged until the whole world becomes one big market. The achievement of this end will greatly facilitate the international division of labor, specialization, and therefore the general expansion of world output. International trade and exchange are, however, more problematical.

Finally, out of this atomistic system, which seems to have all the ingredients of a jungle rather than of an organized society, an overall harmony emerges. The harmonizing force is the competitive market where exchange occurs. The market induces people to exchange goods and services in ways that are mutually advantageous; it is thus a peacemaker. It "forces" uncooperative, antisocial, and combative individuals into tolerable and peaceful relations, contrary to personal impulses. The theoretical accomplishment of such harmony, given the human being's assumed hedonism, rationalism, and atomism, is no small feat. It defines, in fact, a capitalist utopia.

NOTES

1. Lionel Robbins, *An Essay on the Nature and Significance of Economic Science*, 2nd ed. (London: Macmillan, 1935), p. 16.

2. Paul A. Samuelson, *Economics*, 10th ed. (New York: McGraw-Hill, 1976), p. 3.

3. We are not suggesting that mainstream economists agree about the extent to which the economy is *in fact* self-regulating; nevertheless, their common belief is that if it were, a preferred state of affairs would be achieved. For a study of the full implications of the hypothetical self-regulating market system, see Karl Polanyi, *The Great Transformation* (New York: Rinehart, 1944).

4. *Ibid.*, pp. 69, 71.

5. Robert L. Heilbroner, "On the Possibility of Political Economics," *Journal of Economic Issues* 4 (December 1970): 10.

6. Milton Friedman, *Capitalism and Freedom* (Chicago: University of Chicago Press, 1963), p. 15. We are not suggesting here that Friedman's position on this question is acceptable to more welfare-oriented mainstream econ-

omists, who tolerate or favor much more state intervention. Samuelson, for example, has written an excellent critique of Friedman's view of the relationship between freedom and the market. Nevertheless, Samuelson addressed himself to a wide audience of lay people and economists, suggesting that many share beliefs approximating those of Friedman. See Paul A. Samuelson "Personal Freedoms and Economic Freedoms in the Mixed Economy," in *The Business Establishment*, ed. Earl F. Cheit (New York: Wiley, 1964), pp. 193–227.

7. Friedman, *Capitalism and Freedom*, p. 15.

8. Joan Robinson, *Economics: An Awkward Corner* (New York: Pantheon, 1967), p. 14.

9. Kenneth Boulding, "Welfare Economics," in *A Survey of Contemporary Economics*, ed. Bernard F. Haley (Homewood, Ill.: Irwin, 1952), vol. 2, pp. 12–13.

10. *Ibid.*, p. 27.

11. Robert A. Gordon, "Rigor and Relevance in a Changing Institutional Setting," *The American Economic Review* 66 (March 1976): 4.

12. For a discussion of productive and consumer efficiency, see Tibor Scitovsky, *Welfare and Competition*, rev. ed. (Homewood, Ill.: Irwin, 1971), Chapters 4 and 8.

13. Claudio Napoleoni, *Economic Thought of the Twentieth Century* (London: Robertson, 1972), p. 34.

14. Benjamin Ward, *What's Wrong with Economics* (New York: Basic Books, 1972), pp. 24–25.

COMPETITIVE THEORY
AND THE
MIXED CAPITALIST SYSTEM

As we turn from the ideal world of competition to the real world
of concentrated economic power, vested interests, and government involvement in large segments of the economy, it would be
reasonable to expect a decline in the relevance of the pure competitive ideal among mainstream economists. No such decline has
occurred, however; or at least the observed decline has not been
as great as we might initially have expected. The purpose of this
chapter is to show how mainstream economists have managed to
reconcile their commitment to the ideal world of competition and,
at the same time, to deal with the real world of contemporary
American capitalism, the "mixed capitalist system," as it is commonly labeled.

THE MAINSTREAM:
MINORITY AND MAJORITY VIEWS

A small minority of influential conservative, laissez-faire economists believes that our economy does not deviate significantly

from the ideal of pure competition. There are, for example, millions of wholesale and retail establishments that all appear to exist in reasonably competitive relations with one another. This sphere, it is argued, is usually overlooked in discussions about the decline of competition. Instead, monopolistic practices in the manufacturing sector receive most of the attention, although they are not characteristic of the total population of enterprises in the American economy.[1]

Another small group, consisting of those who can be identified as "trust-busting types," would like the real world of imperfect markets to conform more closely to the ideal world of perfect markets; they would give the Federal government more power to enforce antitrust policies. With the zeal of reformers they criticize today's economy in order to return it to a state that presumably prevailed in the past, when the average size of the firm was smaller and competition more rigorous.[2] This group, however, is dwindling.

The majority of mainstream economists is more difficult to classify, for it consists of individuals with widely divergent opinions about specific issues and problems. Nevertheless, regardless of differences, there is an underlying style of reasoning that does in fact define their approach to contemporary American capitalism. As Walter Heller, past president of the American Economic Association and former chairman of the Council of Economic Advisors under President John F. Kennedy, has stated the matter: "Appearances are deceiving. . . . Our areas of agreement and consensus are vastly larger than our areas of differences. . . . What we know . . . is that beneath the visible tip of disagreement and rivalry lies no huge iceberg of divisiveness."[3] The vast area of agreement that Heller refers to primarily involves justifying the existing system without forgoing the competitive ideal. The competitive ideal is believed to be useful for two reasons: It correctly predicts the long-run course of the real economy, despite the unrealistic assumptions on which it is based; and it provides economists with useful analytical tools and categories with which to explain and evaluate the real economy. Although a discussion of the mainstream claim of predictability would take us beyond our present purposes, the second claim will be briefly examined here as the basis for our discussion of how the competitive model has been adapted to fit noncompetitive realities.

THE THEORY OF IMPERFECT COMPETITION

The notion of ideal competition has led to the development of categories that mainstream economists use to classify and evaluate the behavior of the real economy. For example, one important property of a competitive industry is the large number of firms producing highly standardized commodities. The number must be sufficiently large so that no single firm can affect the industry price by its own decisions. Each firm in an industry is a price acceptor. As the number of firms competing in an industry declines and the proportion of the output that each firm produces rises, the ideal ceases to approximate reality. At the opposite end of the spectrum is the industry consisting of a single firm. If such a firm's product is one for which there are no near substitutes, as is true of utility companies, then the industry is characterized by perfect monopoly. It is evident that such a firm is not only a price maker but is also in a position to wield considerable power over consumers.

Between perfect competition and perfect monopoly there are, of course, many intermediate arrangements. A significant portion of the manufacturing sector is characterized by "competition among the few," or oligopoly. In oligopolistic industries, prices are administered jointly through casual collusion strategies or are set by dominant firms in ways carefully patterned so as to avoid price rivalry. In mainstream theory, these firms can be shown to produce less at higher prices than under more competitive conditions. They can be shown to face less than perfectly elastic demand schedules; that is, one firm's small increase in price above that of the nearest competitor does not lead to complete loss of its purchasers.

The competitive model is employed to evaluate the "goodness" or "badness" of such markets, as well as to provide the basis for analyzing them. Similar deviations from other properties of pure competition—for example, the prevalence of barriers to entry and differentiated, rather than standardized, products—can also be analyzed and evaluated from the point of view of the model. The assumption implicit in this analytical framework is that in the real economy corrections guided by the competitive ideal lead to a more desirable state of affairs for the society's members. In the radical view, this assumption is dubious, and the relevance of competitive analytical categories is therefore in doubt also. This doubt, it should be noted, is not completely foreign to mainstream economists. For example, M. A. Adelman has noted, "[Although in competitive theory] output is higher, prices are lower, and resources are better used . . . it is less clear that the *long-run* performance of a competitive market is also superior to one where a small group has market power and controls supply."[4] With this reservation in mind, we can proceed to examine some characteristics of the actual American economy, in order to set the stage for a detailed discussion of how its behavior is interpreted by mainstream economists.

THE CONCENTRATION OF ECONOMIC POWER

The American economy is basically a private-enterprise system; some characterize it as a mixed capitalist system. Whatever the differences over details, there is considerable agreement among economists that the American system is one of the most nearly *private* enterprise systems in the world and that the privately managed sector sets the tone of the whole economy. This is true even though the government's role has grown considerably over the past forty years.

The main decisions on how to produce goods and services and in what quantities are made by private businesspeople and managers in the pursuit of private profit. There are approximately 12 million privately owned producing units, ranging from very small "ma and pa" operations to giant corporations whose sales and incomes are larger than the national incomes of many small countries. These 12 million firms account for about 85 percent of the economic activity of the nation. The remaining portion is accounted for by city, state, and Federal governments. Consistent with these figures is the fact that the private sector employs 85 percent of the labor force and the various levels of government together only 15 percent.[5]

A rough breakdown of the total privately run business units for 1970 reveals that more than 9 million (about 79 percent) were individual proprietorships; fewer than 1 million (8 percent) were partnerships; and about 1.5 million (13 percent) were corporations. This paltry 13 percent of the units accounted, however, for more than 80 percent of total business output and significantly more than 50 percent of the total labor force.[6]

When we look more closely at the 1.5 million corporations, we observe considerable concentration of control. About 200 of the largest manufacturing corporations, representing less than .01 percent of all business units, and about 16 percent of all incorporated manufacturing units, control about 60 percent of all manufacturing assets. This figure represents an increase of 15 percent from that for 1929.[7] If we add 133 corporations to the list of the largest 200, it appears that

> the 333 industrial corporations with assets of more than $500 million had a full 70% of all assets employed in manufacturing. . . . An assembly of the heads of the firms doing half of all the business in the United States would . . . be . . . nearly invisible in a [standard-sized football] stadium.[8]

In 1972, the gross sales of General Motors, with assets valued at $30 billion, were slightly more than $18 billion. This figure is greater than the individual national incomes of at least two-thirds of the countries in the world.[9]

Finally, the extent of industrial concentration is apparent in examination of the four largest firms in each of several selected industrial sectors. In the primary aluminum industry, the most concentrated of all, there were only four firms in total, and they, of course, accounted for 100 percent of the output in 1970. In the same year the motor-vehicle, electric-bulb, telephone- and telegraph-equipment, and locomotive-parts industries were each dominated by four large firms that produced more than 90 percent of the output.[10] At the other end of the spectrum, in contrast, were industries like women's apparel, fur goods, and concrete block and brick, in each of which the four largest firms contributed 10 percent or less to the total output.[11]

When we examine the whole range of manufacturing industries, we find, in the opinion of one untroubled mainstream economist, a *dual* economy consisting of a concentrated center and a weak periphery.[12] Given the value-laden pronouncements generally derived from the competitive model, how can mainstream economists remain untroubled? The answer will be elaborated in detail in the next section. For now it is enough to suggest that mainstream economists have acquired a benign attitude toward big government and big business and believe that the two can cooperate to achieve the common goal of full employment without endangering cherished economic freedom. In the words of Robert Averitt, the author of the dual-economy thesis:

> There is good reason to [believe] that center firms . . . will be amenable to basing their decisions on economic projections

that *assume* a continuation of full employment. . . . We can attain perpetual prosperity while retaining a high level of what the business community calls "economic freedom." In fact, moral suasion by government is much more effective in highly concentrated industries . . . than firms elsewhere.[13]

MAINSTREAM ECONOMISTS' ADAPTATION TO REALITY

We have now arrived at the heart of our discussion. Few mainstream economists deny the fact of concentration. However, most do not receive information about concentration with excessive alarm, even though it seems to contradict their competitive model. Although most of these economists have long ago given up strong preoccupation with breaking up large corporations into smaller units, they have *not* given up the competitive ideal; it is still very much alive in their theorizing and research. The question is, Why do mainstream economists not have more anxieties about concentrated corporate power and its general implications for misuse and for the malfunctioning of the American economy? The answer shows how mainstream economists have adapted the competitive ideal to fit the changing realities of the American enterprise system. Their adaptation is based on seven "observations" about American reality.

INTERINDUSTRY COMPETITION

As the facts of concentration have stubbornly continued to manifest themselves, mainstream economists have gradually adjusted their ideas by redefining competition to include firms from different industries that produce functionally interchangeable commodities or services. Competition thus seems more prevalent than the old competitive yardstick would suggest. The classical illustration of the new form of competition is provided by the trucking and railroad industries. It is now claimed that it was not competition among rail companies themselves that protected the buyers of rail service; rather, the growth of truck transport and interstate highways was sufficient to ensure competition between the two industries. In the same vein, aluminum must compete with copper, plastic, and wood substitutes.

There is no *theoretical* limit to the extent of possible substitution. For example, concentration in the production of golf equipment may lead to the abuse of golfing consumers. But bowling can be viewed as a recreational substitute. To the extent that sporting consumers are price conscious in their recreational spending, they can be driven to a variety of other functionally "equivalent" alternatives. Competitive pressures are said to reign in the supply of sporting equipment, as producers compete for the money that consumers may wish to spend on recreation.

STABILIZATION OF CONCENTRATION

In the mainstream view, the concentration of economic power has become stabilized over the past thirty to forty years in the context of an *expanding* market. There now appears to be little chance that we will someday find ourselves in the controlling hands of one firm in each major industry. As a matter of fact, many industries that were highly concentrated years ago appear to be less so today. The aluminum industry began as one firm during World War II, and now is made up of a small number of competing firms. The concentrated power of the U.S. Steel Corporation, measured by the percentage of the steel market that it supplies, has decreased over the years. Thus there is said to be little hard evidence that concentration is growing.

TECHNOLOGICAL PROGRESS

One of the strong theoretical justifications of pure competition, as we noted in Chapter 2, is that it stimulates rapid technological change, the mainspring of economic progress and material well-being. When each firm in a competitive industry is a price acceptor, it is forced by competitive circumstances to increase its profits or prevent their erosion by reducing costs. Cost reductions occur through technological improvement, the increase in output per man-hour. The competitive system thus in theory *compels* technological progress. Technical change becomes a requirement for survival of individual firms. But competitive theory has never been clear about where relatively small competitive enterprises are to acquire funds for the research and development that precede technological innovation. As a result, the relation between rigorous competition and technological progress becomes theoretically even more tenuous.

With the appearance of large corporations, as well as imperfect and concentrated markets, come surplus profits, which are neither whittled away by competitive forces nor distributed *in toto* to stockholders. Because profits in noncompetitive industries can be protected by price manipulation, they do not, in theory, have to be protected by reductions in costs through technological innovation. Oligopolistic firms are thus not *compelled* to innovate by circumstances beyond their control.

Theoretically, this circumstance should be received as bad news by adherents of competitive theory. But they have accommodated to this difficulty, noting that the long-term excess profits of monopolistic enterprises are often used for investment in research and development facilities, which in turn lead to technological innovations. Large corporations, which in theory are less compelled to innovate, actually do so in practice. Surplus funds, which must be used if large corporations are to keep growing, find their way into research and its applications. One of the "evils" of concentrated power thus turns out to be less an evil than competitive theory would suggest. Mainstream economists therefore contemplate without undue anxiety the fact that the pure competitive model is a bit fuzzy in its explanation of the ultimate sources of technological progress, that is, of research and development.

BIGNESS AND SOCIAL RESPONSIBILITY

Among the presumed political and social virtues of competition is the fact that each firm is relatively powerless to exploit the consumer and influence the government. The growth of concentrated economic power gives the corporation, at least in theory, disproportionate influence in the halls of government and the capacity to take advantage of the unorganized or less well-organized consuming public. Although this possibility has traditionally been a concern of mainstream economists, they now consider that concern somewhat misplaced. Large corporations are said to have learned over the years that size carries responsibilities to other groups, like consumers, employees, and the government itself. In a nutshell, these corporations have become *socially responsible* in making decisions affecting employment, output, prices, and the use of resources; their own enlightened self-interest induces them to consider others who possess less power. Size, in other words, has a logic of its own. Managers of a giant manufacturing unit, for example, may discover that setting a price to maximize short-run profits is detrimental to the firm's long-run position with consumers; they may therefore set the price lower than short-run considerations seem to dictate. This enlightened attitude is said to have developed, not merely as a public-relations gimmick or because of the changing climate of opinion associated with the emergence of the welfare state,[14] but also because size carries with it a sense of responsibility.

COUNTERVAILING POWER

Other groups, like laborers and farmers, have organized themselves into larger units to protect themselves against possible abuses by corporations.[15] Power on one side of the market is believed automatically to beget power on the other side. One common example of this process is the growth of large industrial unions to protect workers in concentrated industries, for example, the steel, auto, glass, oil, rubber, and electrical-appliance industries. When concentrated corporate power hampers efforts to organize a countervailing force, the government can step in to assist the "underdog" to achieve sufficient strength to defend itself.

ALLOCATION OF RESOURCES AND PROFIT SHARES

All theoretical concerns aside, there is no hard evidence to prove that large corporations earn excessive profits that are damaging to the economy. Two claims are relevant here: that concentration has not resulted in serious misallocation of resources[16] and that the corporate share of profits relative to total national income has at most remained constant over the years. The evidence collected by mainstream economists suggests in fact that the relative profit share has probably declined moderately. It is difficult to feel anxious about the consequences of concentration if they do not in fact appear empirically significant.

PLURALISM AND BIG GOVERNMENT

Finally, mainstream economists point out that the government has grown along with the power of the private corporation. Because, in a democratic society like our own, government represents many competing interests, it can avoid being dominated for long periods of time by any particular set of interests, like the giant corporations. Our society seems sufficiently *pluralistic* to prevent concentrated economic power from being misused to an unreasonable degree. The government is viewed as a "protector of last resort" for those who may be exploited by large corporations.

We are prompted to conclude from this brief survey that the more things change, the more they stay the same. Ideological attachment to the competitive theory, when combined with an ambiguous reality, empirically measured, enables mainstream economists to weather many a storm. They see no reason to reject economic analysis based on the assumption of competitive enterprise, because of the considerations discussed:

1. the discovery of competition among industries
2. the stabilization of economic concentration
3. the continued technological progress in the absence of pure competition
4. the rise of social responsibility on the part of big corporations
5. the development of countervailing powers—organized groups to balance the large corporations
6. the failure of monopoly practices to result in serious misallocation of resources and to severely upset the relative profit shares
7. the emergence of a pluralistic political structure, which has prevented big corporations from taking over the government and bending it completely to their own ends.

PRIVATE CONSUMPTION

Mainstream economists believe that private consumers determine *what* goods and services are produced and that consideration of their role is critical in evaluating the performance of the economy. Although collective consumption, in the form of expenditures by the government for schools, libraries, clean air, and so on, has been recognized as necessary and has even been given theoretical justification, mainstream economists assume that private consumption based upon consumers' self-knowledge and the expression of individual preferences best ensures maximum benefits from any given amount of income or constellation of resources. The consumer should be, at least in principle, the king.

Although well-known economists like John Kenneth Galbraith have argued colorfully, if not rigorously, that the consumer is not and cannot be independent of corporation control in today's society, most mainstream economists have not been swept away by their arguments. They share an underlying belief that the influence of producers on individual consumption decisions has been exaggerated, though it is admitted that consumers are much less autonomous than is often assumed in textbook discourses. Again a combination of reasons is cited: the existence of reasonable competition among producers; the consumers' supposed ability to see through advertising, which is itself competitive and therefore self-nullifying; the possibility that purchasing advertised brands perhaps actually even enhances consumer satisfaction and that advertising is therefore not a waste or a fraud; the fact that in the more affluent European welfare states and the European socialist countries consumer patterns similar to our own appear to be emerging even in the absence of the Madison Avenue vulgarity; and, finally, the fact that a significant proportion of advertising may in fact be informative and may serve to enhance consumers' recognition of actual differences in product quality and price.

In a different vein, mainstream economists reason that, however far the consumer may be from approximating his or her theoretically sovereign role, the alternative to private consumption patterns is grim. Governmental authoritarianism and the loss of individual freedoms of all kinds (civil and political as well as economic) are viewed as the almost certain consequences of an economy in which the consumer must surrender his or her freedom to buy land, homes, and automobiles guided solely by individual tastes and priorities. The point was put this way by one prominent mainstream economic theorist:

> The economist's reason for clinging to the assumption of consumer rationality is that the moment he questions it, he lays himself open to the charge of authoritarianism, of claiming to know better what is good for other people than they know themselves. I admit that I too used to find this argument unanswerable.[17]

In essence, centralized planning is viewed a priori as anathema to freedom and freedom a priori as prerequisite for the rational choice that a private-enterprise system requires of consumers. Mainstream economists ask, Who has the right to tell the individual consumer that the legitimate theater is better for him or her than televised cowboy-and-Indian movies? Their answer is self-evident: no one.

THE CHANGING ROLE OF GOVERNMENT

Mainstream economists convey the impression that, "in the beginning" (in the "golden age" when competition was rigorous and enterprise was truly private), self-regulating markets alone allocated human and nonhuman resources among firms and industries; consumers alone spontaneously determined what was produced; and, finally, the distribution of income, in the absence of external meddling, was related to the value of each factor's contribution to the total productivity of society. Full employment was normal; to the extent that unemployment existed, it would have been eliminated in short order by rapidly acting market forces. Wages and prices would have shifted to stimulate increases or decreases in employment or in the demand for output. Essentially, as long as the system could adjust itself, it had not been necessary to go beyond the market.

Then "it" happened. At some point in history, perhaps during the Great Depression of the 1930s, the system ceased to resolve its problems automatically, and faith in the market was shaken.[18] The government had to be called in as a "third force" to supplement the forces of consumers and producers. Initially, the presence of this new actor on the scene was greeted by economists with caution and uneasiness. But eventually necessity was recognized, and theory was adapted: The expanded role of government in the context of private enterprise came to be accepted as permanent and even legitimate. The mixed capitalist economy had arrived.

According to mainstream economists, the government had acquired a new role, which, at least in theory, should not be confused with its more traditional economic role. In the perfectly competitive society, there are four functions of the government:

1. "to protect our freedom from the enemies outside our gates . . .
2. to preserve law and order
3. to enforce private contracts, [and]
4. to foster competitive markets."[19]

We might perhaps add a fifth function: to undertake those few public projects like road construction, that are clearly of general value to the whole society and cannot be readily undertaken under private auspices. Paradoxically, the laissez-faire philosophy essentially conveyed the idea that the best government is one that does not govern.

In reality, to digress for a moment, the facts have always been much different. The government has not only undertaken the minimal functions prescribed in competitive theory, but it has also regulated industry, banks, working conditions, interstate commerce, and international trade through tariffs and export-promotion schemes. More important, the government has provided private owners of the means of production with land, capital, and much of what is necessary to establish businesses and has helped them to remain in business during periods when the market has failed. Capital has always had legal support, protection from excessive competition, and subsidies from the state, yet the long history of government intervention of this kind is not viewed by mainstream economists as evidence for the early presence of a mixed enterprise system in this country. The notion emerged only in the 1930s in the economic thinking of John Maynard Keynes.

These realities aside, the government's prescribed role, in the mainstream view, is that of *balance wheel*. It requires sufficient power to keep the private economy balanced on a razor's edge between avoiding unemployment on the one side and inflation on the other. By preventing either of these contingencies, the government prevents the economy from experiencing extreme swings and breakdowns. It does so through a variety of tax, spending, and credit policies, that is, by regulating the supply of money. This armory of policies must generate the proper magnitude at the right time. The theoretical underpinning of this governmental role will be discussed in Chapter 4. For the present, we shall concentrate on the main assumption implicit in the conception of the balance wheel.

GOVERNMENT AS NEUTRAL FORCE

The assumed ability of the government to function as a balance wheel through appropriate monetary and fiscal policies is related to the belief that government is a neutral entity, which "not only stands above classes, but stands also above the warring interests of particular [business] groups; as an impartial institution which can represent the general interest of society as a whole and hence steer capitalism in the social interest."[20] This point is illustrated in a more concrete way when mainstream economists pose the problem of government decision making. In discussing the question of what to do with concentrated economic power, Fritz Machlup has pointed out that "[capitalist] governments, apparently have never been able to make up their minds as to which they dislike more, competition or monopoly."[21] This phrasing suggests the image of government as thinker, presiding over a large debating society, listening to all sides, in order to acquire information and to make judicious decisions in the best interests of the total population. Systematic biases in the government's decisions do not form part of the mainstream theoretical framework.

This is not to argue that mainstream economists fail to recognize in practice the role of such interest groups as corporations, business associations, and banks (although they devote little time to examining the details of their influence). But, in their discussions of the relations between such groups and the government, they assume that divergent interests of such groups cancel one another out. The government is thus assumed to have independent power, at least in the long run, to stand above the warring parties in a way that justifies belief that it can be free of systematic biases toward powerful moneyed or corporate interests.

PRIVATE ENTERPRISE:
STILL THE PRIME MOVER

However important the growth of government has been in the past thirty to forty years, it should be emphasized that the basic tools, modes of reasoning, and ideological directions of mainstream economics are based on the assumption of privately owned means of production directed toward privately determined goals. As Wassily Leontief, winner of the 1973 Nobel Prize for economics, has stated:

> The pursuit of private economic gains is certainly the mighty power source that propels the American economy forward. Under our system of free enterprise the profit motive in particular promotes and safeguards its unequalled technical and managerial efficiency. This is the wind that keeps the vessel moving.
>
> But to keep it on a chosen course we have to use a rudder. The steering apparatus consists . . . of governmental economic policies. . . . Private enterprise made this country the most prosperous in the world, and our economy will, of course, rely

on it as its main driving force for a long time to come. But to keep on the right course, we certainly have to use the rudder [that is, the government].[22]

Putting pure theory aside for the moment, mainstream economists recognize, as practical people must, that the market system, like life itself, is imperfect. The private sector can be sluggish at times and may therefore need assistance from the government to ensure steady growth at reasonably high levels of employment without *excessive* inflation. And it *will* receive assistance. The government is conceived by mainstream economists as a *deus ex machina*, a power above society, periodically applying its energies and its spending, taxing, and monetary powers to the private sectors of the economy in order to keep it healthy and in good spirits.

Mainstream economists treat the mixed capitalist system as an extremely complex phenomenon. (The term "complex" often means only that generalizations are difficult to make.) As we saw in our earlier discussion of economic concentration, the facts of concentration can be readily identified, but they are quickly cancelled out by other kinds of "facts." The question of concentration, after years of empirical investigation, is still in limbo. "The chief problem," writes one authority, "is why industry concentration has remained so stable for so long, through stronger and weaker antitrust enforcement; through war, depression, and boom."[23]

Although the standard radical position tends toward the view that concentration has steadily increased over the years, the contrasting observations of the mainstream economists cannot be readily dismissed. In our view, the ambiguity of the empirical findings, after so many years of research, makes it easy for economists to ascribe legitimacy to whatever actually occurs. Mainstream economists can remain ideologically "safe" yet play cautious roles as critics, drifting along in the center. This approach involves a sophistication that tends to be absent among die-hard conservatives and socialist radicals. In discussing the war economy, and after eliminating all ideologies of both left and right, Paul A. Samuelson concludes: "One sweeping monistic explanation cancels out another. Alas, there is no substitute for tedious analysis of . . . experience, unsparing analysis of what makes the macroeconomics of the mixed economy tick and sophisticated insight into the checks and balances of realistic power politics."[24] And, of course, the center is the home of the welfare-liberal governing establishment, which accepts the system more or less as it exists. From the radical point of view, the ideological dogma of welfare-liberal economists permits them, in the absence of supportive evidence, to adhere to competitive metaphysics. This metaphysics provides the basis for rhetoric legitimizing an economy dominated by the business system.

LONG LIVE THE COMPETITIVE MODEL

The propositions and observations that constitute mainstream thinking about production and consumption in the mixed capitalist system prompt a word of caution: No one economist would accept all of the statements that we have described. Our point is that mainstream reasons, when viewed in their totality, explain the broad intellectual support of the mixed private-enterprise system. They also explain why most economists cling to the competitive model, which is still deemed valid or useful—however complex the realities of our system—if the time horizon is long enough. In fact, we are encouraged to take comfort in the assurance that "In the long run, many imperfections [in the system] turn out to be transient. The competitive model, therefore, may suggest in its oversimple way some interesting hypotheses that turn out to have a measure of long-run validity."[25] But, even if the competitive model had no pretensions to prediction, it would still be useful because of its similarity to the

> no-friction model of the physicist; it is not a picture of the real world as we know it; [nevertheless, the engineer] does find the frictionless model a valuable tool in throwing light on complicated reality. So it is with our ideal competitive model. . . . This model is extremely important in providing a bench mark to appraise the efficiency of an economic system. [Everyone] needs to study its analytical principles.[26]

The competitive model is thus still the critical factor that shapes mainstream analysis of the American economy.

NOTES

1. Milton Friedman, *Capitalism and Freedom* (Chicago: University of Chicago Press, 1963), pp. 122–123.

2. The thinking of Ralph Nader is partly influenced by this group. Less well known to the general public are the views of Henry C. Simons, *Economic Policy for a Free Society* (Chicago: University of Chicago Press, 1948).

3. Walter W. Heller, "What's Right with Economics," *The American Economic Review* 65 (March 1975): 3–4.

4. M. A. Adelman, "The Two Faces of Economic Concentration," in *Capitalism Today*, eds. Daniel Bell and Irving Kristol (London: Mentor, 1971), p. 139.

5. *Survey of Current Business*, cited by Louis A. Dow, *Economics* (Columbus, Ohio: Bell & Howell, 1974), p. 82.

6. *Statistical Abstract of the United States, 1971*, cited by Louis A. Dow, *Economics* (Columbus, Ohio: Bell & Howell, 1974), p. 79.

7. U.S. Congress, Senate, Committee on the Judiciary. Subcommittee on Antitrust and Monopoly, "Economic Report on Corporate Mergers," 91st Congress. First Session, 1969, pp. 172–173.

8. John K. Galbraith, *Economics and the Public Purpose* (Boston: Houghton Mifflin, 1973), p. 43.

9. Campbell R. McConnell, *Economics: Principles, Problems and Policies*, 6th ed. (New York: McGraw-Hill, 1975), p. 134.

10. U.S. Bureau of the Census, *Annual Survey of Manufacturing*, 1970, cited *ibid.*, p. 574.

11. McConnell, *Economics*, p. 561.

12. Robert T. Averitt, *The Dual Economy* (New York: Norton, 1968).

13. *Ibid.*, p. 200.

14. Earl F. Cheit, "Why Managers Cultivate Social Responsibility," in *The Business Establishment*, ed. Earl F. Cheit (New York: Wiley, 1964), pp. 152–192.

15. John Kenneth Galbraith, *American Capitalism: The Concept of Countervailing Power* (Boston: Houghton Mifflin, 1956).

16. See F. M. Scherer, *Industrial Market Structure and Economic Performance* (Chicago: Rand McNally, 1970), p. 408.

17. Tibor Scitovsky, "A New Approach to the Theory of Consumer Behavior," *The American Economist* 17 (Fall 1973): 29.

18. "Ever since the New Deal, a primary excuse for expansion of governmental activity at the federal level has been the supposed necessity for government spending to eliminate unemployment." Friedman, *Capitalism and Freedom*, p. 75.

19. *Ibid.*, p. 2.

20. Maurice Dobb, *On Economic Theory and Socialism* (London: Routledge and Kegan Paul, 1955), p. 219.

21. Fritz Machlup, *The Political Economy of Monopoly* (Baltimore: Johns Hopkins Press 1952), p. 182.

22. Wassily Leontief, "Sails and Rudders, Ship of State," *The New York Times*, March 16, 1973, p. 41.

23. M. A. Adelman, "Two Faces," p. 147.

24. Paul A. Samuelson, "Taking Stock of War," *The New York Times*, March 14, 1973, p. 41.

25. Paul A. Samuelson, *Economics*, 9th ed. (New York: McGraw-Hill, 1973), p. 630.

26. *Ibid.*, pp. 630–631.

KEYNESIAN WISDOM

Although microeconomics, as suggested in Chapter 2, is concerned with the interrelations among *components* of the economy—markets, firms, and consumers for example—*macroeconomics* is concerned with the total national product and the broad interactions of investment, consumption, and savings in relation to price levels, total wages, and the money supply. Macroeconomics emphasizes the whole forest as viewed from an airplane, rather than the twigs, branches, and individual trees as viewed from the ground.

The measure most commonly employed to determine the absolute size of the nation's output is Gross National Product (GNP), defined as the market value (in constant dollars) of goods and services produced in one year; another common measure is Net National Product (NNP), which is simply Gross National Product minus the value of capital (like plant or equipment) that has been worn out or exhausted in production.

THE ISSUE OF LONG-TERM UNEMPLOYMENT

Microeconomics, as a specialized field, is older than macroeconomics. It is intimately associated with Alfred Marshall (1842–1924), a British economist who was one of the chief architects of the neoclassical school of economics. Marshall's main contribution was to the theory of the firm and how it adjusts the various factors under its control in response to market forces in the short and long run. Economists in the tradition of Marshall believe that the size of GNP is determined on the supply side by the amounts and quality of land, labor, factories, equipment, and natural resources available for production. In the short run, the greatest output occurs when the given inputs are allocated according to the rules of competitive markets. To increase overall output in the long run, however, it is necessary to increase the amounts and quality of the inputs available.

Potential aggregate output and actual output were not distinguished sharply in the neoclassical model; all resources available were assumed to be in use. The possibility that there could be *unused* labor was excluded from the theory, for it was generally assumed that aggregate demand for goods and services would be sufficient to call forth the profitable use of all who were willing to work. To put this point in premacroeconomic terms, full-employment production generates full-employment income, which in turn generates sufficient expenditure to sustain full employment.

We do not suggest that neoclassical economists were oblivious to actual unemployment. But such unemployment was assumed to be a temporary phenomenon. The reasoning of neoclassical economists on this point took three general directions.

First, surplus or unemployed labor in one industry was assumed to be matched by a shortage of labor in another. Unemployment was thus mainly associated with the question of labor immobility—the problem of moving workers from industries where job opportunities were scarce to those where they were abundant.

Second, the competitive theory assumes, it should be recalled, that wages and prices are sufficiently flexible *downward* to stimulate adjustments in the numbers of workers demanded and the quantity of goods produced. If an unemployed labor pool exists, for example, competition among unemployed and employed workers should bring down wages. The lowering of the wage rate, which was seen primarily as a decrease in costs to business firms, would thus have been expected to stimulate an expansion in output and consequently the absorption of unemployed workers.

Finally, it was recognized that all the income generated by production may not be spent. Some income is saved. Unspent income means unpurchased goods, leading eventually to unemployed labor. But thrift—defined as the sacrifice of present consumption in order to enhance future consumption—is not without a rationale; it diverts resources from the production of consumer goods to the production of capital goods. For initiating this process, savers receive a return in the form of interest. If they cannot find capitalists who wish to borrow at the going rate of interest, savers, competing among themselves, will drive the rate down. As the interest rate declines, capitalists will be induced to increase their borrowing, diverting resources from consumption to capital goods. This augmentation of the capital stock requires the use of more labor: precisely the unemployed labor released from the consumer-goods industries.

The general conclusion to this set of reasoning was that involuntary unemployment is theoretically impossible. Actual unemployment was assumed to be of short duration and therefore did not require special government programs to create jobs. Prices, wages, and interest rates were *assumed* to change in appropriate ways and at sufficient speeds to absorb unemployed labor. But John Maynard Keynes and his early converts questioned these assumptions. What if unions, business monopolies, and other institutions prevented wages, prices, and interest rates from changing downward? How then could unemployed workers be absorbed? Their answers to such questions represent the basis of Keynesian economic theory.

When the Great Depression of the 1930s came, Keynes knew that the twilight hour had arrived for laissez-faire and the self-regulating price system. In his book *The General Theory of Employment, Interest and Money* (1936), he shifted the emphasis from supply to demand in explanations of the size of the nation's total product. Keynes's contribution marked a turning point in economic thinking. Not only did a Keynesian school of thought develop, but also the host of English economists upon whose work he based his own contribution was relabeled "pre-Keynesian" or "classical," though such labels encompass a multitude of misunderstandings.

The market's failure to generate its own comeback necessitated a theoretical explanation that would convince the mainstream microeconomists of the time. Keynes provided it by attacking the assumptions upon which traditional microeconomic wisdom rested. He also provided monetary and fiscal prescriptions by which a growing governmental bureaucracy could try to save the collapsed economy. When, after World War II, the storm of the 1930s could finally be viewed from the perspective of history, Keynes's theories and practical policy recommendations produced a veritable revolution in economic thinking. The essence of that revolution will be summarized in this chapter.

PRODUCTION, INCOME, AND EXPENDITURES

Imagine an economy consisting of one firm that produces the total output, for which it also sets the prices.[1] The value of the output would be measured by multiplying the quantities produced by their prices. The firm has to use laborers and pay them wages, rent land, and pay interest on capital. To the extent that the value of net output is greater than these and other costs, the firm will show a profit, which will be paid to the businesspeople who co-orinate the production process. Profits can also be viewed as income, a return for ownership or the "entrepreneurial"—risk taking—function. The sum of the incomes paid to all individuals participating in production is equal to aggregate income. If aggregate income is, by definition, equal to the net value of aggregate output, how can there be insufficient demand, as Keynes argued there was in the 1930s? His answer has two interrelated parts.

First, *potential* national product, the potential output of the nation under full employment, is not necessarily equal to *actual* national product. It may be equal to or greater than actual output. If actual output is significantly smaller, large numbers of available workers are unemployed. "Unproduced national output," measured by the number of available man-hours not being used, is output that is permanently lost to society; it is part of the *social cost* of unemployment.

Second, although income is equal to the actual value of output, the proportion of national income that people wish to spend may *not* be equal to the value of national output. If it should prove to be less, then both income and output will decrease, thus causing unemployment and a further gap between potential and actual output.

The critical import of the Keynesian theoretical edifice was to show how the value of potential output tends to be permanently greater than the equilibrium values of actual output, income, and expenditures. Full-employment output cannot be sustained. Although measured saving and investment are necessarily equal by definition, *planned* investment geared to expectations of profit may often be less than *actual* savings. This reflects overproduction (unintended short-run investment in inventories). Investment cutbacks result, followed by decreases in output, income, and employment. The process ends when the aggregate supply and demand forces of the economy are balanced at a level significantly below the full-employment equilibrium mark. In the longer run, Keynes's "entire intellectual effort," in the words of Joan Robinson, "[was with the insufficiency of] investment outlets to absorb available funds."[2] Acceptance of the theoretical possibility of "unemployment equilibrium" compelled capitalist governments to reject their laissez-faire traditions.

CONSUMERS, ENTREPRENEURS, AND SPECULATORS

In the Keynesian view, there are three main groups of actors in the economy: consumers, business entrepreneurs, and financial speculators. The adjustment of each of these groups to particular variables and to one another is at the heart of the Keynesian explanation of why mature capitalist systems fail to work as pre-Keynesian, or neoclassical, economists had believed that they would.

CONSUMERS AND THE MARGINAL PROPENSITY TO CONSUME

Consumers, by far the most numerous of the three groups, receive incomes for supplying services in the production process. They are preoccupied with how much of their current income should be spent on the output produced; they are thus simultaneously deciding how much of their current income should be saved (current income minus current consumption equals current savings).

As the general level of income in society rises, so does the level of consumption. The rise in consumption, however, is less than the rise in income. As a society becomes wealthier, there is a distinct possibility that the overall tendency to save will also rise, a critical factor in understanding why full employment eludes richer capitalist nations without positive government programs for creating jobs.

Derived from this income-consumption relation is the concept of marginal propensity to consume, the MPC. The MPC is equal to the change in consumption divided by a unit change in income (see Table 4.1, column C). Its value can range from 0 to 1. A value of 0 means that a unit change in income, for example, $10 a week, begets 0 change in consumption: The whole increment in income is saved. A value of 1 means that the total increment in income

Table 4.1 • *The Hypothetical Relations Among Income, Consumption, and Saving*

A INCOME	B CONSUMPTION	C MPC	D SAVING	E SAVING/INCOME
75	100		−25	−.33
		$\dfrac{150 - 100}{150 - 75} = \frac{2}{3}$		
150	150		0	0
		$\dfrac{200 - 150}{225 - 200} = \frac{2}{3}$		
225	200		25	.11
		$\dfrac{250 - 200}{300 - 225} = \frac{2}{3}$		
300	250		50	.17
		$\dfrac{300 - 250}{375 - 300} = \frac{2}{3}$		
375	300		75	.20
		$\dfrac{350 - 300}{450 - 375} = \frac{2}{3}$		
450	350		100	.22

In column A the unit change from one level to the next is $75; in column B consumption associated with consumption level changes by $50. The fractions in column C show the changes in consumption divided by a unit change in income. Column D is the difference between income and consumption. The figures in column E represent the average propensity to save, that is, saving divided by income.

is spent. The value of the MPC for any nation is an empirical question, the answer to which must be obtained through consumer-budget studies. In the United States the MPC is about ⅗. The precise importance of the MPC will be investigated when we discuss the investment multiplier. For the moment, it is enough to note that the value of the MPC is related to the stability of the economy.

In any event, income, once determined, begets responses from consumers that simultaneously determine the level of consumption and the level of saving. Saving is, in the Keynesian system, considered simply as the residual income that is not used in consumption—a relatively passive variable.

ENTREPRENEURS
AND THE EXPECTED RATE OF PROFIT

Business entrepreneurs are the volatile agents in the Keynesian model of the economy. They mobilize real goods and services. When the system works, it is because of their energy; when it fails, it is because of their lack of energy. Entrepreneurial moods fluctuate considerably and therefore represent the main source of capitalist instability. Business decisions affect both fluctuations in investment activity and, in any given time period, the level of private investment. As the Keynesian time frame (at least as interpreted by most American Keynesians) is the short run, production involves increasing or decreasing inventories. There is generally not sufficient time to change the given stock of capital machinery or to introduce alterations in plant and equipment, alterations that incorporate technological changes. In the Keynesian analysis, the basic technological structure of the economy is assumed constant.

Two aspects of entrepreneurial decisions should be underscored: the way in which big changes in income and output are associated with relatively small changes in investment levels and the ways in which expectations of profit and the interest rate become the critical variables that determine the level of investment.

First, small changes in the level of investment produce magnified changes in income, output, and employment through the "investment multiplier." Technical considerations aside, the value of the multiplier reflects the relationship between incremental income and consumption expenditures, that is, the marginal propensity to consume.

Suppose that a family's weekly income increases from $150 to $225, an increment of $75. If the family was spending $150 a week when its income was $150 and is now spending $200, the ratio of the change in consumption to the change in income is $50/$75 or ⅔. This incremental ratio is the value of the marginal propensity to consume. It should be noted that the process is reversible: When a family's weekly income decreases $75, from $225 to $150, consumption is assumed to decrease by $50 (⅔ of $75).

For illustration, let us assume that a community has a marginal propensity to consume equivalent to the family in our example, ⅔, and that it experiences a decrease in investment of $5 billion. By how much do income and output fall? Given certain assumptions —for example, a closed economy and no price changes—the theoretically "exact" answer is $15 billion; less exact but nevertheless in the right direction is an answer of some multiple of $5 billion. The explanation is that the immediate impact of a $5 billion decrease in investment spending is a decrease in output and income of $5 billion dollars and a rise in unemployment. Unemployed workers, finding themselves with less income, decrease their aggregate consumption expenditures by ⅔ of $5 billion, or $3 billion. But such a decrease in expenditures by workers generates a secondary round of decreases in income, for workers are purchasing fewer goods and services supplied by others. These others also experience a decrease in their aggregate income of $3 billion. A third round is now set into motion, and workers' expenditures decrease by ⅔ of $3 billion, or about $2.2 billion. The chain reaction continues until the amounts become negligible in their impact. If this process were carried to its last fraction of a cent and the sum of all the decreases were calculated, the total decrease in income would be $15 billion. A permanent decrease in the level of investment by $5 billion thus generates a much larger decrease in income and output. The process also works in reverse; a $5 billion increase in investment generates a $15 billion increase in aggregate income.

The second result of entrepreneurial decisions is determination of the level of investment itself. Keynesians emphasize the relation among net investment, profit expectations, and the cost of borrowing money. The expected profit rate is the margin of return above the cost of a unit of capital. Suppose that an entrepreneur is trying to decide whether or not to produce more work aprons and that an increase in production would require the purchase of an additional heavy-duty sewing machine costing $400 and having a useful life of one year. If the price of the machine were the entrepreneur's only cost, then the *rate* of net expected profit would be equal to net revenue from the sale of aprons divided by the cost of the sewing machine. If net revenues were $40, the profit rate would be 10 percent of cost. Whether the sewing machine is purchased depends on the market rate of interest (the cost of capital), for the $400 must be borrowed. An interest rate greater than 10 percent would discourage investment in the sewing machine; one less than 10 percent would encourage investment. Keynesians see the typical investor "as being in the grip of a major objective influence and a major subjective influence. The objective element is the price of the [sewing] machine and the subjective one is the investor's best guess of the machine's impact upon his flow of receipts."[3]

If at any time there is a whole range of possible investment projects—some of which have expected returns well above the 10 percent cost of borrowing money, others below it, and still others equal to it—it is clear that entrepreneurs should be willing to borrow funds to invest in those projects that promise profits greater than (or even equal to) 10 percent. Projects with anticipated returns below 10 percent would not be undertaken, for investors could earn more money by lending it to others at the market rate of interest than by investing in their own less remunerative projects.

There are thus three variables that can affect the level of investment or changes in it. First is the entrepreneur's own expectations about his or her chances of making money. In the Keynesian view, typical businesspersons are creatures of mood and habit, controlled by fears and hopes. Their reactions to the market can be readily whipped into a state of manic hyperactivity or depressed to a complete standstill. Second, the cost of capital goods may change, affecting the entrepreneur's estimation of profitability. For example, a lowering of the prices of plant, equipment, and natural resources would positively affect the profit horizons of business. Finally, the interest rate—the cost of borrowing money—can decrease or increase. This would affect the willingness of entrepreneurs to borrow money to undertake investment in new projects.

In examining how the interest rate is determined and its relation to aggregate output and income through investment, Keynes was able to integrate theoretically the financial markets and the real commodity markets. The notion of money as a *store of wealth* was thus added to the classical notion of money as mainly a medium of exchange. Money, in other words, was not simply an instrument to lubricate spending, but one that could be held to assist speculators. Speculation, and its relation to the determination and fluctuation of interest rates, leads us to the *third* group of actors on the Keynesian stage, the financial speculators.

SPECULATORS
AND THE PREFERENCE FOR LIQUIDITY

To understand the role of financial speculators, in contrast to that of business entrepreneurs, we must digress briefly to discuss some definitions and the way in which, according to Keynes, the interest rate is determined. As we have indicated, interest, in the view of pre-Keynesian economists, serves to induce people to forgo present consumption; it is considered a payment for "waiting," for sacrificing the present to the future. This explanation assumes, of course, that there is full employment and that resources not used to produce consumer goods mean the permanent loss of such goods to society. Keynes, theorizing in a context of mass unemployment, could not see that anything was being sacrificed in a society in which there were both unemployed capital and unemployed labor, for using resources in *any* way, even wasting them to build pyramids, involves no sacrifice or "waiting" period. This was possible because investment, by means of the multiplier effect, created the saving needed to finance itself.

To Keynes and the Keynesians, the interest rate seemed a monetary phenomenon, a payment for the use of money, "a reward to a wealth-holder who parts with the control of money in exchange for a debt, e.g., for a bond . . . or a mortgage, for a stated period of time."[4] By emphasizing this "purely" monetary component in the determination of the interest rate and by linking it to the stock of money (defined as the sum of bank checking deposits, paper money, and coins), Keynes integrated the notion of money as a means of payment and store of value into the theory of output and income determination for the economy as a whole. Closely related to Keynesian views of the interest rate and its determinants is thus a view of monetary policy.

To understand some of these matters, we must examine why money is held. We begin with the simple observation that people do not spend all their money. Generally, they put part of their income into banks or the stock and bond markets. Perhaps a few people still put their cash holdings under the mattress.

More important, however, is the question, What motivates people not to spend all their income and to hold some portion of it in cash? Without introducing too many complications, Keynes emphasized two main incentives for such behavior: transaction motives and speculative motives.[5]

The *transaction* motive poses no problem, since holding for transaction reasons is short-lived. People hold cash for the purpose of making regular payments that are built into their living routines: to meet food and transportation expenses, and to pay monthly bills and rent. The transaction motive was recognized by pre-Keynesian economists; in fact, it was the *only* motive for holding money that they recognized explicitly and integrated into their theory of the production and circulation of goods and services.

The other reason for holding money is *speculation*. There are people with surplus wealth who have the choice of holding their wealth in one of two forms, interest-bearing bonds or cash. Bonds, although they bear interest, are risky because they fluctuate in price. One can suffer capital losses with price declines. Money, while bearing no interest, has the advantage of being perfectly liquid. Why would anyone choose to hold money rather than bonds? The answer is *uncertainty*, guessing about the unpredictable and incalculable future.[6] Because holders of wealth can speculate on the terms of purchase of debts, a market arises that produces a group of speculators who win by outwitting majority opinion. "Thus," wrote Keynes, "certain classes of investment are governed by . . . expectations of those who deal in the Stock Exchange as revealed in the price of shares, rather than by the . . . professional entrepreneur."[7]

Putting aside for a moment the role of the money supply in determining the interest rate, we must keep in mind that the interest rate itself is the cost of borrowing money for purposes of investment. When speculators move in and out of the market, they produce fluctuations in interest rates that cause changes in the levels of investment and thus even greater changes in output, income, and employment as a result of the investment multiplier. In the Keynesian view, speculators can cause investment to act in perverse ways: for example, interest rates may be forced up or prevented from declining at times when more investment is needed to achieve more employment. Speculators can do serious harm "when enterprise becomes the bubble on a whirlpool of speculation. When the capital development of a country becomes a by-product of the activities of a casino, the job is likely to be ill-done."[8]

To neutralize, or even nullify, the speculator's impulses, Keynes recommended control of the money supply, which is connected to both the interest rate and the hoarding of cash, as described in a liquidity-preference schedule (Figure 4.1).

The demand for money (Md) is the liquidity preference schedule. It is determined by the rate of interest and is negatively sloped: The lower the rate of interest (vertical axis), the larger will be the amount of money demand indicated on the horizontal axis. The economic reasoning underlying this relationship is as follows: At high interest rates (low bond prices) holding money involves forgoing considerable income. High interest rates also involve negligible risk of dropping bond prices, for presumably they are already as low or nearly as low as they are likely to go. At high interest rates people tend to *avoid* holding cash but, as interest rates decline, there is an incentive to shift from bonds to cash. Lower interest rates mean not only that less income is forgone by holding cash but also that the risk of capital losses from decreasing bond prices is greater. Finally, at very low interest rates (below 2 percent), the income forgone by hoarding cash be-

Figure 4.1 • Liquidity Preference and the Supply of Money

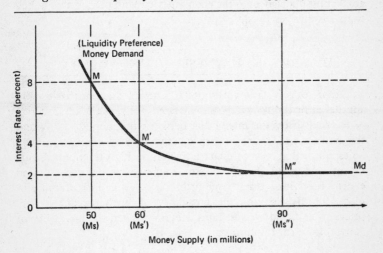

comes negligible, and the risk of capital losses (given the high prices of bonds and the possibility of their dropping) becomes great. It is this trade-off between the possibility of capital gains or losses from price changes and the loss of income through holding cash that determines the special shape of Keynes's notion of demand to hoard a certain proportion of the total stock of money in the form of cash.

The supply of money (Ms) in the Keynesian system is determined exogenously by the central banking authorities. When the supply of money is M, the equilibrium rate of interest is 8 percent; that is, the supply of money at M equals the amount of money people wish to hold. A shift of the money to M' leads to an equilibrium rate of interest at 4 percent. If the money supply should shift to M'', other factors remaining unchanged, the interest rate would reach its practical limit, 2 percent. At this interest rate, the desire to hold cash becomes *limitless* as the money supply expands. Further expansion in the money supply does not induce financial speculators to buy more bonds with their additional cash. Rather, additional increases simply enhance the willingness to hoard cash.

By demonstrating the possibility of the flattening out of the liquidity preference schedule—the Keynesian liquidity trap—Keynes was able to define the limits of a workable monetary policy. The lowest possible interest rate in a depressed period may simply not be low enough to generate demand for investment adequate to achieve full employment. The conservative hope of correcting imbalances in the economy by manipulating the money supply is thus removed.

SUMMARY OF KEYNESIAN FUNDAMENTALS

The more or less static version of Keynesian thought that usually appears in textbooks can be summarized. First, as the interest rate is determined by the interaction between the money supply and the desire to hold money for speculative reasons, equilibrium may be established at an interest rate that is too high to stimulate sufficient investment. Then the sum of investment and consumption expenditures may reach equilibrium at a level short of full employment. By denying the possibility of further reductions in prices, wages, and interest rates, Keynes proved the possibility of "unemployment equilibrium."

Second, assuming stable habits and attitudes, consumption is determined by the level of income. From this relationship, the marginal propensity to consume is derived; its value is assumed to be relatively stable and is expressed in fractions of 1.

Third, the relationship between consumption and income is assumed to be reasonably stable; the source of economic instability lies in the volatile character of private investment. Expenditures in this domain are determined by expected net rates of profit and the rate of interest. Investment is undertaken by entrepreneurs, the main source of enterprise in the economy.

Fourth, financial speculators, alternately hoarding cash and holding bonds, can cause erratic changes in the interest rates. These changes can affect the level of investment adversely; the speculator's liquidity preference may have a destabilizing effect on the economic system because of the investment multiplier.

Fifth, monetary authorities can control the money supply; in conditions of unemployment they should expand it in order to reduce the interest rate to its lowest possible level. If such a rate should still prove an inadequate stimulant to investment, it will in theory become necessary to go outside the private market to increase aggregate demand. Government deficit spending, financed through the creation of money, is then the only route out of a profound depression. Government expenditures thus become the third critical component of aggregate demand.

Finally, although Keynes preferred sensible government spending programs to nonsensical ones, he understood that the latter may be the only politically feasible kind. In his words:

> If the Treasury were to fill old bottles with banknotes, bury them at suitable depths in disused coalmines which are then filled up to the surface with town rubbish, and leave it to private enterprise on well-tried principles of *laissez-faire* to dig the notes up again . . . there need be no more unemployment. . . . It would indeed be more sensible to build houses and the like; but if there are political and practical difficulties in the way of this, the above would be better than nothing.[9]

For radicals, this final point is one of the main deficiencies in the Keynesian system. There are not, in the radical view, enough productive opportunities for government spending that are politically feasible; warfare expenditures and waste therefore become the practical Keynesian solutions (see Chapter 10).

KEYNESIAN DYNAMICS

It can be argued, however, that Keynes was really interested not in how unemployment equilibrium can be achieved but in how unemployment disequilibrium can continue for a very long time. The multiplier was relevant, not because it would enable economists to predict the exact decline in output and income that would result from an initial decline in investment, but because it emphasized the cumulative consequences of interactions among businesspeople and consumers under conditions of imperfect knowledge (such as lags in price and wage changes, and uncertain profit expectations).

Joan Robinson, a leading English economic theorist and student of Keynes, has propounded the view that American economists have "bastardized" the Keynesian contribution.[10] The more correct observation, in our judgment, is that they have "nationalized" it by omitting the discussion of Keynes's contribution, which suggests that capitalism is inherently unstable. Be that as it may, there is a view that "real" Keynesian thinking is unlike that found in American economics textbooks and therefore unlike that described so far in this chapter. The "real" Keynesian contribution falls in the category of "economic dynamics," in which historic time and decision making under conditions of uncertainty are emphasized. In this view, the course of the economy cannot simply be reversed in mechanical ways to satisfy equilibrium conditions. On the contrary, the economy moves on an irreversible path through time, so that self-defeating decisions may also have long-term effects. Moreover, decisions in one direction foreclose alternative lines of development. Technology is not infinitely flexible; once a certain technique has been chosen, other present possibilities are eliminated, and future choices are already partly determined. What follows here is a bird's-eye view of the "real" Keynesian contribution, which appears to be experiencing a renaissance in popularity among some economists.[11]

In the short run, major decreases in the quantity of output are associated with relatively small changes in demand, especially investment demand; these small changes cannot be corrected by price and wage decreases because such decreases do not occur or follow only very slowly. A chain reaction sets in as a result of an initial disturbance, which feeds upon itself and leads to significantly larger disturbances. A decline in investment spending leads to a decline in income, which leads to a further decline in spending and a still further decline in income. This process, of course, has practical, as well as theoretical, limits. The instructional value of the multiplier is that it underscores the short-run instability of capitalism associated with the volatile nature of investment demand.

More generally, once the economy begins to contract, profit expectations may sink much faster than the interest rate can be pushed down. Changes in the interest rate are then unable to attract business investment very quickly. Even if prices and wages were assumed to be flexible in the downward direction, they would be unlikely to decline once and for all, given the existence of unions and monopolistic business practices in concentrated industries. In reality, wages would decrease spasmodically, and expectations of further decreases might lead employers to postpone investment decisions in order to reap even lower cost advantages later on—at least until they were certain that wage decreases had reached bottom. Such postponements of investment decisions, however, would operate to extend the downward spiral. In the same way, once prices began to decline, consumers, in the expectation of further decreases, might postpone demand, causing further decreases in output. Finally, as both prices and wages moved downward in spurts, the value of cash balances would increase in the same way and would thus affect the speed at which hoarders would release cash. This would dampen the rate at which people would purchase goods and services or shift to bond holdings. In the event of too much hesitation, interest rates could not be lowered quickly enough to assuage the gloomy expectations of businesspeople struggling to cope with the downward trend.

Even if businesspeople understood that wage increases represent increases in the demand for the products that they make, such increases would represent themselves to individual businesses as increased costs *before* being translated into demand for more goods and services. The whole economy is not visible to each business unit. Moreover, decreases in demand for consumer goods may occur at a faster rate than the fall in wages, and then the decreases in costs associated with falling wages may not appear sufficient to stimulate reemployment and the expansion of output. All these factors are *dynamic*, fundamental to the Keynesian analysis of possible causes of long-run unemployment disequilibrium.

THE NECESSITY FOR GOVERNMENT SPENDING

At various points in his thinking, Keynes emphasized the interaction, over time, among a number of variables that generate expectations that may operate on the economy in perverse ways. Whether the Keynesian contribution is most valuable for having proved the possibility of unemployment equilibrium or for having proved that disequilibrium is dynamic and can last a very long time, it eventually became clear to neoclassical economists that something outside the market had to go to work. That "something" was, of course, the government. At the risk of repetition, we note that Keynes's analysis of the private sector led him to state the necessity of, and the rationale for, a specific kind of governmental action: deficit spending, designed to prevent adverse side effects on the private sector. What seemed needed was financing that would not produce a decrease in demand by businesspeople or consumers. The net impact of an increase in government demand depends upon how the government chooses to finance its expenditures. Keynes thought that, to be effective, deficit spending must be financed by borrowing from big private savers, whose spending propensities will not be seriously affected by such lending, or by creating new money for the purchase of goods and services from the private sector, without alteration in the tax structure. Whatever the specific means adopted, the critical idea is that the government's participation in the spending process is not neutral or negative. On the contrary, by spending more than it receives in taxes, it can stimulate the rehiring of unemployed labor. Government spending must therefore be taken into account as an element in aggregate demand.

Aggregate demand may now be viewed as equal to consumption plus investment plus net government expenditures. To the extent that tax receipts are less than governmental expenditures, governmental actions tend to stimulate increases in income, output, and employment. The task of the government is thus to estimate the size of the deficit necessary to employ the unused portions of the labor force fully. Moreover, in a period of unemployment such a deficit would necessarily be smaller than the resulting increases in income and output because of the multiplier effect, which we have discussed in relation to changes in investment. As government spending will generate the use of unemployed labor that is not contributing to government receipts in the form of taxes, government revenues will automatically increase and can be used to pay off debts incurred initially. As full employment is approached, it may even be necessary for the government to acquire *surplus* revenues (tax receipts greater than expenditures) in order to prevent aggregate demand from becoming excessive and setting off an inflationary spiral. The latter possibility is not a "Keynesian problem" and therefore takes us beyond our present discussion. The problem of inflation implicit in the Keynesian analysis of an upward swing was understood simply as one in which aggregate demand would tend to exceed aggregate output at full employment. If such a state were reached, national product would rise in *money* terms, rather than in real ones. In the short run, real changes in output are limited by the extent to which resources are in use. Excess demand in a full-employment economy generates higher prices, rather than larger outputs. But chronic inflation is strictly a "post-Keynesian" phenomenon, which mainstream economists have not fully dealt with in analytical terms. This matter will be discussed at greater length in Chapter 13.

CONCLUSION

The general Keynesian assumption that has guided government policy is that the "micro" elements of the economy will respond in appropriate ways to positive government action. It has been further assumed that the government can participate in ways that will support the entire private-enterprise system and the market calculus.

In the eyes of mainstream economists, the formulation of Keynesian economics and its acceptance by capitalist governments have destroyed once and for all the possibility of mass unemployment. Belief in this accomplishment, perhaps the most important economic fact of the thirty years following World War II, has permanently crippled (if not completely discredited) the socialist critique of capitalism. The Achilles heel of capitalism in the radical view, it should be noted, is mass unemployment, which can presumably be eliminated only by means of imperialist expansion, wars, or exploitation of underdeveloped countries. The issue was put by one mainstream economist in the form of two questions: Must capitalism break down if it does not find foreign markets in which to spend money and rid itself of domestically produced surplus goods? Can the high living standards characteristic of the few capitalist nations of the West be "maintained only by the exploitation of the teeming billions who live in the impoverished underdeveloped nations?"[12] His answer to both questions was an unequivocal "no":

> This is 1973, not 1903 or 1933. We are almost forty years into the Age of Keynes. I believe that [the radicals] were right to worry about the sustainability of full employment in William McKinley's balanced-budget *laissez-faire* [days]. However, not a single mixed [capitalist] economy has had any problem these last thirty years with chronic insufficiency of purchasing power. . . . Nor in the century to come—1973–2073—will the ancient scourge of intermittent-shortage-of-purchasing power reoccur in the old form.[13]

To achieve its leverage role and sustain high employment levels, the government must examine carefully the magnitude and movement of the basic variables that make up the aggregate system. Mainstream economists have thus become involved in measuring aggregate levels of income, output, and employment, as well as the individual components of each. This has led to a concern with national income accounts and with the components of national income: consumption, investment, and government spending. It has also led to the construction of statistical models that can be used to predict overall production and its various elements.

The Keynesian legacy has accomplished much more. It has brought the complexities of the welfare state with its host of subsidies—the dividends of giant corporations, deficits and debts of the Federal government, the moderately progressive Federal income tax, and the waste of resources in military spending and make-work projects—into a unified theoretical framework in which the parts seem "reasonably" consistent with the whole if we do not insist too rigorously on clarifying the full meanings of "consistency" and "relationship." Worries about "boom-bust-depression" have become old-fashioned, replaced by such empirical concerns as economic fluctuations and high-level plateaus.

In substance, the mixed capitalist system has been perceived by economists and other social scientists as possessing a social logic that no longer requires serious theorizing in the context of history. Keynes is believed to have produced all the theoretical boxes necessary for the foreseeable future. What remains are details to be sorted out by practitioners of the economics trade. Lest this judgment strike the reader as reflecting merely the strong biases of an unsympathetic critic, let us examine the following statement by Robert Solow, a prominent Keynesian economist from the Massachusetts Institute of Technology:

> I think that most economists feel that short-run macroeconomic theory is pretty well in hand. . . . The basic outlines of the dominant theory have not changed in years. All that is left is the typical job of filling in the empty boxes, and that will not take more than 50 years of concentrated effort at a maximum. . . .[14]

A good deal of such "filling in the empty boxes" involves evaluating—and celebrating—the empirical performance of the economy.

NOTES

1. Arnold Collery, "Macroeconomic Theory," in *Perspective in Economics*, eds. A. A. Brown, E. Newberger, and M. Palmatier (New York: McGraw-Hill, 1971), p. 53.

2. Joan Robinson, "Michal Kelecki: A Neglected Prophet," *New York Review of Books* (March 4, 1976): 30.

3. Robert Lekachman, *National Income and the Public Welfare* (New York: Random House, 1972), p. 37.

4. Dudley Dillard, *The Economics of John Maynard Keynes* (Englewood Cliffs, N.J.: Prentice-Hall, 1948), p. 166.

5. There is a third type, the precautionary motive, which involves holding cash to satisfy some unexpected need or desire. For the purpose at hand, however, the transaction and speculative motives are the critical ones, and they are the only ones that we shall discuss.

6. Joan Robinson, "What Has Become of the Keynesian Revolution?" *Challenge* (January–February 1974): 8.

7. John Maynard Keynes, *The General Theory of Employment Interest and Money* (New York: Harcourt, 1936), pp. 150–151.

8. *Ibid.*, p. 159.

9. *Ibid.*, p. 129.

10. Robinson, "What Has Become of the Keynesian Revolution?" p. 8.

11. The "dynamic" side of Keynes's thinking has been elaborated with considerable force by an American economist, Hyman P. Minsky, who has concentrated on Keynes's view of the financial system and the possibility that debt deflation might induce a serious depression. See Minsky, *John Maynard Keynes* (New York: Columbia University Press, 1975); see also Axel Leijonhufvud, *On Keynesian Economics and the Economics of*

Keynes (New York: Oxford University Press, 1968).

12. Paul A. Samuelson, "Taking Stock of War," *The New York Times,* March 14, 1973, p. 43.

13. *Ibid.*

14. Robert Solow, "Economic Growth and Residential Housing," in *Readings in Financial Institutions,* eds. M. D. Ketchum and L. T. Kendall (Boston: Houghton Mifflin, 1965), p. 146.

WORLD WAR II:
AN INTERLUDE

The Great Depression of the 1930s, which gave birth to Keynesian theory, also gave birth to institutional reforms and changes in social attitudes that were conducive to the assimilation of the new theoretical wisdom. Although these two levels of change, institutional and theoretical, were largely independent, they did reinforce each other after World War II. Gradually, the business community became converted to a conservative version of Keynesian thinking, which was employed to rationalize government fiscal policies.[1] The details of this conversion will be discussed in Chapter 6. For the moment, we focus attention on the way in which World War II provided a ladder by which the country climbed from the depths of the Great Depression to an unprecedented period of prosperity.

CHANGES IN THE GREAT DEPRESSION

Under the banner of the New Deal headed by Franklin Delano Roosevelt, numerous changes were instituted in the 1930s. Among his reforms were unemployment compensation, aid to the aged, laws guaranteeing workers the right to organize unions, minimum-wage legislation, and tax policies designed to modify, however slightly, the unequal distribution of wealth and income. On another level, the New Deal accelerated the rise of a national bureaucracy, a centralized government with more economic power to influence the national economy. The dimensions of the Federal government were changed and enlarged to conform more closely to those of the corporate giants, with their national and international market links. The growth of these giants had been more or less completed by the 1890s. The political lag was a "mere" forty years.

As seen from a radical perspective, Roosevelt's reforms and programs tended to alleviate "the suffering of the depression's hardest-hit victims,"[2] but they did not provide avenues to a new, productive life commensurate with people's abilities and desires. As for the government's power to change the course of the business cycle, the measures that were taken over the decade of the 1930s had little effect. Again, in the radical view, "The normal business-cycle upswing of the 1930's, which lasted from 1933 to 1937, naturally brought the unemployment rate down, but only from 29.9 percent in 1933 to 14.3 percent, after which it shot up again to 19 percent in the sharp recession of 1938."[3] The seven years (1933–1940) of New Deal efforts can thus not be considered an overwhelming success in aggregate economic terms. Alvin Hansen, Harvard University's liberal Keynesian and key disseminator of the new economics, caught the mood of the depression decade with his "stagnation thesis."[4] He expressed the view that there are forces shaping the fate of the American economy that cannot be overcome simply by short-run government-induced deficits. Although the details of Hansen's interpretation have been rejected by most of his own colleagues, his thesis did reflect the spirit of the day.

THE FUNCTION OF GOVERNMENT

What would have happened to the American enterprise system in the absence of World War II is impossible to know. There are reasons to suggest that its history since then would have been very different. What we do know is that World War II abruptly terminated faltering New Deal economic policies. It was only after the injection of *warfare*, rather than *welfare*, expenditures that the economy was stimulated to full recovery. The wartime deficits ran to about $45 billion annually, in stark contrast to the

Table 5.1 • *Federal Taxes, Expenditures, and Deficits: 1942–1945 (in Millions of Dollars)*

YEAR	TAXES	EXPENDITURES	DEFICIT
1942	12,547	34,037	21,490
1943	21,948	79,368	57,420
1944	43,563	94,986	51,423
1945	44,362	98,303	53,941

SOURCE: *Economic Report of the President*, January 1965, p. 260.

$2–4 billion deficits that had seemed the "solution" promising full recovery throughout most of the 1930s (see Table 5.1).

Although most Keynesians refer to the World War II period to demonstrate that deficit spending, if large enough, will work, radicals see the New Deal failure and war period in a different light. They argue that the kind of massive governmental intervention that was really necessary during the depression, when real GNP was extremely low relative to the full-employment potential, would have further shaken the public's commitment to the already depressed and defensive private sector. Even the limited reforms and modest deficits of the New Deal, most of which fell within the confines of capitalist relations, tended to bump into all kinds of private business interests, which felt threatened. Joseph Schumpeter, a conservative in spirit, argued this point. He suggested that the reform tone of the New Deal, general governmental meddling, and specific intrusions into the domain of the private utilities in the form of the Tennessee Valley Authority (TVA) worsened the condition of an already uncertain and demoralized business class.[5] Businesspeople themselves confirmed this view when they expressed a preference for government deficits resulting from handouts to the poor over deficits that would create productive jobs. In their view, the government's paying the "dole" would not challenge the ideology of the private-enterprise system, "whereas government prevention of unemployment [through governmentally created jobs] threatens the businessman's position in the economy."[6]

In the radical view, the government's capacity to respond rationally in a crisis is always circumscribed by the needs of the private sector. That is, even when the government is not being narrowly manipulated by the dominant segments of the business class because of the presence of countervailing popular forces, the boundaries of governmental action are nevertheless determined by the capitalist economic structure. These boundaries involve a network of agencies, regulatory commissions, contracting procedures, and legal arrangements that have as their raison d'être the growth of private capital and its profitability or, when conditions are adverse, at least the minimization of their decline. If the government intentionally acted otherwise, it would worsen the state of the economy, produce more social unrest, and threaten the very fabric of the social order. A derivative function of the government is thus to legitimize the existing economic system through various kinds of social expenses. This entails a commitment to private enterprise, the pursuit of policies that do not compete with the mixed capitalist system, and the prevention of social unrest. Efforts in this last direction can take a variety of forms, ranging from co-optation by creating unproductive government jobs and political harassment to the use of direct force.

THE WAR AND ITS ECONOMIC SIGNIFICANCE

When the exigencies of World War II were upon us, large governmental deficits were mandated. But, for radicals, the big war deficits do not prove the Keynesian argument. They prove that deficits can bring about full employment without inflationary chaos *if* they are accompanied by price and wage controls, rationing, the establishment of enforceable production priorities for both the civilian and military sectors, and particularly an ideological commitment to planning machinery and planned levels of output and distribution. This commitment was assisted by the patriotism developed by the war. These elements, of course, are not included in the pure Keynesian vision of a government that guides private capitalism *indirectly* by means of deficits incurred during depressions, deficits that are "automatically" liquidated by budgetary surpluses during prosperous periods. But the Keynesian strategies for coping with depression, when rigorously applied, require a degree of state planning and intervention far removed from the formulations found in mainstream textbooks and journal articles. Recognition of this fact has actually still not penetrated the theoretical deliberations of mainstream economists.

Although, as practitioners of a trade, they yield to various kinds of income-control policies, in theory, they still oppose moves in such a direction.

It is not our aim to evaluate the relative success or failure of the government's specific mobilization efforts during World War II, the degree of corruption that prevailed, or the extent to which private businesspeople were able to maneuver themselves into position to advance their own interests and corporate connections. From the radical perspective, the experience of World War II revealed something more important: the extent to which the American economic system had failed, on the one hand, and its enormous potential for eliminating economic misery, on the other. In World War II we observed the incredible gap that prevailed between our actual economic performance just before the mass mobilization efforts and what we could have achieved with a different method of mobilizing resources and people.

Even in the absence of technological change, Robert Lekachman, a radical Keynesian, has pointed out that between 1939 and 1944

> the real value of the nation's output rose over 70 percent. Still more remarkably, private production expanded by over a half at the same time that the value of the government's ouput more than trebled and its share of total output rose from slightly more than 10 percent in 1939 to between [20 and 25 percent] in 1944.[7]

The American standard of living, measured in terms of civilian goods, had risen tremendously, despite the fact that large proportions of our human and material resources had been mobilized for military uses. Again, as Robert Lekachman, has observed:

> At the cessation of hostilities in 1945, some 11,410,000 men and women were in uniform. Nevertheless, the total civilian labor force numbering 55,230,000 individuals in 1939 dropped only to 53,860,000 in 1945. The numbers contain no mystery. The elderly, the maimed, and the drunken housewives, pensioners, and students turned out in millions at the call of patriotism and high wages. And suddenly there was no unemployment problem. By 1942 the rate was 4.7 percent, but in 1943 it was 1.9 percent and in the succeeding year a wartime low of 1.2 percent.[8]

We could add that thousands of rural, semiliterate southern black tenant farmers quickly responded to the call of the job market and located themselves in northern industrial war plants, without manpower studies and programs initiated and directed by government professionals.

Essentially, the unused resources of the American economy, which the price system could not mobilize, were of magnitudes beyond comprehension and imagination at the time. The war served as a real laboratory for demonstrating what economic planning, even in the context of capitalism, can accomplish.

The war economy, whatever its costs in human lives and anxieties to individual American families, was a boon to the American people as a whole. It provided economic mobility for many and rescued still more from starvation, destitution, and total demoralization. The hardship suffered by the Russian people, the horrors experienced by the European Jews, and the terror injected into the Japanese community at Hiroshima somehow bypassed the ordinary American. Here, at home, too many of us witnessed the military comeback of the Allied military forces like we watch the hometeam score a touchdown from its own five yard line. As we rooted for our side on the European and Pacific battlegrounds, we also ate more food and drank more beer than we had been accustomed to.

Whatever other factors may also have entered into our postwar attitudes toward the rest of the world, it was important that World War II was associated with the emergence of our "affluent society." The war and its aftermath, contrary to general expectations, launched the American economy on a remarkable boom. The 1950s marked, in a phrase coined by sociologist C. Wright Mills, a "Great American Celebration." And it was in this context that Keynesian wisdom was largely assimilated by the American presidency and the American business community. The culmination of this assimilation was reached in 1964, when President Lyndon Johnson's Keynesian economic advisers consciously maneuvered a tax cut without simultaneously decreasing government spending. This event, however, leads us to the subject of Chapter 6, in which we shall explore the contours of the post–World War II period.

NOTES

1. For a detailed history of this process, see Herbert Stein, *The Fiscal Revolution in America* (Chicago: University of Chicago Press, 1969).

2. Paul M. Sweezy and Harry Magdoff, "The Economic Crisis in Historical Perspective," *Monthly Review* (March 1975): 4. Copyright © 1975 by Monthly Review, Inc. Reprinted by permission of Monthly Review Press.

3. *Ibid.*

4. Alvin Hansen, "Economic Progress and Declining Population Growth," in *Readings in Business Cycle Theory* (Philadelphia: Blakiston, 1944).

5. Joseph Schumpeter, *Capitalism, Socialism and Democracy,* 3rd ed. (New York: Harper Torchbook, 1962), pp. 64–65.

6. Sidney S. Alexander, "Opposition to Deficit Spending for the Prevention of Unemployment," in *Income, Employment and Public Policy: Essays in Honor of Alvin H. Hansen* (New York: Norton, 1948), p. 197.

7. Robert Lekachman, *The Age of Keynes* (New York: Random House, 1966), p. 149.

8. *Ibid.*, p. 150.

THE GREAT
AMERICAN CELEBRATION: 1950–1964

In the post–World War II period from 1946 to 1950, considerable skepticism prevailed about the American economy's capacity to continue its performance at wartime levels. This skepticism was expressed by Congress in the Employment Act of 1946: In order to allay popular fears, the government assumed responsibility for maintaining full employment. As the bill provided no specific machinery to accomplish this purpose, it served merely as a moral commitment.

Among individuals there was the extreme example of Sewell Avery, who, as chairman of Montgomery Ward's Board of Directors, had absurdly piled up the liquid reserves of the company in preparation for the assumed imminent depression. His hope was that Montgomery Ward would be in an advantageous position to buy up its defaulting competitors as they went down with the crash, which only Avery himself would have had the foresight to withstand. A more common reaction was the admonition by Dean Acheson, Secretary of State under President Harry S. Truman:

> We cannot go through another ten years like the ten years at the end of the twenties and the beginning of the thirties. . . . We have got to see that what the country produces is used and

sold under financial arrangements which make its production possible. . . . We cannot have full employment and prosperity in the United States without . . . foreign markets.[1]

The general skepticism, although misguided in anticipating depression, was not totally ill founded. The cold logic of the Keynesian model, as we have already suggested, had failed as a practical weapon to pull the country out of its doldrums in the 1930s. Nevertheless, the war had established a new base upon which the national government could proceed to influence the economy. When the war had ended and the dust had settled, a new period in the history of American capitalism began.

THE BASIS FOR PROSPERITY

Many factors were operating to prevent a return to prewar economic conditions. They included the monetization of the national debt by converting the bonds held into an expansion of the money supply, the backlog of consumption needs unfilled during the war, the high rate of capital investment (especially in the Far West), the dramatic increase in military spending for the Korean War, and particularly Marshall Plan aid, which ensured extensive market opportunities for American capital in Europe. All these factors converged to generate and sustain a high level of aggregate demand relative to the system's production capabilities. By 1950 the realities of a prosperous and viable economy had finally overcome the public fixation on depression; the decade of the Great American Celebration was launched.

In crude statistical terms, the Gross National Product (in constant 1958 prices) rose from $355 billion in 1950 to $581 billion in 1964, an increase of 64 percent. In the same period, population increased only 26 percent. Real per capita GNP thus increased 29 percent, representing an average real growth of about 2.1 percent a year. This growth resulted in changes in real disposable income, which increased from $1,646 per person in 1950 to $2,123 in 1964.[2]

What had emerged was a new American economic profile. It had begun with the New Deal, in the form of partial innovations, and was fully developed by the mid-1950s. Guided by his Keynesian economic advisers, theory and practice combined by 1964 in the policies of the President.

For the typical mainstream economist, with his or her cautious, eclectic, and pragmatic outlook, the profile reflected basic structural changes: emergence of a more liquid economy associated with centralization of the banking system, elimination of reckless speculation on the stock market and the development of the Securities and Exchange Commission, the rise of a host of built-in stabilizers that acted to modify the business cycle, and the establishment of a high level of government spending and a set of fiscal policies conceived as independent of fluctuations in national income generated by the private sector. These institutional changes, along with the Keynesian revolution in economic knowledge, permitted the average technically oriented economists to put their faith in the short-run tinkering process, that is, in manipulation of the interest rate by means of the money supply and moderate adjustments in government spending and taxes. They enabled governmental authorities to proceed as if they could readily control the levels of employment and output through manipulation of a few aggregate variables and could thus control indirectly, or at least contain, any social unrest that might occur.

More popular versions of the new optimism emphasized the culmination of 100 years of industrial growth in a context of private enterprise.[3] According to this historic view, it was this growth that had produced more goods and leisure, sources of communication, cars and other means of transportation, and educational opportunities than existed in any other country in the world. Although some of the evils associated with industrial capitalism were admitted, it was argued that they had been corrected by such developments as social legislation, public services, trade-union activity, changes in the attitudes of businesspeople, and the logic of mass production itself. These developments had presumably produced a more nearly classless society, one in which income and status differences between rich and poor had narrowed to the point where the majority could be deemed members of the great middle class. Specific versions of this view were focused on such themes as the "corporate soul,"[4] "countervailing power,"[5] "new competition,"[6] and "people's capitalism."[7] Popular pundits drew optimistic conclusions, projecting their pet postwar "discoveries" into the indefinite future.

These views all reflected the development of a new "welfare liberalism" that was, in the radical view, essentially a rationalization of what had actually occurred. It was closely associated with the development of what we have already identified as the "mixed capitalist system." The political and social brokers of welfare liberalism generally argued that the "good society" had arrived, at least in the mundane sense of material comfort and related amenities, and that no valid argument could be made for fundamental change. To former political radicals, who were perhaps seeking to justify their own rapid assimilation into mainstream academia, the new state of affairs spelled the "end . . . of domestic politics for those intellectuals who must have idealogies or utopias to motivate them to political action."[8] The evidence justifying this new mood of domestic tranquillity was encapsulated not only in Keynesian logic and its derivatives but also in the new welfare institutions and optimistic "climate of opinion."

THE KEYNESIAN LEGACY AND WELFARISM

A purely theoretical model requires institutional soil in which to take root. As we suggested briefly in our concluding remarks in Chapter 4, Keynes's theory did much more than simply furnish a new theoretical edifice. It also provided an intelligent rationale for the existing institutional arrangements of the welfare state. Many seemingly unrelated matters—like subsidies, the dividend policies of large corporations, the moderately progressive Federal income-tax structure, and the waste of resources in the form of military spending and make-work projects—became unified in theory.

In addition, the Keynesian legacy did much to undercut the apparent social relevance of some concepts that had a great deal of ideological respectability among conservative business leaders and financiers. Such symbolic mainstays as thrift, budget balancing, and minimizing the national debt lost much of their political clout. Finally, notions like "taxing the rich and giving to the poor" and built-in welfare stabilizers were elevated from the status of moral affirmations to that of analytically sound procedures. The latter achievement, of course, met the practical needs of liberal Keynesians and social administrators. A brief discussion of both the conservative and liberal notions will perhaps serve to clarify the nature of the grand socioeconomic synthesis associated with the assimilation of Keynesian ideas and the development of a welfare society.

THE VIRTUE OF THRIFT

The "fallacy of composition"—the idea of saving for a rainy day, for old age, or out of habit—was attacked in the first chapter of almost every postwar economics textbook. It was pointed out that, when everyone seeks to save more of his or her current income, the result is decreased spending and therefore decreased income. A decrease in income induces less, rather than more, saving. The propensity to save was thus transformed from a social virtue into a general vice, at least under conditions of unemployment. What seemed rational for each individual was defined as irrational for the whole; hence the term "fallacy of composition."

BALANCING THE FEDERAL BUDGET

The ideas of symmetry and balance are deeply rooted in the "wisdom of the folk." Government deficits (unbalanced budgets) have often been associated with runaway inflation, fiscal irresponsibility, and gross waste of resources.[9] Keynesian reasoning undermined the fixation to balance the budget on a regular basis. Why must the fiscal budget be balanced every year? Why not every month? Every week? Every day? In fact, why does the government have to balance the budget according to guidelines from the planetary system? To Keynesians, the budget must be seen in relation to the overall state of the economy. The concept of a countercyclical budget emerged from Keynesian reasoning, and it nurtured the faith that the mixed capitalist system can achieve economic stability. It was to provide automatic guidelines for what are called "discretionary policies," that is, policies that do not operate automatically (as a thermostat automatically controls room temperature at some preestablished norm). Discretionary policies require deliberate spending decisions by the Federal government at appropriate times and in magnitudes appropriate to achieving economic stability at high levels of employment.

Although in principle it would be good if government deficits designed to mobilize unused resources were employed in useful projects—for example, in schools, hospitals, and libraries—in practice it is not necessary. In the view of mainstream Keynesians, the building of tanks to be stored in armories is functionally equivalent to the construction of hospitals: Both stimulate demand and employment opportunities through the multiplier.

The main point is that budgets do not have to be balanced at any particular point in time; reason dictates that they be balanced over the business cycle. Deficits at one stage and surpluses at another create a financial rhythm that can achieve a more stable and more smoothly performing economy. The budget, in other words, must be viewed as a means to a balanced economy and not as an end in itself. The Achilles heel of old-fashioned capitalism, its boom-bust-depression cycle, could presumably now be eliminated.

THE NATIONAL DEBT

Closely related to budgetary deficits are the concern about the size of the national debt and the popular fear of its alleged burden on future generations. Again, the common sense of the "folk" was transformed, in the hands of Keynesians, into common nonsense.

First, it was noted that it is not the absolute size of the debt that matters but its size relative to national income. When the national debt is viewed as a proportion of national income, that is, as part of a debt/income ratio, it becomes clear that over time the debt declines in quantitative importance in a growing economy. This point was made clear in the line charts printed in the President's annual economic report. Just as corporations with larger incomes can afford larger absolute debts, bigger countries with expanding outputs can supposedly afford absolute increases in the national debt.

Second, the folks who feared that big debts would eventually lead to bankruptcy were assured that no such thing would happen. A private debt is different from a public one. There are several reasons for this distinction: the Federal government has discretionary taxing power to raise income, it has many more sources of income than an individual corporation or family, and it has the power to create money. All these factors enable the Federal government to meet debt obligations in ways that are not available to private businesses or individuals.[10]

Third, Keynesian economists made a distinction between internal and external debts. Debts owed to a foreign country do put a burden on those future generations that politicians were customarily concerned about. Had we borrowed money from Mars in order to acquire resources to fight World War II, the postwar generation would have had to forgo income in order to repay the

Martians. But our actual internal debt is merely a debt owed to other Americans. The government borrows from Peter to pay Paul; it taxes Paul to repay Peter. Because we live in a democratic society and do not impose taxation without representation and because the "loans" are voluntary, internal debts cannot be conceived as a burden on anyone. Given these Keynesian rationalizations, the issue of the national debt ceased to generate much political heat.

INCOME EQUALITY

Keynesian wisdom taught that soaking the rich and giving to the poor is "functional"; it can be defended on "scientific" grounds, in addition to moral, ethical, or sentimental ones. That is, a move toward a more equal distribution of income can be justified because of its instrumental role in facilitating the performance of the economy. Given the need to maintain a high level of aggregate demand, Keynesians claim that a moderately progressive tax is good for business, as well as for the poor. Because the poor are assumed to have a higher marginal propensity to consume than the rich, changes in the tax structure that redistribute income in favor of the poor shift the consumption schedule upward. Such shifts stimulate business activity and the growth of national income by means of the multiplier. The poor should thus be helped, not only for ethical reasons, not only because the utility of a poor person's last dollar is greater than that of a rich person's dollar, but also because it is *functional* to help them. Economic conservatives can thus be appealed to on logical and "scientific" grounds and not solely on emotional and "value-laden" ones.

BUILT-IN STABILIZERS

The progressive income-tax structure, along with employment-compensation insurance and large corporations' dividend policies, were viewed by Keynesians as working in the same way as our thermostat. These stabilizers seem good, not only because they provide income security to various segments of the population, but also because they go to work *automatically* in ways that will allegedly prevent business recessions from turning into depressions and business upswings from turning into uncontrollable inflationary booms.

In analyzing the moderate nature of the first post–World War II recession (1948–1949) and what prevented it from being more severe than it was, R. A. Gordon, a well-known mainstream student of the business cycle, pointed to the effects that stabilizers had on sustaining disposable income:

> First, corporations maintained dividends despite a decline in profits. Second, some increase in unemployment . . . led to a rise in government transfer payments. And third, personal taxes were lower. Thus, disposable income declined much less than did the GNP. Consumption, however, did not fall at all. Instead, consumers reduced their savings and maintained their current rate of spending.[11]

Each of these stabilizing mechanisms will be explained briefly here. Corporations, because they tend to retain earnings, tend also to maintain steady dividend policies. Rather than paying maximum dividends in prosperous periods, when profits are high, and no dividends in recession periods, when profits are down, corporations generally pay moderate dividends at all times.[12] The dividend policies give corporations a source of capital and, at the same time, allegedly modify inflationary pressures during upswings and excessive deflation during downswings. In this way, during upswings demand is modified to prevent excessive inflation, and during downswings it is sustained to prevent excessive deflation.

In peak periods, when the work force is fully employed, workers have less money to spend because of their contributions to unemployment-insurance funds. In recessions, when they find themselves unemployed, insurance enables them to maintain their spending at higher levels than would be possible otherwise. Again inflationary-recessionary cycles are dampened.

Finally, because the Federal tax structure is moderately progressive, periods of boom mean that more people move into higher tax brackets, which holds down spending rates. In recessions, more people fall into lower tax brackets, and thus more money is available for spending.

What must be emphasized is the *automatic* way in which these mechanisms are presumed to counteract swings in the economy. Each functions without deliberate intervention by state managers. Mainstream economists have a great propensity to view such mechanisms in highly positive terms, since their automaticity avoids the lead-lag problems often characteristic of discretionary policies.

THE SOCIAL CLIMATE:
SELECTED IMPRESSIONS

The general acceptance of the welfare state, Keynesianism, and the emergence of the giant corporation as an enterprise run by clean-cut reasonable managers with M.B.A. degrees from Ivy League graduate schools converged in a postwar social atmosphere in which those from the vast middle layers of American society struggled energetically to climb career ladders. For adults who had managed to avoid being drafted in World War II, the period between 1941 and 1945 was an economic blessing, especially in contrast to the 1930s. They found lucrative occupations and established businesses that elevated their economic status and eliminated their de facto insecurities—however psychologically doubtful they may have felt about their economic fate at the war's end. As for the returning young veterans between the ages of twenty and forty years, they displayed a compelling drive to make up for time lost during the war. Given these predispositions, the traditional lure of success and material gain worked with a vengeance to produce a very narrow and limited social ethos for the vast majority of the American people from all walks of life.

In the context of relative affluence, some observers saw in this development the arrival of the bland society. Teamwork and "groupishness" replaced or seriously modified traditional values of "rugged individualism" and the willful madness of lonely genius. The price demanded for success was a calculated drive to belong and to work cooperatively with others, especially when "others" meant authorities. The ordinary citizen sought security. The formerly "rugged businessman" was now caught in an organizational complex. Surburbanites competed with other suburbanites in the game of imitation. Last, but not least, the younger generation was observed as being silent. In general, the 1950s were either periodically celebrated or simply described in terms of caution, careerism, and conformity. Few mainstream social scientists imagined that the mood would change precipitately and in ways that would challenge the institutions associated with the welfare-liberal capitalist state.

The picture sketched here is admittedly a caricature, and it could be radically altered by the inclusion of such events and phenomena as the Korean War (1949–1953), McCarthyism, the Berlin blockade, the Hungarian revolution, the media cynicism concerning President Eisenhower's inadequate grammatical syntax and golf course escapades, the U-2 incident, the impact of Sputnik, and the general fear of nuclear war. In the radical view, however, mainstream social scientists of the 1950s greeted these events and phenomena as exogenous to the American system. Except for the Russians' launching of their Sputnik satellite, events rarely stimulated serious examination of the internal workings of any major American institution.[13] In spite of many particular reasons for gloom or social action, the central domestic tendency of the 1950s, was at best one of general complacency. At worst it enabled a consequential minority of conservative groups and individuals to discard any serious criticism of the American social order as being subversive or communist inspired. In this regard, we must momentarily digress to discuss the alleged "communist menace" that haunted this period.

THE ANTICOMMUNIST CONSENSUS

A strange paradox of the 1950s, one that deeply influenced the history of the following decade, has not been, and perhaps cannot be, explained by writers who celebrate the period. In the midst of this complacent and prosperous decade, in which most Americans were preoccupied with the pursuit of material success and in which the Communist party, radical action groups, and radical thought in general declined to near oblivion in the United States, there was widespread obsession with an alleged subversive menace. This obsession was so incongruous with the reality that it becomes necessary to treat it as a kind of inexplicable myth that "somehow" gripped the American political mind. Carey McWilliams's observations on this point are most apt:

> The alleged communist issue has been investigated at every level, state, federal, and local, and in every walk of life, law, science, the ministry, education, the military, labor, industry, the arts, entertainment, the mass media—not once but again and again. . . . It has been "exposed" *ad nauseam*. . . . The phoniness of the issue has been ridiculed and satirized so often, and so widely, that our obsession with it has become an international stock joke. All the while . . . the sleuths of HUAC . . . [have] enormous difficulty in flushing out a few relics now and then to exhibit at [their] hearings.
>
> The American consensus on communism [was] so massive that the issue [was] not debatable; there [was] no "opposition" to debate it. The fact is that we debate[d] only the degree of

hatred that all proper Americans are expected to exhibit when the subject [is] mentioned. "Liberals" and "conservatives" alike campaigned on the "anti-communism" issue, which . . . [was] a cover for the lack of platform or program. . . . Yet in volume and weight it remain[ed] the most massive one in American politics—undebated, unchallenged, and meaningless. No better proof is available of the fatuousness of American politics [in the 1950s] than our underlying obsession with this non-issue.[14]

Although a detailed explanation of this deranged preoccupation with a nonissue is beyond the scope of our discussion, the matter cannot be entirely neglected. As we have indicated, the preoccupation with communism was a sort of collective pathology in American politics; it was not related to the actual threat of any domestic communist or even radical activity. In fact, in the radical view, it was the absence of a significant left-wing movement following World War II that made it possible for the American people to become obsessed with a fiction in their political and social lives! Nevertheless, this obsession served a very important function in ensuring consensus. It partially satisfied conservatives and nascent fascists who opposed the welfare state and so-called New Deal socialism. It partially satisfied anticommunist socialists, radicals, and reformers, all of whom had become completely disillusioned with the Soviet Union, Stalinism, and the Communist party of the 1930s. Anticommunism also partially satisfied postwar welfare liberals, who gave in to anticommunist pressures on the foreign front and supported right-wing tyrants in the Third World, in exchange for a few domestic welfare programs of limited scope. Last, but not least, it partially satisfied the needs of the military and business establishments, whose interests converged in the desire to police Third World nations, protect international trade patterns and investment interests, and maintain high levels of domestic demand.

SOME MAINSTREAM CRITICS: A BRIEF DIGRESSION

It is not our intention to argue that all mainstream economists viewed the postwar performance of the American economy with complacency. A few began to express some doubts in the late 1950s and early 1960s. They represented, for the most part, the liberal, left of center part of the mainstream. Although they were critical of specific aspects of American society, in the radical view, they never transcended the boundaries of the system and therefore never got to the root of the ailments that they identified and described.

Some professional economists, for example, doubted our apparent economic well-being and began to review the pattern of unemployment that had characterized the labor market from at least 1955. From approximately the mid-1950s to the end of the decade the peaks of prosperity were accompanied by abnormally high rates of unemployment, which suggested a tendency toward stagnation associated with a long downward swing in the economy. The problem was suggested by Moses Abramovitz, a highly respected economist of business cycles, at the 1959 hearings of the Congressional Joint Economic Committee:

> The rate of growth of output . . . has not been great enough to absorb the growth in the labor supply and in the stock of capital. We are passing through a period of low rate of growth, after allowing for business cycles, and it is in that sort of period that we begin to accumulate idle resources, both of labor and capital.[15]

Other professional economists, less concerned with the business cycle or creeping stagnation as such, focused on the issue of structural unemployment, unemployment that cannot be absorbed simply by the standard procedure of increasing aggregate demand. On the popular level, the structural question was presented as the possibility that automation would make less skilled members of the labor force completely superfluous. A more precise statement of this notion was provided by Charles Killingsworth, an economist who developed the structuralist view:

> The fundamental effect of automation on the labor market is to "twist" the pattern of demand—that is, it pushes down the demand for workers with little training while pushing up the demand for workers with large amounts of training. The shift from goods to services is a second major factor which twists the labor market in the same way. There are some low-skilled, blue collar jobs in service-producing industries; but the most rapidly growing parts of the service sector are health care and education, both of which require a heavy preponderance of highly trained people. . . . These changing patterns of demand would not create labor market imbalance, however, unless changes in the supply of labor lagged behind.[16]

Chronic long-term unemployment was observed to be a permanent condition for a significant part of the black population. The statistics showed that prosperous "full"-employment peaks did not absorb many of the blacks in the total labor force. Also economists discovered that many blacks were dropping out of the labor force and were therefore statistically unaccounted for in measures of black joblessness. This phenomenon resulted in serious underestimation of the precarious position of the black community. Welfare rolls often appeared to increase unabatedly in both prosperous and depressed periods.

To some social scientists, writing as general critics, the corrosive influence of affluence, which they associated with an over-developed private sector and an underdeveloped public one, became a critical issue. The epitome of this view was presented by John Kenneth Galbraith in *The Affluent Society*.[17] In one sense, this book represented an extension of the complacent mood established in the early 1950s; in another, it projected some doubts that proved justified in the middle and late 1960s. On one level, Galbraith was saying that the American system had "arrived"; we had solved all our broad domestic problems, although there remained specific pockets of misery. But these pockets were unique and did not lend themselves to general solutions; political or social movements would not eradicate them; rather, they called for the delicate instruments of specialists, for example, social workers and mental-health professionals. Galbraith was thus in tune with the "end of ideology" school, which tended to view most domestic problems in narrow technical terms.

On another level, however, Galbraith was arguing the views of a "creeping socialist" and succeeded in raising some very serious questions. The public sector needed bolstering, according to Galbraith, not because capitalism had failed but because it had succeeded. The private sector had produced such abundance that additional goods generated in this sector could not really provide satisfaction. In the jargon of the economist, he suggested that the marginal utility of goods produced in the private sector was approaching zero. Although most economists sneered at this assertion, Galbraith demonstrated his proposition by pointing out that producers have to use advertising to create wants that would not occur or be sustained naturally or spontaneously. The need to nurture such wants, to maintain a process of conditioning them, results from the "fact" that capitalism has fulfilled its historic mission, that is, the abolition of scarcity of the basic and urgent requirements for economic survival. From this reasoning, Galbraith mounted an attack on the conventional preoccupation with production to overcome scarcity. Unfortunately—and herein lies Galbraith's particular insight—affluence is created in the private sector at the expense of the public sector, which had now become critical to the survival of an overcrowded urban civilization. The public sector has a vital role and mission, and further increases in the productive capacity of the system must be absorbed for use by the state, which means that the public sector must grow both absolutely and relatively, thus increasing its control over the resources of the nation.

When Galbraith turned to the question of how this goal is to be accomplished, however, he became completely indecisive. He did not even recommend curbing, let alone eliminating, the influence and power of the private corporations, the main source of the artificial creation of demand and the resulting malaise that he had identified. Nevertheless, by relating the deficiencies of the public sector to the corporations that dominate the private sector, Galbraith touched the critical nerve center of the system.

Eventually, social scientists began to deal in more dramatic terms with such urban issues as school segregation, housing, and poverty. The level of anxiety escalated, at least among the more sensitive critics. Some of the better-known social scientists of the early 1950s who, though ritually critical of American complacency, had mainly concentrated on why and how our country had "made it," became preoccupied, in the 1960s, with foreign crises, nonconformity, violence, black poverty, and militarism. Moreover, the treatment of these issues more frequently took into account the "system," or structural rigidities in society, though the "system" itself was not always defined clearly and was never viewed as inherent in capitalism.

THE KENNEDY-JOHNSON YEARS

The terms of John F. Kennedy and Lyndon B. Johnson (1960–1968) represented the bringing together of all the main threads in the economic and political fabric of the 1950s: the culmination of anticommunist militarism, moderate liberal-left reformism, and conservative fiscal Keynesianism. It was welfare liberalism's postwar "moment of truth," but it was only a moment.

John F. Kennedy (1960–1963) opened the decade with campaign speeches that emphasized the need to "get the country moving again." This need arose from the fact that the country was in the midst of its fourth postwar recession, or "slow-growth period." Brought together in Kennedy's Council of Economic Advisors were the leading Keynesian economists of the nation, eager to test their ideas. The unemployment picture was, as we have indicated, mixed. Some unemployment was believed to be owing to a deficiency in aggregate demand; some was explained in terms of structural imbalances. To this domestic picture must be added the mythical "missile gap" and ferment developing in some Third World nations, which appeared threatening to American business interests abroad. An increase in military spending, moderate domestic-reform programs, and deficit spending reflected the political and economic pressures emanating from a public in conflict. A comment on each is warranted.

MILITARY SPENDING

Although purchases of military hardware had previously increased because of the "missile gap" (which, once safely inaugurated, Kennedy admitted did not exist), it was the Cuban revolution that was used to justify Kennedy's own appeasement of the military-industrial complex. "Pentagon capitalism," as Seymour Melman has called it, has an insatiable appetite for larger and larger budgets,[18] which help to feather the bureaucratic nest and seem most easily obtainable when the labor market is slack. There was also, perhaps, a truly felt need to confront directly the threatening insurgent nationalism of many underdeveloped countries. In any event, the now defunct Alliance for Progress was Kennedy's answer to the Cuban revolution. The Alliance represented an effort to lend vitality to the center in a polarized context; in the radical view, the center was not a viable position. This position was articulated by Walter Lippmann:

> We cannot compete with Communism in Asia, Africa, or Latin America if we go on doing what we have done so often and so widely, which is to place the weak countries in a dilemma where they will stand still with us and our client rulers or start moving with the Communists. This dilemma cannot be resolved unless it is our central and persistent and unswerving policy to offer these unhappy countries a third option, which is economic development and social improvement without the totalitarian

discipline of Communism. For the only real alternative to Communism is a liberal and progressive society.[19]

As if not wanting to take any chances, Kennedy supplemented rhetoric about the middle way with an interest in and growing endorsement of counterinsurgency warfare. He gradually came to see Vietnam as a place in which to test our capacity to block the revolutionary path to reform and nation building. He thus set in motion the bureaucratic momentum that would make direct, large-scale military intervention (which he was purportedly against)[20] inevitable.

Military spending, beginning in the short-lived Kennedy administration, continued to increase and, of course, escalated sharply as a result of our large-scale involvement in Vietnam, which commenced in 1965 during Johnson's presidency. By that time, the American social order was in the throes of dramatic conflict and change, which will be discussed in subsequent chapters. Our main object here is simply to underscore the ease with which military spending became the mainstay of a fiscal policy designed to maintain and increase aggregate demand. In the radical view, this consequence was no accident, nor did it reflect genuine threats from enemies abroad.

DOMESTIC REFORMS

On the domestic front, specific pockets of misery and the growing number of permanently unemployed workers in central-city black ghettos led to area-development programs and the Manpower and Training Act. Both were surpassed in importance by the passing of the 1964 Civil Rights Act and the launching of the Office of Economic Opportunity (OEO).

These programs were not radical, but they did capture the interest of various publics, like labor unions, blacks, welfare liberals, and some enlightened members of the business community. The job-retraining programs gave unions funds and *control* over aspects of retraining unemployed workers, especially those who were members of minority groups. The funds for these programs were carefully administered by union bureaucrats so as not to upset their rank-and-file white workers.

The OEO, which served mainly the black community, was more experimental. It was concerned not only with job retraining in the narrow sense but also with the whole gamut of instruments under the rubric "ghetto economic development." It brought together at various levels black proletarians, white and black middle-class professionals, and enlightened members of the business community.

Finally, the area-development programs boiled down to traditional outlays for highway construction. Their main virtue was that they met with few objections from the business community in the Appalachia region. Funding such programs required no new political avenues in Congress.

It is not our purpose to evaluate the relative success or failure of these varied programs. From a radical perspective, they represented only modest efforts by the welfare-liberal establishment to forestall a more radical approach that was emerging in the black communities and among the nation's college youth as a result of growing American involvement in the Vietnamese civil war.

DEFICIT FINANCING AND THE 1964 TAX CUT

According to Herbert Stein, chairman of former President Richard Nixon's Council of Economic Advisors, a fiscal revolution developed during the period from the early 1930s to 1964.[21] Contrary to the impression that is frequently conveyed in mainstream literature, this revolution was *not* in the American public's gradual acceptance of the Keynesian wisdom that deficits are the proper means of stimulating the economy and eliminating unemployment. As Stein has meticulously documented, the stimulating impact of deficits was understood reasonably well by economists and politicians even before Franklin Delano Roosevelt and the New Deal. Even when it was not understood and despite balanced-budget rhetoric among politicians, in actual practice there was reasonable tolerance of deficits during periods of unemployment. The real fiscal revolution, according to Stein, was a

> change in the content of deficit policy. The policy to which business objected in the 1930's was a *spending* policy, which carried with it both the fear and the fact of higher taxes. The policy of the 1960's was a *tax reduction* policy, coupled with the promise of expenditure restraint which would permit more tax reduction later. The opposition of conservatives, and particularly of businessmen, to tax increases and their support for tax reduction has been one of the reliable constants. The revolution was as much a switch of policy to conform to this constant

conservative thinking as it was a change of conservative thinking.[22]

The 1964 tax cut without a corresponding change in government spending was the culminating event in the fiscal revolution. It represented not a change in basic ideas and the conception of fiscal deficits per se but a change in the way that deficits can be generated and made palatable to conservatives and businesspeople.

In a cautious speech before the conservative Economic Club of New York in 1963, President Kennedy's chief economic adviser, Walter Heller, had celebrated the success of Keynesianism: "I gave them straight Keynes and Heller, and they loved it."[23] But Stein, a man much closer to the conservative and business community, had another (and, in the radical view, more nearly correct) interpretation of Heller's success:

> [Heller erroneously thought] that the main issue with the conservatives related to budget-balancing and Keynesianism. . . . But by 1962 this was not the issue, at least not with the conservatives of the business community to be found in the Economic Club of New York. The issue was tax reduction, particularly reduction of those taxes which affected the return from investment most directly, and expenditure restraint as a means to future tax reduction. In these terms . . . the Economic Club was getting not only congenial language but also some real benefits.[24]

For our purpose, the details that led to the actual tax cut in 1964 are not important. The principle had been endorsed by President Kennedy before his death. Deficits were more or less commonly recognized as a practical necessity and had been tolerated by a long line of presidents since 1930. But they became ideologically "official" when businesspeople finally endorsed their use. In a peculiar way, the conservative Stein unwittingly confirmed the power of a simplified Marxian view of the relationship between ideology and the business class. In any event, it was conscious acceptance of a deficit achieved by means of a tax cut, articulated by President Kennedy and implemented by President Johnson, that capped the postwar performance that we have chosen to call the Great American Celebration. What followed this celebration represents a different phase of American economic and social history and will be examined in subsequent chapters. At this juncture, we shall proceed to tie some of the elements of our exposition together and to make some concluding observations.

THE MIXED VOLUNTARY SYSTEM

The heart of the mainstream justification of the mixed capitalist system is the belief that it is shaped by relatively free and *voluntary* decisions in an open society in which monopoly power is not so excessive as to warrant breaking it up or allowing the government to take it over. People who produce and sell services do so voluntarily and possess alternatives. Private owners of the means of production operate under sufficient competitive pressure to check *extreme* abuses of power, at least in the long run. The government's purchases of goods and services are ultimately determined by an election process in which individuals are reasonably free to mandate such purchases. Workers are free to change their occupations, and, perhaps more important, individuals as consumers are free to allocate their incomes to suit their autonomous value systems. However imperfect these processes are, the possible alternatives all appear worse. Critical *moderation* is the best of all alternatives.

What this view often means in practice is an endorsement of "realistic" measures, which appear, in the radical view, to mean simply expediency and opportunism. The "reality" syndrome is perhaps best illustrated by the attitude of many mainstream economists toward inflation and growth. Recognizing that it is impossible to achieve simultaneously steady growth, stable prices, and full employment and recognizing that a redistribution of income involves many difficulties, they have opted for inflation and growth. It has been observed by Robert Lekachman that:

> Inflation benefits the more enterprising members of the community, among them housing developers, land speculators, industrialists happy to borrow dollars and repay their property and mortgage burdens which are a diminishing percentage of the rising value of land and structures, and stock-market investors eager to share the gains to be derived from a bull market. By contrast, deflation dampens business activity and discourages assumptions of new risks. Old debts become more burdensome and new ones less desirable . . . unsold inventories decline in value. For new investment the outlook darkens, economic growth stutters and stops, [and] . . . unemployment spreads through the economy.[25]

It is no accident that emphasis on inflationary growth is often seen by mainstream economists as the only *practical* alternative to "solving" problems within the system. As Leonard Ross and Peter Passell have pointed out:

> [D]uring the 1960's continuous economic expansion raised more men and women above the poverty line than all the Great Society programs lumped together. If a steady dose of inflation is the only recipe for growth, and growth the only hope for the poor, then men of good will may opt for inflation—if they are convinced that the costs of inflation are really lower than those of slower economic growth.[26]

Inflationary growth thus appears to eliminate the struggle among various segments of the population over the distribution of the national product, for it enables the *absolute* size of each individual share to rise. In the radical view, it provides a way of removing the dirt from the house by sweeping it under the rug.

Mainstream economists are essentially saying: "As long as the economy appears to be functioning reasonably well (it was never expected to function perfectly), we shall find reasons to justify its continuation and to dampen our criticisms. Although inflation is still an unresolved problem, it does not appear to be out of hand. Although there is room for change and criticism, our recommendations, in view of the absence of proven alternatives, will be moderate and more or less within the boundaries of the given system." Working within the institutional and ideological boundaries of the system is, of course, what it means to be a mainstream economist.

NOTES

1. Dean Acheson, quoted by W. Appleman Williams, *The Tragedy of American Diplomacy* (Cleveland: World, 1959), p. 148.

2. *Economic Report of the President*, 1974.

3. See F. L. Allen, *The Big Change* (New York: Harper & Row, 1952).

4. A. A. Berle, Jr., *The 20th Century Capitalist Revolution* (New York: Harcourt, 1954).

5. J. K. Galbraith, *American Capitalism: The Concept of*

Countervailing Power (Boston: Houghton Mifflin, 1952).

6. D. E. Lilienthal, *Big Business: A New Era* (New York: Harper & Row, 1952).

7. V. Perlo, "People's Capitalism and Stock-Ownership," *The American Economic Review*, 48 (1958): 333–347.

8. S. M. Lipset, *Political Man* (Garden City, N.Y.: Doubleday, 1960), p. 443.

9. J. K. Galbraith, *The Affluent Society* (Boston: Houghton Mifflin, 1958).

10. It should be pointed out that local and state governments also do not enjoy these advantages; their deficits may thus be more serious.

11. R. A. Gordon, *Business Fluctuations* (New York: Harper, 1952), p. 443.

12. John Lintner, "Distribution of Incomes of Corporations Among Dividends, Retained Earnings, and Taxes," *The American Economics Review*, 46 (May 1956): 97–113.

13. The Russian Sputnik was the first satellite to encircle the earth. It became a symbol of Russian technological sophistication and the quality of the Russian educational system. Given the tension and competition in relations between the United States and the Soviet Union at the time, Sputnik stimulated a profound examination of the American educational system. This examination led to frequent attacks on "progressive education" and its alleged nefarious influence on the public school system; Sputnik became the excuse for a right wing attack on welfare-liberal social scientists whose intellectual roots went back to the New Deal period.

14. Carey McWilliams, "Time for a New Politics," *The Nation*, May 26, 1962, p. 461.

15. Testimony of Moses Abramovitz, in U.S., Congress, Senate, Joint Economic Committee on Employment, Growth and Price Levels. Hearings Before the Joint Economic Committee, 86th Congress, 1st session. April 7–19, 1959, pp. 406, 412, 414.

16. Testimony of C. Killingsworth, in U.S., Congress, House. Committee on Education and Labor. Subcommittee on Employment and Manpower, 88th Congress, 1st session, September 20, 1963, pp. 1475–1479.

17. Galbraith, *The Affluent Society*.

18. Seymour Melman, *Pentagon Capitalism* (New York: McGraw-Hill, 1970).

19. Walter Lippmann, quoted in Norman Podhoretz, "America and the World Revolution," *Commentary*, October 1963, p. 278.

20. R. J. Barnet, *Intervention and Revolution* (New York: World, 1968), p. 212.

21. Herbert Stein, *The Fiscal Revolution in America* (Chicago: University of Chicago Press, 1969).

22. *Ibid.*, p. 74.

23. Walter W. Heller, *New Dimensions of Political Economy* (New York: Norton, 1967), p. 35.

24. Stein, *The Fiscal Revolution*, p. 420.

25. Robert Lekachman, *Inflation* (New York: Random House, 1973), p. 76.

26. Quoted in *ibid.*, pp. 86–87.

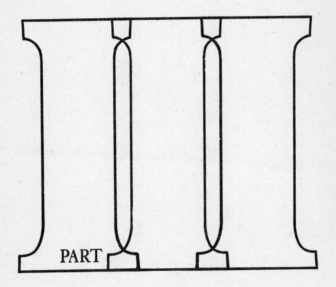

PART III

ORIGINS OF CONTEMPORARY
RADICAL POLITICAL ECONOMICS

Radical political economics has deep roots that go back, at least, to the socialist writings of Karl Marx. We shall undertake a more detailed discussion of Marx's contribution in Chapter 9. First, however, we think it is appropriate to develop a counterview on some of the broader issues and ideological questions raised in our discussion of mainstream economics. In this chapter we are concerned with some of the factors that have brought about the recent revival of radical political economics. Admittedly, our discussion is concerned mainly with the events and issues that have forged a "climate of opinion" conducive to critical thought. In Chapter 8 we shall address ourselves specifically to the question: What is the scope of radical political economics?

RACE AND METROPOLITAN AREAS

As far as the black people's drive for equality is concerned, the decade between 1954 and 1964 can be described as having begun with a struggle for civil rights and a belief in integration and having concluded with civil disorder and a commitment to some form of racial separatism. The years following the Supreme Court school-desegregation decision in 1954 were marked by such events as the bus boycott in Montgomery, Alabama, led by Martin Luther King, Jr., in 1956; the dispatch of Federal troops to Little Rock, Arkansas, in 1957; the organization of the 1958 and 1959 civil-rights marches on Washington, D.C., by Bayard Rustin; the lunch-counter sit-ins in Greensboro, North Carolina, in 1960; the emergence of organizations like the Student Nonviolent Coordinating Committee (SNCC) and the Mississippi Democratic Freedom Party; the organizing of the Lowndes County, Alabama, voter-registration drive; and finally, the mushrooming of the highly publicized freedom rides, accompanied by "blood and death."[1] These efforts culminated in the 1964 Civil Rights Act, a measure aimed at improving the legal and social status of the black people.

Although these civil-rights struggles were by no means in vain, they fell short of their target. There soon developed an awareness that the problems facing the black people and other oppressed minority groups were deeper than the questions of voting rights and illegal discrimination in the market. As disillusionment with the aftermath of the civil-rights movement grew, black militancy took the form of calls for black power and nationalism. Paralleling these ideological and political tendencies, black violence on a large scale erupted against the authorities and established routines in almost all the major cities of the nation. These violent eruptions (or "rebellions" as they were sometimes called) brought to the attention of the public and the government the plight of inner-city black workers: their low levels of employment and income and their sense of general alienation. All these problems formed the subject of an historic document, *Report of the National Commission on Civil Disorders*,[2] in which American society was indicted for institutional racism.

An indirect consequence of the riots and of this report was a more general indictment of the pattern that had come to define the American city and its surrounding suburbs, known as "the metropolitan area." The distribution of economic activities (industries and job opportunities) between the older central cities and the newer suburbs had produced a great imbalance, which in turn led to much greater problems than urban sprawl, commuting, and peak-load congestion at rush hours. The exodus of wealth from the central cities had destroyed their tax bases, but the necessity for local revenues had meanwhile increased. Many major cities were approaching bankruptcy. Differences in class and race were now viewed as intertwined with institutional divisions that deeply influenced the functioning of local government. Social scientists of various persuasions began to envision the possibility of a complete breakdown of urban life as it then existed.

THE STUDENT MOVEMENT

In 1958 there had developed at the University of California at Berkeley an undergraduate radical activist group called SLATE. Imitators soon sprang up at a number of other major colleges and universities throughout the country.[3] Shortly after, the Fair Play for Cuba Committee was formed for the purpose of preventing the United States from destroying the Cuban revolution that had been led by Fidel Castro. At about the same time, a massive and successful demonstration was conducted against the House Un-American Activities Committee (HUAC) hearings in San Francisco. Although the demonstration ended when students were hosed and "dragged by the hair down the marble steps of the . . . courthouse,"[4] the committee never recovered to carry on its smear tactics again. As a by-product of this struggle against HUAC, "a lurid documentary . . . produced by the committee in cooperation with the F.B.I." appeared. It was "countered by a very different version by the American Civil Liberties Union."[5] When the two films were shown together on campuses throughout the country they had considerable educational impact.

In 1962 the Students for a Democratic Society were organized and drafted their now famous Port Huron statement, which had a socialist message. Although the Vietnam War was not at that time a primary concern among students, it did receive some attention. But as more students had their lives interrupted by the military draft to participate in a war effort that was perceived as unjustifiable, the war's escalation in 1965 triggered the involvement of large numbers of middle-class white students and graduates, many of whom had already been active in various protest movements in the late 1950s and early 1960s. Students throughout the nation were suddenly faced with interruptions of their career plans. The unpopularity of the war combined with other negative feelings about American society and college life to produce campus explosions.[6] Consequential numbers of students and younger faculty members at major universities and colleges debated in public basic questions about the viability of the American social order and its relation to the private-enterprise system. In the process, a minority of students and teachers turned, or perhaps returned, to the socialist writings of Karl Marx for inspiration. Some of the teachers were economists trained at the best graduate schools in the nation. Book publishers, witnessing a change in the academic climate, wasted little time. In their haste to capitalize on new market opportunities, they eagerly sought out radical economists and published a flood of books on corporate power, military uses of resources, poverty and racism, and the role of government in reflecting, rather than checking, the interests of the dominant business class at the expense of workers and the underprivileged. Whatever else the radicals may have accom· plished, they certainly widened the arena of public debate on economic and social problems, especially in the major universities and colleges.

THE ECOLOGY QUESTION

In the late 1960s an ecological concern about the whole preoccupation with growth economics that dominated the post–World War II years (1946–1970) developed. Mainstream economic reasoning that comfortably equated material standard of living with general happiness or welfare was seriously scrutinized. The ideas of zero population growth and negative, or "ill fare," output like noise, air, and water pollution as by-products of normal production began to capture the interest of larger audiences. Although some maverick mainstream economists reacted rather dramatically to the ecological problem by projecting the possibility of planetary disaster in the next fifty to one hundred years under present growth rates,[7] the more cautious reacted by developing a new statistical calculation of GNP that involved subtracting the ill fare goods and services produced.[8] Their emphasis on growth was not altered; the new calculations of GNP meant simply that real growth is less than apparent growth.

The concern for ecology produced even greater despair when mainstream economists began to contemplate the industrialization of underdeveloped countries. During a good part of the 1950s and the early part of the 1960s, these same economists had blissfully assumed that the Third World would solve its basic problems by means of growth and development, preferably along capitalist lines. Suddenly, in the late 1960s, this optimism turned sour. It was not uncommon to read admonitions

> that in all probability the presently underdeveloped countries are not going to develop. There is not enough of everything. There is not enough copper. There is not enough of an enormous number of elements which are essential to the developed economy. If the whole world developed to American standards overnight, we would run out of everything in less than 100 years.[9]

The author of this prediction concluded his pessimistic deliberations with a poem:

> With development extended to the whole of planet earth
> What started with abundance may conclude in dismal dearth.
> And it really will not matter then who started it or ran it
> If development results in an entirely plundered planet.[10]

Radical economists reject the way in which many critics of growth raise the ecology question. In the radical view, Third World social scientists are correct when they note bitterly: Having exploited us for more than two centuries, having made us into dependent territories, having destroyed our traditional societies without replacing them with modern ones, you now inform us that modernizing to solve our problems of poverty and misery will be detrimental to the survival of the already modernized capitalist countries.[11] Radicals view the mainstream approach to ecology as expressing a desire, explicitly or implicitly, to "freeze" present relations between capitalist and Third World nations, without asking whether the capitalist mode of production is inherently antithetical to serious ecological considerations.

In retrospect, the total impact of these developments—the black upsurge in the context of urban structural problems, the Vietnam War, the growth of the student movement, the emergence of radical economics, and the rise of sustained anticapitalist insurgency movements among Third World nations—has affected the deliberations of mainstream economists. Their doubts about numerous theoretical matters and practical remedies have deepened and spread.

THE CONFIDENCE FACTOR

The final reason for the growth of radical political economics has been a decline in confidence among mainstream economists themselves. This decline has been noted by Nobel Prize-winning Wassily Leontief:

> . . . an uneasy feeling about the present state of our discipline has been growing in some of us who have watched its unprecedented development over the last three decades. . . . The uneasiness . . . is caused . . . by the palpable *inadequacy* of the scientific means with which [economists] try to solve [practical problems]. . . . The weak . . . empirical foundation clearly cannot support the proliferating superstructure of pure . . . economic theory.[12]

It is a bit ironic that an empirical, pragmatically oriented, and problem-solving economic profession should find itself in a state of tension over the fact that its theorizing has grown very far from empirical validation and problem solving. Although the explanation of this state of affairs is complex, we believe it consists of at least three parts.

First, as mainstream economics has become increasingly specialized and distinct from other disciplines (even to the extent that its subdivisions create further specialties), mainstream economists have tended to talk more and more to themselves about less and less. What constitutes a problem, or a way of talking about an issue, has increasingly been determined within the professional club. The club itself, moreover, has become highly stratified, so that ways of handling issues tend to be determined by a small elite group at the top of the pyramid; those of lesser rank follow as obedient troops.[13] Ways of looking at issues or problems (relevant as well as irrelevant) have thus grown independently of public scrutiny and debate. Economic modes of reasoning have taken on a life of their own, a life somewhat insulated from the actual economy.

Second, economists, like other professional groups, have been eager to acquire scientific status for themselves and their discipline. They have thus sought to define their subject matter in ways that would give it logical rigor, make it value-free, and lead to quantitative research with high-powered statistical tools. This last preoccupation has involved defining economic problems to fit the means of measurement or the method, rather than developing measuring devices and methods to meet the problems. As a result, quantitative procedures and tools, which should be viewed as means, have become ends in themselves. In fact, the very way that data were processed and refined by methodological devices to test models derived from pure theory has itself become a theoretical game about processing data; even so-called mainstream empiricism has become less empirical.[14]

Finally, both the first two tendencies are "safe," in that they tend to avoid the complexity of the real economy and discussion of the power element implicit in economic life.[15] To talk about oligopoly or monopoly power in very narrow market terms, as mainstream economists are prone to do, is to ignore a great deal of what is necessary to understand the actual American economy and its relation to the social order.

In any event, our concern here is not about whether the theoretical edifices of mainstream economics will remain more or less intact with many cracks or will come tumbling down in a dramatic crash. That some basic aspects of mainstream theory are being doubted by leading members of the economic establishment affords radical political economists an opportunity to reach a larger audience than at any time since World War II. Thus it is not insignificant that the *Wall Street Journal* (February 11, 1972, p. 1) entitled a recent lead article "The Unorthodox Ideas of Radical Economists Win a Wider Hearing" or that *Business Week* (March 18, 1972, p. 72) featured a piece headed "Radicals gain professional chic. Their academic status rises as their critique of capitalism gains depth and new listeners."

Whether or not radical economists are gaining professional chic or acquiring more status is less important than the fact that they are challenging mainstream views about the subject matter of economics and how the American economy works. To understand this point, we must delve into the subject matter of radical political economics itself.

NOTES

1. See Charles Perrow, *The Radical Attack on Business* (New York: Harcourt, 1972), pp. 8–9.

2. U.S., National Commission on Civil Disorders, *Report of the National Commission on Civil Disorders* (New York: Bantam, 1968).

3. Perrow, *The Radical Attack*, p. 9.

4. *Ibid.*

5. *Ibid.*

6. The causes of campus unrest in those years were far more complex than we have suggested here, but it would simply take us too far from our main focus to explore the matter further.

7. See Kenneth Boulding, "Fun and Games with the Gross National Product," quoted in *The Environmental Crisis*, ed. Harold H. Helfrich, Jr. (New Haven: Yale University Press, 1970).

8. See Paul Samuelson, *Economics*, 10th ed. (New York: McGraw-Hill, 1976), p. 4.

9. Boulding, "Fun and Games," pp. 166, 170.

10. *Ibid.*, p. 170.

11. See Hans-Magnus Enzensberger, "Critique of Political Ecology," *New Left Review* 84 (March–April 1974): 3–31.

12. Wassily Leontief, "Theoretical Assumptions and Nonobserved Facts," *The American Economic Review*, 61 (March 1971): 1.

13. Benjamin Ward, *What's Wrong with Economics* (New York: Basic Books, 1972), pp. 8–9.

14. See Barbara Bergmann, "Economist, Poll Thy People," *The New York Times*, November 3, 1974, p. 14.

15. John K. Galbraith, "Power and the Useful Economist," *The American Economic Review* 63 (March 1973): 1–11.

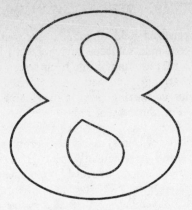

THE SCOPE OF RADICAL
POLITICAL ECONOMICS

Defining the scope of radical political economics is more complex than identifying some of the events and conditions that have stimulated its emergence. For purposes of clarity, we have divided our discussion into seven parts.

HISTORICAL DYNAMICS

Unlike their mainstream counterparts, who accept the broad institutional constraints of the existing system, radical economists are interested in the structural *transformation* of society. They have a strong interest in what is known as "historical dynamics," the "framework within which the economic process takes its course. This kind of historical dynamics lies outside [mainstream] economic theory. . . . In historical dynamics one is interested in different types of environment, and in problems of the transition from one type of environment to another."[1]

Because radical political economists assume the inevitability of change and the transformation of systems, they are necessarily preoccupied with comparing systems (socialism versus capitalism, slavery versus feudalism, preindustrial versus industrial capitalism, and so on). Such comparisons are not a peripheral interest relegated to a specialized field of inquiry and ranked low in the hierarchy of economic subjects; they reflect an interest arising from the belief that it is impossible to understand any particular set of economic arrangements without comparing them to alternatives or without comparing present developmental stages with previous ones. For this reason, radical economists tend to view many aspects of the economic process as transitional: Systems, evolutionary phases within systems, even programs advocated by radicals themselves are frequently viewed as transitional, appropriate to particular stages of social development.

As a result, radicals see themselves as on a historical journey to end, rather than to stabilize, capitalism; they are working for the establishment of a socialist society that will involve participatory planning, public ownership, elimination of production for profit, and a genuinely egalitarian redistribution of income and wealth. They view theorizing, not as an end in itself or as a ritual of rigorous elegance, but instead as integral to their advocacy of fundamental change and to their analysis of barriers obstructing such change. Economic analysis must deal with problems of political and economic power; rarely are solutions only technical in nature, unrelated to the established goals of given institutional arrangements. Radical economists are therefore devoted to providing a theoretical basis for social transformation; their politics is aimed at producing a political and ideological climate that will stimulate institutional changes.

INTERDISCIPLINARY KNOWLEDGE

Most radicals believe that understanding the economy requires a knowledge of history, including not only economic data but also the relation of those facts to noneconomic data and thus to the social sciences in general.[2] The social and political structures of society impinge upon the economic variables. Without knowledge of these noneconomic spheres, our analysis of the economic processes would be seriously limited.

It is not surprising, then, that contemporary radical economists have been shaped by influences of a different type from those that have shaped mainstream economists. In addition to a handful of older Marxists or radicals, like Paul Baran, Paul Sweezy, Harry Magdoff, Maurice Dobb, Joan Robinson, and Ernest Mandel (all of whom bring interdisciplinary knowledge to their analyses of the economy), a number of thinkers in other fields—for example, Herbert Marcuse (philosophy), William Appleman Williams (history), and C. Wright Mills (sociology)—have had important influence on contemporary American radical economists.

PLANNING

Whereas mainstream economists tend to view planning, especially centralized planning, as authoritarian and antidemocratic, radicals find such a view to be a gross oversimplification. They argue that we already have a great deal of planning and regimentation in the economy but that it is mainly corporate planning for private ends by an oligarchy that is hierarchical, self-perpetuating, and largely invisible.

The role of private corporate planning has been the subject of the most recent best-selling books by John Kenneth Galbraith.[3] Although radicals do not accept many details of Galbraith's thesis, they do accept its general contours. He argues essentially that the economy is dominated by large corporations that are responsible only to themselves. Because the magnitude of output and of investment necessary to production are enormous, corporations *must* plan future sales and prices; the planning is carried out by the corporation's organizational bureaucracy, which Galbraith calls the "technostructure." Planning in this instance also means manipulating consumers, by means of advertising, to want what they do not need.

The goal of the technostructure is growth, and success brings power, status, and large salaries. To ensure growth, the technostructure must further plan (and use its influence) to persuade the government to establish foreign and fiscal policies designed to ensure adequate demand and to provide abundant funds for technological research. The overall consequence of the totality of private corporate planning is a society in which environmental quality and human decency have been obliterated in favor of the commercial needs of corporations.

Radicals argue that public planning, in contrast to the present corporate variety, would broaden both participation and the arena of public control over the economy. Most radicals favor decentralized forms of socialist planning, with decisions being made as much as possible at the local level and with citizen-consumer and worker-producer groups deciding what and how to produce. Many radicals fear centralized control—whether by large corporations, wage-price control boards, or a GOSPLAN under state socialism. Decentralization is, in fact, a critical element for many radical political economists because they believe that the concept of "production" should encompass not only goods and services but also the work process itself and how enterprise relates to the environment. They believe that a socialist government acting as a mediator among various groups and sectors can bring about a social harmony that will lead to a more humane and less oppressive society.

POLITICS AND ECONOMIC POWER

Radicals see an intimate relationship between the political apparatus that governs society and the economic concentration of private power. Except in periods of mass agitation, the typical role of government is not to direct but instead to reflect or further the interests of wealth and concentrated economic power.

As competition has declined and been replaced by forms of oligopoly and monopoly, it has become necessary not only to talk about price policy in terms of collusive market strategies and tactics (which mainstream economists do) but also to explore systematically how oligopolies and monopolies use their economic power outside the market (which mainstream economists do not do) in order to "circumvent the market," "alter the data of the market," "modify the principle of market behavior," and "influence the scope for extra-market operations."[4]

The need to shift the focus in analyzing the nature of giant oligopolies and monopolies was stated effectively some years ago:

> The fact is that when we enter the field of rivalry between oligopolistic giants, the traditional separation of the political from the economic can no longer be maintained. . . . [Given the world scale of oligopolistic interests] we have . . . to conclude that a theory of oligopoly can be complete and relevant only if its framework includes *all* the main aspects of the struggle for security and position. It follows: *The oligopolistic struggle for position and security includes political action of all sorts right up to imperialism. The inclusion of these "non-economic" elements is essential for a full explanation of oligopoly* [and monopolistic] *behavior and price.*[5] (emphasis in the original)

In essence the link between the business and political spheres cannot be treated incidentally (as mainstream economists are prone to treat it) if economic relations and their consequences are to be understood.

DISTRIBUTION OF INCOME AND WEALTH

Because the connection between economic and political power is regarded as crucial, radical political economists assert that any basic understanding of the American social order requires careful analysis of the distribution of income and wealth, as well as of its generation and transmission over time. Radical analysis reveals gross inequities in distribution, as suggested by statistics frequently reported not only in professional journals but also in more popular business publications:

> . . . in almost every year since 1947, the poorest fifth of American families has received only about 5% of the country's total family income while the top fifth got 42%—an 8:1 ratio. . . . From 1949 to 1969 . . . the gap between average real incomes of the poorest and richest fifths of the population widened from less than $11,000 to more than $19,000 in constant 1969 dollars. . . . According to the latest available survey, the top 20% of consumer units . . . owned 77% of all wealth. . . . The richest 2.5% of U.S. families own 44% of all private assets, while the poorest 25% have, on the average, no net worth at all—their total debts just equal their assets.[6]

The relationship between income and wealth is shown more systematically in Table 8.1, which shows not only that wealth increases with income but also that the proportion of the wealth invested in income-earning assets also increases steadily. One well-known student of the distribution process has noted that

> Nearly all the current large incomes, those exceeding $1 million, $500,000, or even $100,000 or $50,000 a year, are derived in fact from old property accumulations, by inheritors—that is, by people who never did whatever one is required to do . . . in order to assemble a fortune.[7]

To radicals, differences in income and wealth are more than mere facts reflecting differences in command of goods and services among individuals and groups. They also provide an overall

Table 8.1 • Income Levels, Wealth, and Investment

INCOME	WEALTH	PERCENTAGE OF WEALTH INVESTED IN INCOME-PRODUCING ASSETS
$10,000–14,999	$ 28,021	28
15,000–24,999	62,966	37
25,000–49,999	291,317	42
50,000–100,000	653,223	43
Over 100,000	1,698,021	69

SOURCE: Dorothy Projector and Gertrude Weiss, *Survey of Financial Characteristics, Federal Reserve Technical Papers,* August 1966, p. 10. Cited by Howard P. Tuckman, *The Economics of the Rich* (New York: Random House, 1973), p. 10.

measure of status. Sustained differences suggest human experience that statistical tables obscure.

Stated in the broadest possible terms, sustained differences in levels of income and wealth mean differences in life chances that prevail in a particular society. Life chances, in contrast to "things," include health care, education, longevity, information about employment opportunities, acquisition of knowledge unavailable through general education, and superior social contacts. Most important, they include the ability of the ruling class to transmit its position of power from one generation to another. In Marxian terms, sustaining differences in wealth, as well as accumulating further wealth, involve reproducing the class relations that define the system itself.

Sustained differences in income also suggest differences in individual power to initiate change and manipulate the environment in ways that would eliminate myriad obstacles that clutter normal individual living arrangements. They mean variations in the ability to withstand unpredictable disturbances in the economic and social environment. The *quality* of an individual's reactions—his or her range of alternatives—is tempered by his or her current and expected future income. If there is a threshold of inability to react to disturbances and to make correct decisions, a threshold of despair, it is reached sooner at lower levels of income and wealth.

The notion of threshold is important in radical thinking; it changes the meaning of Paul A. Samuelson's Eiffel Tower image of our income-distribution profile: "If we made an income pyramid out of child's blocks, with each layer portraying $1,000 of income, the peak would be far higher than the Eiffel Tower, but almost all of us would be within a yard of the ground."[8] The general impression conveyed by such imagery is that 99 percent of the American people are in very much the same boat, one in which distinctions in social rank are minuscule, and the remaining 1 percent exist in some rarefied atmosphere above us all. Although the latter impression may well be true, the differences among the 99 percent who do not rise more than a yard from the ground are far greater than implied.

The income profile of a nation can be viewed from another perspective. Is a difference of $1,000 in income between two families much to worry about? Should a difference of $5,000 be of concern? No answers can be formulated unless such questions are raised in a more elaborately defined context. To use an analogy, suppose that two children measure respectively 4 feet 7 inches and 4 feet 9 inches from the floor to nose level. Is this a big difference? As numbers and averages go, the answer may be no. Suppose, however, that the two children are tied to a pole inside a tank in which the water level is expected to rise to the level of 4 feet 8 inches; what does the difference mean now? In the context of a rising water level, it may well mean the difference between drowning or not.

It should be clear from our discussion that the meaning of sustained differences in income and wealth can easily be obscured unless we transcend a purely statistical presentation. Differences at some levels are not simply differences between whether a family buys a car every four or every two years. At some threshold levels they are differences between being socially viable or not. It may be that the majority of the American people are within one "income yard" in statistical terms, but if one-third of the population is a foot below the water line and two-thirds are a couple of feet above it, there is nevertheless a significant difference between the two groups. Being a little above rather than a little below the poverty level can mean a large qualitative difference in the real lives of people.

From reasoning of this kind radical economists argue that the unequal distribution of income associated with an unequal distribution of wealth begets an unequal distribution of political power. The government, in behalf of the state, is not a neutral entity standing above warring interest groups; instead it displays systematic biases. Radicals find it necessary to examine not only what questions are raised but also what questions are omitted if the boundaries of a system dominated by business and property are to be understood.

Radicals think it is necessary to point out that American businesspeople typically come from business, rather than from professional, farming, or working-class families. This fact does not, of course, mean that there is zero upward mobility in the United States, but it does mean that those who are black, chicano, Indian, or of working-class origin have very limited chances of achieving business success. Even in the realm of the equal opportunity to become unequal (an idea that is not in principle anathema to American capitalism) rules of social inheritance arising from stratification and differences in power (an area that mainstream economists tend not to explore) are critical, for they help to determine the allocation of people in the job market.

Inequities in the economic sphere not only influence the political values, objectives, and policies of the government in ways that curtail social and economic justice; they also obstruct the ability of the economic system to recognize and solve its problems. In the radical view, the system is intrinsically flawed by the nature of its hierarchical structure, associated with differences in wealth and income, and not simply by the absence of "good" people in Congress or the presence of a "bad" president who does "wrong" things. Because mainstream economists either ignore or treat casually the relationship between political power and economic concentration, they do not come to grips with the nature of the system's policy failures. Deliberately overlooking such interconnections, radicals believe, leads to *poor*, not *pure*, social science.

MASS PARTICIPATION

The normative goals that guide the thinking of most radical economists are mass participation in decision making and the equal sharing of society's income and wealth. In practical terms, these goals imply different social relations in the spheres of production and minimum economic differences within a framework that recognizes variable aptitudes, tastes, and temperaments among individuals. This vision of society involves rejection of the idea of individual gain without general gain or loss for the group; it stresses the importance of moral over economic incentives.

This notion is probably best expressed in terms of a principle of "solidarity." The individual works to further group interests that he or she *consciously* understands. In the radical vision, group competition is not completely eliminated; it is assumed that political and social restraints can be devised to prevent such competition from resulting either in anarchy or in the domination of some groups by others.

Radicals argue that community solidarity is impossible under capitalism for a variety of reasons. The single and most important one is the division of society into a distinct economic sphere, on the one hand, and a political one, on the other. Moreover, the economic sphere is dominated by a relatively small elite that owns and controls the means of production, viewing all other aspects of society as instruments and therefore as objects of manipulation to sustain and enhance the economic position of the elite itself. As the economic sphere is private, fragmented, and characterized by continuous rivalry, a common ideology necessary for governing never enters into the psychic life of individuals. In a capitalist society, relations in noneconomic spheres are viewed as means (rather than ends) in the production of commodities for profit. In this way, capitalism as a system obscures the importance of social relationships and enhances the significance of "things." Competition for "things" becomes the determinant of the community's fate.

Moderate social critics of the American scene often ascribe the American people's obsession with "things" to "materialistic" values, a proposition that is manifestly true. But these values, it must be noted, are not viewed as determined by the nature of the economic system. A serious analysis of the source of the value system is simply outside the boundaries of mainstream economic thinking.

From a radical perspective, values are a product of relationships people form at the point of production, which in turn affect income distribution, whether consumption styles are individualistic or collective, and the division of society into rival status groups. If consumption decisions were less private and more collective, if the distribution of income and wealth could be more nearly equal, if political and social life were integrated with motives for work and economic existence, then the consumption habits of the American people would be fundamentally altered.

Their attachment to "things" would be different. Moderate mainstream critics do not take their argument this far, and therefore their criticism (however harsh in tone) is limited and deficient.

In a different vein, the "rational" use of private profit by the owners of capital, given the maturity of our economic system, perpetuates an ever-widening gap between our technical means of providing a healthy and sane life for everyone and the alienating social relations that thwart more humane use of these technical capacities.

The solidarity principle leads radicals to reject the mainstream conception of efficiency, which is defined in purely economic and technical terms and which necessitates inequality as a stimulant to work. In contemporary American capitalism, the important force that keeps the system functioning "efficiently" is the maintenance of inequities, which generate fears of falling behind and stimulate desires to get ahead. In the radical concept of a good society, "efficiency" has far more than an economic meaning. It also involves self-realization through the work process, the worker's control over his or her own work space, and a belief that the consumer goods being produced are necessary and important to a good life. Economic efficiency is not conceived as a separate dimension completely divorced from other critical elements that make up the social system. Private economic motivation, which is divorced from the question of distribution and from other noneconomic matters, breeds great social inefficiency ("diseconomies" in the mainstream jargon), which mainstream economists consider only incidentally. In the radical view, a reconstructed set of economic arrangements would require the meshing of economic and noneconomic motives.

THE QUESTION OF HUMAN NATURE

Many of the beliefs described here arise from a more encompassing view among radicals of the process by which individuals are socialized, what motivates them, what defines their welfare and well-being, what constitutes their potential for development and growth. Simply put, the rock upon which almost all mainstream economic thinking rests is the belief that individuals are naturally acquisitive and motivated primarily by their narrowly defined economic interests. What is lacking in this view is a recognition of the extent to which each individual's emotions and values are also socially determined. Because of these beliefs, mainstream economists obscure both the true potential of the individual and the social nature of economic problems in our society.

Human nature, in the radical vision, has a general and a specific component that must be understood if the individual's full potential is to be realized. On the general plane, the human being is viewed as a social animal. This does not mean that he or she is by nature "good" or "groupish." It means that the human organism is not born with all the biological equipment necessary to survive and grow as an independent entity. A relatively long maturation period is necessary for him or her to learn the "rules of the game." The acculturation process comes from and is sustained by intense interaction between the individual and organized society, with its language, symbols, customs, rewards and punishments, and modes of control. Motivation and patterns of activity are nurtured *through* social relations. The vulnerable infant thus requires a "social life and a system for learning correct behavior. . . . The group is the locus of knowledge and experience far exceeding that of the individual member."[9]

Although individual assimilation of the social equipment necessary to survive is dependent upon the socialization process, the collective capacity for survival is not—at least in the mechanical sense—limited by the characteristics of the natural environment, especially as the group accumulates superior modes of social organization, knowledge, and better tools and artifacts for coping with the exigencies of nature. As nature becomes an object of control and the group acquires a surplus significantly greater than what is necessary for minimum subsistence, nature becomes less a determinant in the mechanical sense. Social limitations become increasingly related to the nature of the society itself, which leads us to the specific component of human nature that concerns radicals.

Every system has a historically specific structure that breeds a historically specific notion of human nature that the dominant classes generalize as universal. In this way, the system acquires justification in terms of the "natural" characteristics of people rather than in the more tenuous and changing structure of the system. In other words, the particular concept of human nature under capitalism serves to maintain its class characteristics. But this maintenance of the system is not without its contradictions. As the structure of capitalism evolves and changes into a more independent system, its original notion of human nature tends to remain fixed for reasons of ideological necessity. Thus, radicals typically argue that mature capitalism is now racked by tension that involves a highly socialized and integrated system of production, on the one hand, and an individualistic notion of human nature, on the other. In the radical view, the ramifications of this discrepancy will eventually nurture alternative notions of human nature as the struggle to change capitalism unfolds.

Implicit in the radical argument is the assumption that "man . . . is infinitely perfectible. Man's *essential* powers—his latent and potential human powers—are unlimited in their capacity for development."[10] Why, the radical asks, are an individual's potential humaneness, generosity, and lovingness greater than his or her display of such qualities? The answer lies in the nature of social relations determined by the economic system. Changing the economic system will thus change the nature of social relations, which, in turn, will close the gap between the individual's actual and potential development. In this sense, most radicals display a utopian streak in their approach to the world.

In a market-dominated society not only are cars deliberately produced with built-in obsolescence in order to keep the wheels of profit rolling, not only is the environment polluted without regard for its value to those who want to breathe clean air and love the beauty of a natural terrain, not only are the "mere" sentimental value of landmark buildings and the security associated with stable neighborhoods destroyed for the construction of "efficient" superhighways needed by industry—but also human morality, sexuality, and sensibility are all manipulated for the purpose of selling commodities. American capitalism destroys human relations in order to maintain purely economic ones involving gain, "getting ahead," and the private accumulation of things. To allow the market so much importance in the determination of each individual's lifestyle is to acquiesce to a one-dimensional view of human nature.[11]

DEFINING RADICAL POLITICAL ECONOMICS

On the basis of the seven propositions described, radical political economics is defined. We can do no better than to reproduce Karl Marx's oft-quoted passage from *A Contribution to the Critique of Political Economy:*

In social production which men carry on they enter into definite relations that are indispensable and independent of their will;

these relations of production correspond to a definite stage of development of their material powers of production. The sum total of these relations of production constitutes the economic structure of society—the real foundation, on which rise legal and political superstructures and to which correspond definite forms of social consciousness. The mode of production in material life determines the general character of the social, political and spiritual processes of life. It is not the consciousness of men that determines their existence, but, on the contrary, their social existence determines their consciousness. At a certain stage of their development, the material forces of production in society come in conflict with the existing relations of production, or—what is but a legal expression for the same thing—with the property relations within which they had been at work before. From forms of development of the forces of production these relations turn into their fetters. . . . With the change of the economic foundation the entire immense superstructure is more or less rapidly transformed.[12]

But an abstract definition of economics can acquire flesh and blood only in the context of a real economy. As a preliminary to this effort, we must familiarize ourselves in detail with the Marxian schema itself. Because the influence of Marx has been so important in the shaping of the views of radical political economists, we shall first develop a reasonably orthodox statement of his contribution before examining it in relation to the contemporary contours of American capitalism and its various specific problems.

NOTES

1. Erich Schneider, *Pricing and Equilibrium* (New York: Macmillan, 1952), p. 186.

2. See Paul M. Sweezy, "Modern Capitalism," *Monthly Review* 23 (June 1971): 1–2.

3. John Kenneth Galbraith, *The New Industrial State* (Boston: Houghton Mifflin, 1967);

John Kenneth Galbraith, *Economics and the Public Purpose* (Boston: Houghton Mifflin, 1973).

4. E. Ronald Walker, "Beyond the Market," in *Power in Economics*, ed. K. W. Rothchild (Harmondsworth, Eng.: Penguin, 1971), p. 44.

5. K. W. Rothchild, "Price Theory and Oligopoly," in *Readings in Price Theory*, eds. George J. Stigler and Kenneth E. Boulding (Chicago: Irwin, 1952), pp. 462–463.

6. *Business Week*, "More Money, But the Shares Stay the Same," April 1, 1972, p. 56.

7. Ferdinand Lundberg, *The Rich and the Super Rich* (New York: Bantam, 1969), p. 155. Cited by Howard P. Tuckman, *The Economics of the Rich* (New York: Random House, 1973), p. 9. This statement is somewhat misleading. According to Lester C. Thurow, among fortunes of more than $1 million, "about half are inherited and about half are what [is called] instant wealth." Instant wealth, it should be noted, is derived not from hard work or patient saving and reinvestment "but by operating in the financial markets to take advantage of 'disequilibrium' in rates of return on capital investment." It is a matter, first, of a lucky strike and then of capitalizing on it in markets that are not competitive. Thurow, "Tax Wealth, Not Income," *The New York Times Magazine*, April 11, 1976, p. 32.

8. Paul A. Samuelson, *Economics: An Introductory Analysis*, 10th ed. (New York: McGraw-Hill, 1976), p. 84.

9. Joan Robinson, *Freedom and Necessity* (New York: Pantheon, 1970), p. 15. We do not mean to imply that biological variations are irrelevant or that the infant is infinitely malleable. The extent of individual variations within relatively homogeneous groups or larger societies cannot be explained completely by the social context in which learning occurs. Infants display at birth significant variations related to biological endowment, which may manifest themselves as variations in behavior and thinking within a general social order. Our point here is that the factors that differentiate basic lifestyles connected with different modes of seeking a living are not biologically determined.

10. Irving M. Zeitlin, *Ideology and Development of Sociological Theory* (Englewood Cliffs, N.J.: Prentice-Hall, 1968), p. 84.

11. See Karl Polanyi, *The Great Transformation* (New York: Rinehart, 1944), Chapter 6; Herbert Marcuse, *One-Dimensional Man* (Boston: Beacon, 1965).

12. Karl Marx, *A Contribution to the Critique of Political Economy* (Chicago: Kerr, 1904), pp. 11–12.

THE SPIRIT AND LOGIC
OF THE MARXIAN SCHEMA

Joseph Schumpeter has pointed out that Karl Marx was not only an economist but also a sociologist, a philosopher, a historian, and a prophet.[1] Although Schumpeter justifies compartmentalizing Marx's contribution into these various specialized parts, he recognizes that in so doing we may be denying the unity of Marx's view of the world. We will explore this question of unity at the conclusion of this chapter.

Understanding the Marxian schema is not easy. There are several reasons other than its obvious complexity; Marxian analysis is multidimensional, interdisciplinary, and concerned with the dynamics of whole systems as they change over time. We shall begin by designating the four major areas of Marx's endeavors, which made him the most important and influential social scientist of the nineteenth century.

First, Marx explored the evolution of human society from its primitive state to the present. This perspective leads Marxians to interest themselves in the nature of precapitalist systems and transitions from one stage to another. It forces them to take history seriously, for incorporating evidence about early societies, their evolution, and their breakdown determines the universality

127

of some Marxian propositions and the validity of Marxist notions about capitalism itself.

Second and more important than the general evolution of civilization is the actual historical transition from feudalism to capitalism. Marxists believe it is more important because understanding the genesis of capitalism as a system is critical if its nature and functioning are to be understood in the profoundest sense. This view is analogous to the Freudian view that the adult personality, although influenced and shaped by contemporary events, cannot be properly understood without analyzing the first five years or so of the person's life. Predictions about a system cannot be made simply from current variables. We need to know the history of past reactions and adjustments under a variety of circumstances.

Third, Marx was concerned specifically with the historical unfolding of capitalism itself, a focus that manifested itself in concrete examination of particular capitalist countries and their characteristic features. He developed an abstract model of the inner workings of capitalism, in which we find a rich interplay between the theoretical and the concrete, the economic and non-economic elements.

Finally, Marx was interested in changing capitalism, in abolishing it. His specific notions about how systems change led him to concentrate on basic contradictions within capitalism, for such contradictions, he believed, lead to breakdowns and the emergence of new systems. There is thus a tendency in Marxian reasoning not only to note contradictions but also to press them to their logical limits in order to "prove" the inevitability, or at least the strong probability, of the breakdown of the system. For purposes of clarity, countervailing tendencies are often left out of accounts.[2]

Marx anticipated that the breakdown of capitalism would bring socialism, a system whose seeds had already been sown. In this sense, his conception of socialism was not simply a moral creation or an abstract idea. It was, of course, both of those things too, but above all it was a vision spawned by the conditions of alienation and periodic breakdown assumed to be inherent in capitalism. Marxian programs and forms of agitation are thus aimed not at restoring the health of capitalism or at improving its normal functioning but at directing workers and their allies toward conscious pursuit of a socialist system, the presumed next stage in society's development.

The metaphors used in Marxian thinking to illuminate underlying relations in the four areas that we have emphasized are taken from biology, mechanics, and chemistry. First, systems are viewed in developmental terms: birth followed by stages of growth, maturity, and decay. Second, every system operates according to laws that can be abstracted from concrete relationships. The parts of the machine are believed to work in accordance with a few logically consistent principles. Marx's claim to have discovered the "laws of motion" controlling the capitalist system is explained by the metaphor of the clock, a familiar and popular image in the eighteenth and nineteenth centuries. Finally, he emphasized how the elements of a system are related and combined to produce something qualitatively different, how they can be exploded or synthesized to form compounds in which they are no longer recognizable in their original form. Dialectics is basically a process by which contradictory quantitative relationships are transformed qualitatively.

It was not without reason that Schumpeter remarked, in reflecting upon the Marxian framework, that it is the only one that has sought—even if not always successfully—to inject life into the "ghostly concepts of theory." The Marxian schema, Schumpeter wrote,

> without losing its logical quality . . . is no longer a mere proposition about the logical properties of a system of abstractions; it is the stroke of a brush that is painting the wild jumble of social life. Such analysis conveys not only richer meaning of what all economic analysis describes but it embraces a much broader field—it draws every kind of class action into its picture, whether or not this class action conforms to the ordinary rules of business procedure. Wars, revolutions, legislation of all types, changes in the structure of governments, in short all the things that non-Marxian economics treats simply as external disturbances do find their places side by side with, say, investment in machinery or bargains with labor—everything is covered by a single explanatory schema.[3]

What is the Marxian framework? What are its parts? How does it explain the details of the capitalist process? In answering these questions we shall find a kind of counterpoint to the orthodox, or neoclassical, economics developed in the nineteenth century, the modern version of which we discussed in Chapter 2.

The Marxian schema is, in the most general sense, derived from

Marx's definition of political economy (see Chapter 8). It consists of three elements: superstructure, relations of production, and forces of production (see Figure 9.1). These elements, it should be noted, can be used to discuss any economic system: feudalism, slavery, socialism, and so on. We shall discuss them in connection with competitive capitalism only as it is generally assumed to have prevailed in the nineteenth century.

Our procedure will be to discuss each part of the Marxian schema separately in order to elucidate some basic concepts. These concepts will then be used to explain the motion of capitalism as a whole, especially as Marx expected it to evolve through time.

THE SUPERSTRUCTURE

The superstructure consists of the state, with its network of government agencies—executive, legislature, judiciary, police, army, and so on—and socializing instruments of society—mass media and educational institutions—that produce legitimizing ideology.

THE STATE

The capitalist state has both defensive and offensive functions vis-à-vis the business system and society. It seeks to prevent the economic system from self-destructive conflict among individuals and businesses by mediation through the judicial system and, if necessary, by enforcing judicial decisions through the police. The state serves as a "power of last resort" in maintaining general commitment to the social order.

The state's offensive function includes furthering conditions enabling the business system to expand. For example, it generates property rights, provides subsidies, and finances development of the infrastructure needed to carry on business. The capitalist state, viewed from the Marxian perspective, is a weak and relatively dependent structure. Its power, as we shall argue, is linked to the business system, which dominates the economy, which in turn dominates society.

The notion of the state should not be confused with the substantive activities of government, in the same sense that the notion of God should not be confused with the workings of the church. As an idea that carries ultimate authority, the state transcends the

Figure 9.1 • The Marxian Schema

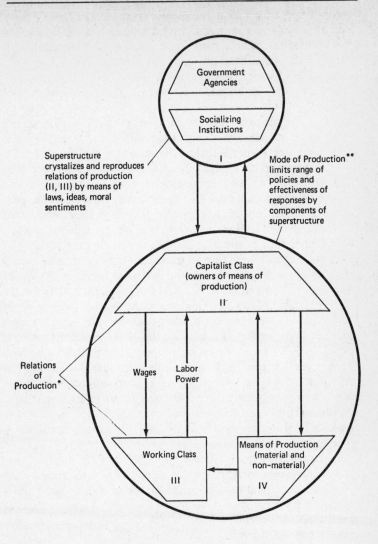

Superstructure crystalizes and reproduces relations of production (II, III) by means of laws, ideas, moral sentiments

Mode of Production** limits range of policies and effectiveness of responses by components of superstructure

Government Agencies

Socializing Institutions

I

Capitalist Class (owners of means of production)

II

Relations of Production*

Wages

Labor Power

Working Class

III

Means of Production (material and non-material)

IV

*Interaction between capitalists themselves; between capitalist and workers; between workers themselves

**Consists of interaction among II, III, and IV

ebb and flow of actual governmental routines. The overall function of the capitalist state is to reproduce conditions conducive to the survival and development of the business system that dominates the economy. In so doing, it also helps to maintain the larger social order of which the economy is a part.

Even in the democratic state, which presumably draws its power from the electorate, claims to legitimacy and ultimate monopoly rights over the instruments of violence to maintain the social order are connected with the needs of the dominant capitalist class (see Figure 9.1, II). The laws that the state enforces, laws that tend to crystallize relations between dominant and subordinate classes in the economy (see Figure 9.1, I), are commonly said to be adopted on behalf of the community, society, the general welfare, and the national interest. However they are justified in principle, they tend in practice to promote conditions necessary to maintain class relations in production (see Figure 9.1, II and III). State agencies are thus instruments of the propertied classes that dominate the social order. In this view, Marx was in agreement with John Locke, who defined political power "to be the right of making laws . . . for the regulating and preserving of property," and Adam Smith, who claimed that "civil government . . . is in reality instituted for the defense of the rich against poor, or of those who have some property against those who have none at all."[4] Yet the instrumental role that some Marxists emphasize should not be interpreted—as mainstream economists are prone to do—to mean that the state has no life of its own, that it simply mirrors class relations and cannot initiate contradictory policies, or that it always favors the capitalist class in its decisions. The reality is more complex.

Although the agencies of the state are interested in preserving and maintaining a social order that is conducive to the functioning of the economy and its domination by the capitalist class, at various junctures there may develop some variance between requirements for the general stability of the social order and the particular economic needs of the capitalists. For example, in the administration of justice it may sometimes be necessary to deny capitalists some market freedoms because such denial may be essential to preserve a general commitment to the social order among the population.

In a slightly different vein, when serious differences arise within the capitalist class, the state is called upon to act as mediator. In this role, it may acquire a certain degree of functional autonomy and may therefore initiate laws and rules to expand its own power, as well as to serve the interests of the capitalist class. Although there is no simple relationship between the ways in which the state perceives and acts and the needs of the dominant class, Marxists assume that, in any period of time, there is some identifiable limit beyond which the capitalist state—however democratically run by elected representatives—cannot be pushed without drastically upsetting the basic class relations defining the economic system. Insofar as the state functions to preserve the social order or acts as mediator, it has a degree of autonomy. But this autonomy is circumscribed, and the state is compelled to manifest systematic class bias in its policies and execution of them. It should be noted that the state does not always recognize the objective interests of the capitalist class. Some of its behavior may prove in retrospect to have been detrimental.[5] Our point is simply that the *intention* behind the state's activities is generally to preserve capitalist relations.

On those occasions when the state appears to have intervened in behalf of the subordinate classes, a type of occurrence that Marxists do not deny, it does so in order to maintain the conditions necessary to the capitalist system. Legalizing the eight-hour day is an example. Many capitalists opposed it, yet most of the working class desired it. The intervention of the state on behalf of labor was aimed not only at preventing class tensions from disrupting social stability but also at increasing the general productivity of labor and thus the efficiency of the entire capitalist system. The latter result is not something that any single capitalist could have accomplished alone. The change in the work day had to apply to everyone simultaneously if each individual was to achieve his or her portion of the benefits.

It should be emphasized that Marxists make no claim that every state action can be explained in terms of class relations. Some problems are only minimally connected with the functioning of the capitalist system, for example, enforcing laws about which side of the street automobiles must drive on. But, insofar as the state is concerned with laws and practices affecting the status of the capitalist class, Marxians seek to describe its central tendencies, on the one hand, and the causes of certain changes in those tendencies, on the other. What is defined as threatening or permissible for the dominant classes changes over time. Universal suffrage, for example, was perceived at various points in the nineteenth century as a threat to property and capitalist hegemony. When this perception proved incorrect—or, rather, when the situation changed so that the implications of universal suffrage were altered—permissible political reform was seen as possible.

IDEOLOGY

The superstructure is also the source of dominant values and prevailing ideas, cultural and religious sentiments, and educational practices, which are promulgated by institutions like the mass media, churches, schools, and universities (see Figure 9.1, I). This part of the superstructure nurtures the ideological climate in which individuals are socialized to the economic relations that define the capitalist system. To say, for example, that the woman's role is to produce in the home (outside the market system) is another way of saying that the economic system does not require her services at the point of production. As class relations alter the needs of the dominant class, socializing institutions also change; old ones are modified, and new ones are created to reflect changes in production relations.

Sometimes old ideas that have been dormant acquire new life. In the early part of the nineteenth century there were not too many New England textile-mill owners who publicly expressed concern about women who were neglecting their children by being away from the home. Women were too important a source of cheap labor. Even though forging a new view of working women was "not . . . appealing to a largely agrarian population with a coherent conception of women's role," the emerging manufacturing system lost little time in developing a new rationale for its labor needs.[6] But, at a later juncture, when consumer demand became a more important focus of capitalists, pious statements about the role of women in their homes became more common among those who dominated the economy.

The superstructure can thus be viewed as the factory in which the propertied classes produce, nurture, assimilate, and perpetuate ideas, which are embodied in the "language of politics, law, morality, religion, [and] metaphysics."[7] These ideas are derived from and used in connection with actual social processes, in particular, the relations that define capitalists and workers at the point of production.[8] They are used both analytically and morally to legitimize the behavior of the economic system.

RELATIONS OF PRODUCTION

Production relations (Figure 9.1, II, III) consist of the exchange by the property-owning classes of wages for labor power, the workers' capacity (mental and physical) to perform services. Two aspects warrant particular attention here: the interaction between capitalists and workers, on the one hand, and among capitalists themselves, on the other.[9] Although these two kinds of inter-actions are distinct and governed by different rules, they influence each other. Competitive pressures among capitalists themselves, for example, determine the intensity of the conflict between capitalists and workers.

CAPITALISTS VERSUS WORKERS

In the Marxist schema attention is focused on only two classes: those who receive their income from owning and controlling the means of production (like land, factory buildings, and machinery; see Figure 9.1, II) and those who receive their income from selling their labor power (Figure 9.1, III).

Before proceeding further we note that the term "class" will be reserved here for workers and capitalists; all other segments of the population will be designated as groups, as strata, or by oc-cupational labels (doctors, lawyers, teachers, self-employed, and so on). A full explanation of this scheme would take us too far astray at this juncture. Suffice it to say that, for Marx, class was inseparable from the *conflict* that he believed inherent in the very nature of capitalist relations. Class is not a mere descriptive cate-gory of possible positions that an individual might occupy in an economic system. On the contrary, it reflects a *relation* that defines the historically unique qualities of the system. Many dif-ferent systems may have doctors, lawyers, petty shopkeepers, and so on, but only capitalism has propertyless workers whose incomes take the form of wages paid by private owners of the means of production.[10]

To emphasize the two classes is not to suggest that Marx ignored the existence and relevance of other strata of the popula-tion: craft workers, small shopkeepers, peasants, self-employed professionals, salespeople, clerks, and the like. In real economic and political turmoil, he knew, these segments, along with the wage-earning class, *have* to be taken into account.[11] His two-class model was not meant to be a description of capitalist society; on the contrary, it was intended as an analytical tool employed to show how the exploitation of workers by capitalists in the sphere of production helps to explain the origin, growth, and function of complex reality.[12] For the purpose of explaining the broader dynamics of the system and its logical properties, Marx focused his attention on the relation between the owners of capital and propertyless workers. He saw the capitalists dominating an alienated laboring class. The businessperson's capacity to dominate the relations between himself or herself and the workers is derived from the control of production through ownership of capital or the means of production (Figure 9.1, IV). Even the worker's initial employment opportunity is determined by a capital advance from such an owner.

Ownership enables the individual capitalist to appropriate the surplus output, defined loosely as output greater than what is necessary to reproduce the working class. For example, a laborer who works eight hours may receive a real wage equal to that for four hours' work, if that is all that is necessary to maintain his or her working energy and abilities. The additional four hours of work are unpaid labor time, the proceeds of which are appropriated by the individual capitalist. The ratio of unpaid labor time to paid labor time is, in Marxian terms, the rate of exploitation, or the rate of *surplus value*. "Surplus value" is a technical term, not a moral statement about the condition of the working class. A laborer's wage may be high or low; what is critical is that he or she works more hours than necessary to sustain himself or herself. The amount of real income received is equal to some average sustenance necessary for reproduction and not to the amount produced from the hours worked. Private ownership, in addition to allowing the individual businessperson to exploit the worker, also permits him or her to make the numerous decisions associated with the production process, that is, to set the pace (intensity) of work, establish work conditions, choose whether to hire or fire, determine the rate at which capital will be accumulated or new techniques introduced, and decide whether to move or to remain in any given location.

The relationship between capitalists and workers, as indicated in Figure 9.1, II, III, is only the surface reality, based on the visible, quantitative exchange that takes place in the marketplace; exchange relations—for example, the wages that labor receives for services rendered and the price of X relative to Y—are the typical preoccupation of mainstream economists. But, for Marx, the exchange relation conceals the fact that the average worker employed in a representative firm is a source of unpaid surplus, which is appropriated by the capitalist because of the power derived from ownership of the means of production. This ownership is a right that is legally sanctioned and maintained by the superstructure. For Marx, it was more essential to explore the source of the surplus and the nature of its appropriation than to explain exchange relations among business enterprises and between workers and capitalists. The extraction of surplus is a *qualitative* dimension in the worker's relation to the capitalist. It is, as we shall discuss in more detail later, the source of added value to output and of capital accumulation. Accumulation, in the Marxian schema, is a relation between capital and labor that is obscured in mainstream economic thinking.

Within the confines of the typical firm, the individual entrepreneur is conceived as being autonomous, whereas workers are assumed to adjust passively to the entrepreneur's commands. The aggregation of all the positions of power derived from ownership of capital ensures domination by the capitalist class of the working class and therefore of the whole economy. The notion that the business class dominates the economy as each individual capitalist dominates his or her firm assumes that all elements of society are passive or subservient to the power of the capitalist class. Social institutions, mores, and values must not obstruct the functioning of the capitalist class and the system that it dominates. This does not mean that any single capitalist necessarily has the power to dominate the whole economy or even one industry. To say that the capitalist class rules through economic relations is to state an abstraction based on decisions made by capitalists. It does not imply that individual capitalists necessarily act in unison. The state protects and cultivates the general interests of the capitalists *as a whole*, but it has no obligation to protect any specific capitalist. Although individual capitalists come and go and some may have more power than others, the network of legalized positions defined in terms of property ownership gives those who occupy positions of ownership a commanding role over workers. The state's function, as we have already suggested in our discussion of the superstructure, is to ensure the power of property to dominate, not necessarily to sustain any individual person in his or her position. The state creates and enforces rules necessary to the functioning of the capitalist order and its corresponding market relations.

ALIENATION

The disproportionate power held by owners of capital enables them to dominate their relations with labor in at least four ways that are *inherently* alienating.

First, the workers are alienated from the commodities they produce. In contrast to the craft workers who own their tools and work at their own pace under conditions that they control to produce objects in which they can take personal pride and for which they can achieve recognition from the consumer, the nineteenth-century propertyless industrial worker felt no connection with the goods produced. Their labor was so fragmented, the product so standardized, the individual contribution to each standardized item so minimal that the sense of involvement and pride in the product was completely destroyed.

Second, the workers are alienated from the machine itself. The workers sometimes mistake alienation arising from their relation to the capitalist as being caused by their relation to the machine; they are not fully aware of the fact that the production process does not involve simply an individual and a machine. The machine does not recreate itself, subdivide labor routines ad nauseam, and destroy the workers' control over their work; the machine is only *part* of the relations formed at the point of production, and it is these overall relations that determine the workers' perception and valuation of work. Under capitalism the workers became instruments, not unlike machines. Their view of work was affected accordingly.

Third, workers are alienated from one another. A competitive labor market is one in which each worker is pitted against the others in order to survive. Although there is an objective interdependence among workers, each is imbued, in a competitive context, with the notion that one must look out for oneself, that no one else will, and that one must face the market or starve. Given these circumstances, each worker must be willing to undersell his or her fellow workers, in the process, becoming distrustful of and alienated from them.

Finally and most important, the worker is alienated from himself or herself. As the system reduces workers to the status of an ordinary commodity, it separates their labor power (capacity to work) from their existence as physical, cultural, and psychological entities. Once separated from the human individual, this capacity to work can be regarded as an object to be bought and sold, shifted from place to place, and not infrequently forced into idleness. But, it should be emphasized, it is technically impossible to harm the working capacity of an individual without simultaneously injuring the other dimensions that define him or her as a human being. The institutionalization of this alienation tends to destroy the moral, psychological, and social elements of the worker's humanity. Alienation from self becomes a social phenomenon.[13] It is not without reason that mainstream economists view work as a burden; from the Marxian perspective of capitalism, it can be viewed in no other terms.

The sum of these specific components of alienation presumably leads to general alienation from the system as a whole. It is this general alienation, when it becomes intolerable, that Marx expected to induce workers to organize collectively against the system. His expectation of the workers' revolutionary role was partially related to the assumed experiences of workers themselves in their everyday struggle to survive, and partially viewed as a necessary result of the capitalists' main preoccupation, the pursuit of profit. Simply because workers are human, Marx expected them to respond to their condition by taking up a struggle against capitalism. Those unhurt or less hurt by the system would have less interest in challenging it. But he went beyond this expectation. As workers are the direct source of surplus that capitalists appropriate to sustain their power and privileges, not only is the alienation of workers inherent in the system but also the working class becomes the only group that can attack the system at the point of production, at the very point where capitalism as a system is centered. Other segments of the population may become revolutionary at various intervals in the system's history, but because of their significantly less essential position in the economy they have no capacity to prevent it from functioning. Marx's preoccupation with the working class as an instrument of revolution was thus not sentimental, romantic, or utopian; it was based on his general analysis of the way in which capitalism actually works and has developed.

CAPITALIST VERSUS CAPITALIST

The capitalist mode of production can be summarized in Marxian terms: $M \longrightarrow C \longrightarrow M'$, in which M is an initial stock of money (capital in liquid form), C stands for the quantity of labor power and nonhuman resources purchased with this money (capital in commodity form), and M' is the increment in value (surplus value from the labor process itself) that must eventually be realized in the form of money. Each capitalist begins the production process with a stock of money (M). He or she puts it into circulation in order to produce commodities to be sold, expecting to have at the termination of the process more money ($M' = M + \Delta M$) than when he or she started. As his or her motive to produce is incidental to consumption needs, he or she immediately puts the realized increment of value (M') back into the market to buy more labor power.

The process reflects the essential rationality of the capitalist mode of production and can be elaborated sequentially:

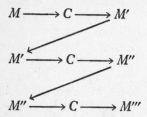

If there is to be a motive for keeping the economy in motion and expanding, M' must be greater than M, M'' must be greater than M', and so on. The end for the capitalist is profit and the expansion of value, which must continue indefinitely, or the whole process will lose meaning. That is, the ebb and flow of the capitalist's activity are determined by profit considerations alone; the greater his or her profits, the greater is the amount of productive activity (employment of labor) that is called forth. If the capitalist does not realize profits, his or her motive to increase or even to continue production is undermined, and the continuity of the capitalist process is broken. Workers are thrown out of work, capital values are destroyed, and misery ensues.

What regulates the relations among capitalists themselves is the competitive market structure. A large number of competing capitalists struggle for economic *survival* in a business jungle. Although Marx's notion of competitive structure is not radically different from the more elegant definition developed by later neoclassical economists (see Chapter 2), his emphasis is primarily on large numbers of competing units, the sizes of the firms, and the mobility of capital among industries. More important, he emphasizes competitive processes, not to demonstrate stability and equilibrium; not to show how abnormal short-run profits are eliminated in the long run, resulting in optimum-sized companies; and not to prove that prices and costs (reflecting the utility of goods and the burden of work) will eventually be equated. In the Marxian schema, the working out of a competitive process has bred chronic instability and disequilibrium; a permanent gap between the capacity to produce and the capacity to consume, which has led to intervals of boom and bust; a continuing disparity between the development of the material and technical side of human beings and the underdevelopment of their social, psychological, and "human" side. Understanding why these consequences have occurred requires an understanding of the forces of production (Figure 9.1, IV) and how they interact with productive relations (Figure 9.1, II and III).

THE FORCES OF PRODUCTION

The forces of production fall into two categories. On the material side, there are the instruments of production—factory buildings, machinery, tools, and natural resources—used to make commodities. On the nonmaterial side are science, technical knowledge, and the stock of skills that together make up the "know-how" of the labor force. The material instruments of production represent "frozen," "dead," or "congealed" labor of the past. The nonmaterial stocks of scientific and technical knowledge belong to the living labor force and are not always separable from human beings themselves.

The forces of production provide an index to the potential magnitude of society's surplus, by which we mean the maximum output obtainable when the forces of production are fully in use, minus the amount of output necessary to maintain the work force and the means of production. The larger the forces of production, the larger the economy's capacity to produce, the greater the division of labor, and the greater the degree of interdependence among individuals, various strata of the population, and regions within a country. The size of the surplus, in contrast to its particular uses, not only reflects the extent to which the forces of production are developed; it also indicates the extent to which the natural environment is under control or is potentially controllable with available technology.

The forces of production also reflect in objective terms the degree of socialization that has taken place in the process of producing goods and services. Marx, not infrequently, noted that the forces of production in his day were becoming increasingly socialized and interdependent while the control of production and the appropriation of surplus production were individualistic and private. He viewed this disparity as a basic contradiction and as a source of chronic disequilibrium.

One final point should be emphasized: To Marx, in contrast to mainstream economists, the forces of production were not "things," neutral objects that can be shifted into any situation for use; more important, they cannot readily be remolded as portions of the capital stock become obsolete. The capital stock, in its varied forms and concrete shapes, has a "fixity" to it. Portions of it used to produce some goods cannot readily be remodeled or transferred to absorb unemployed or new workers into the labor force. The path of technological change is not easily reversible. Technical innovations thus necessarily result in less than transient unemployment problems. Imbalance does not last only through a temporary waiting period until old capital can be converted or unemployed workers absorbed through the mobilization of fresh capital.

THE MODE OF PRODUCTION

The mode of production consists of interaction among the relations and forces of production (see Figure 9.1, II, III, IV). It is an analytical category that focuses attention on the *relations* among classes, technology, and the superstructure. None of these entities have any meaning in themselves. Classes are compelled to establish definite relations that will determine and be determined by the forces of production. These relations, in turn, affect the superstructure, which, as we have already suggested, is connected symbiotically to the changing character of the mode of production. This interaction (between I and II, III and IV) is two directional: The mode of production establishes general limits of a historical nature; with such limits, the superstructure can determine specific aspects of the modes of production, a fact that produces differences among capitalist nations themselves.

To understand any historical or social formation, for example, tribalism, slavery, or feudalism, it is necessary to examine the prevailing mode of production. To understand the breakdown of old formations and the emergence of new ones, it is necessary to examine both changes in existing modes of production and how new modes rise to dominance. The latter point suggests that, in any given society, there may exist more than one mode of production. Under feudalism, for example, independent farmers, who produced for their own direct consumption, operated in a mode of production very different from that of the landed aristocracy and peasants, who were related to each other in the control and working of the land. In this particular instance, the feudal mode was dominant and therefore determined the character of the whole social structure. Marx described this complex web of inter-relations in the following way:

> In order to produce, [people] enter into definite connections and relations with one another and only within these social connections and relations does their action on nature, does production, take place.
> These social relations . . . will naturally vary according to the character of the means of production. With the invention of a new instrument of warfare, firearms, [for example], the whole internal organization of the army necessarily changed; the relationship within which individuals can constitute an army . . . were transformed and the relations of different armies to one another also changed.
> [To put the case more generally], *the social relations within which individuals produce, the social relations of production, change, are transformed, with the change and development of the material means of production, the productive forces. The relations of production in their totality constitute what are called the social relations, society and specifically a society at a definite stage of historical development,* a society with a peculiar, distinctive characer. *Ancient* society, *feudal* society, *bourgeois* society are such totalities of production relations, each of which at the same time denotes a special stage of development in the history of mankind.[14] (emphasis in the original)

In order to understand the concept of mode of production in more concrete terms, we shall discuss it in the context of a competitive capitalist system. This will be followed by a more systematic and detailed discussion of Marx's theory of capitalist economic development.

ACCUMULATION AND CONSOLIDATION

Because individual capitalists operate in a competitive market structure, their economic survival requires that they accumulate and control as much as possible. Accumulation, it should be emphasized, has a quantitative dimension unrelated to power, prestige, or other qualitative goals. Accumulation is infinite; and, for the capitalist, it is his or her raison d'être. For any individual capitalist, the pressure to accumulate is continuous; not to accumulate is to jeopardize his or her chances to survive. Survival requires that the capitalist maximize the surplus value extracted from labor and that capital be circulated to realize maximum profit. The competitive market relations that govern capitalists are thus readily extended to relations between capitalists and workers, for the real wages of the latter affect the size of the surplus available for appropriation by capitalists.

The drive to accumulate leads to dramatic increases in the *scale of production*—the ratio of fixed capital to the number of workers employed. Marx called this process the *concentration* of capital. Accumulation also causes more and more capital to fall into fewer and fewer hands. Marx called this process the *centralization* of capital. Both tendencies together can be viewed as a sort of consolidation process. The growing scale (concentration) of capital results from the need to reduce costs by perpetually introducing labor-saving means of production. Increases in scale are assumed to be intimately associated with increases in the profit rate—or at least with preventing it from falling. Whenever profit is threatened, the concentration process moves forward as the result of efforts to arrest the threat. As technological scale is enlarged, it requires ever greater amounts of liquid surplus (money capital) to mobilize it. This change in turn requires further *centralization* of capital; that is, more independent firms must be brought under the control of a single financial authority, or more centralized financial institutions must be organized to tap the liquid surplus of individual capitalists and other strata of the population. Both the concentration and centralization tendencies accelerate the *socialization of production*—the growth of interdependence among various parts of the economy through extensions of the division of labor and specialization.

As the material forces of production change, they call forth changes in the nonmaterial forces: for example, new skills and new uses of science. In this way, changes in the stock of capital in the form of new machines (dead labor) impinge upon the status of living labor that must be retrained or deployed elsewhere because of the needs of the capitalist class that owns and controls the instruments of production (Figure 9.1, II——→IV——→III). The task of the superstructure in this context is to provide the "social climate" and legal framework necessary to persuade workers and technicians to accept the exigencies of changes in the capitalist mode of production (see Figure 9.1, I, as it interacts with II, III, IV). The mode of production can thus stimulate the superstructure to act, and the superstructure can influence the various elements that enter into the mode of production.

How are class relations between capitalists and workers affected by these inherent tendencies toward concentration and centralization? Why should the interaction between production relations and forces of production lead to chronic instability—booms, crises, busts, and depressions? What can be expected from the superstructure as the mode of production evolves? Marx sought to answer these questions in his analysis of nineteenth-century capitalism. If we are to answer them ourselves, we must understand his theory of capitalist development in more detail.

THE THEORY OF CAPITALIST DEVELOPMENT

The aim of this section is to develop a logical exposition of Marxian economic theory. We shall begin by defining some general terms and then proceed to show how they can be used to explain the pattern of the system's growth. Our emphasis is selective; we focus on those theoretical constructions and hypotheses corresponding to Marx's expectations of capitalist tendencies as they actually appeared in the nineteenth century.

THE VALUE OF OUTPUT

In Marxian terms the value of the gross output for one year is equal to $c + v + s$, in which $c = $ constant capital (the value of raw materials plus the value of the depreciation of physical capital), $v = $ variable capital (the amount of socially necessary labor time recompensed by wages), and $s = $ surplus value (the value embodied in goods beyond what is socially necessary to reproduce the working class; it is appropriated by the capitalist class and represents the source of capitalist income).

The value of net product per year is derived by subtracting the value of constant capital c from the value of gross product. What remains can be expressed as $y = v + s$, in which $v = $ the worker's share of income, $s = $ the share appropriated by the capitalist, and $y = $ the value of the net product or income. The sum of $v + s$ equals unity, in that it exhausts the total net product. With this formula in mind, we can examine the tug of war over distribution of income between capital and labor through the interrelations among three concepts: the rate of exploitation, or surplus value; the organic composition of capital; and the rate of profit.[15]

THE RATE OF EXPLOITATION

The rate of exploitation (s') is the ratio of unpaid labor time (s) to labor time socially necessary to reproduce labor (variable capital, or v). This ratio can be written algebraically: $s' = s/v$. Whatever the length of the working day (six–eight–ten hours), the workers receive a real wage equal to the amount necessary to reproduce themselves, that is, the physical energy and skills to continue his job routine. Commodities produced in excess of those that the worker can command with his or her wage embody surplus value, the remaining portion of net product, which is appropriated by the capitalist; his or her right to expropriate it is legalized and enforced by the state.

The laborers do not recognize their contribution of free (unpaid) labor. If they work eight hours and receive $2 an hour, a day's pay is $16. They receive compensation for every working hour. In the Marxian framework this notion is only an illusion. Although workers each receive $16, the value of their output is assumed to be greater. It is as if part of their day was *donated*, in order to produce output to support the capitalist.

Extracting surplus value is the means by which the value of total output is increased. Although elements of production other than labor impart only their own value to current output, workers are hired to produce, in addition to their own reproduction costs, *added* value. Surplus, or added value, is the ultimate source of increments to the capital stock (the accumulation of capital), the raison d'être of capitalist activity. But capital accumulation does not occur by itself or automatically; that is, it is not the capitalists per se or the machines per se that are relevant. It is the relations among classes of people, in particular between capital and labor, that constitute the basis of Marx's view of the accumulation of capital.

Although labor is productive, although the machine that embodies past or dead labor facilitates production of goods by current labor, the private ownership of the means of production does not in itself contribute to the total value (or size) of output. Ownership, in the Marxian view, is simply a mechanism for *distributing* output, not for producing it. In this sense, the capitalist is functionless; his or her capacity to claim a share of the output is based on the power of ownership, legalized and enforced by the state apparatus. The amount of surplus appropriated (output of unpaid labor time) varies with the intensity of work, the length of the working day, the quantity of goods necessary to reproduce the worker as an energy-expending organism that sells labor power, and the productivity of labor.

For any given technological mix, assuming that the existing stock of factories and machinery and the dexterity of the average worker are constant, the intensity of work and the length of the working day will be determined by the continuing class (political) struggle between capitalists and workers within the confines of the business enterprise itself. The quantity of goods necessary to reproduce the worker is mainly, if not completely, dependent upon the particular period of time and the particular country, that is, upon the variable social and cultural standards established at different historical junctures.[16] If technological change is assumed, as it is in the Marxian schema, the productivity of labor is measured by the average amount of time it takes for a typical worker to produce the consumer goods necessary to reproduce his or her own labor power. The more productive labor becomes, the less time is necessary to produce the goods needed for its own reproduction, and the greater is the potential time available to produce surplus output to be appropriated by the capitalist.

When all four of the processes that determine the ratio s/v are examined together, they reveal the relative proportions of income going to labor and the owners of capital. In contrast to the neoclassical productivity theory discussed in Chapter 2, the Marxian theory views the distribution of income as evolving from the continuing power struggle between capital and labor. Although this struggle can and frequently does manifest itself in the political arena, around such issues as tax legislation and minimum-wage laws, it is *always* present in day-to-day relations within the confines of the capitalist-owned enterprise. The struggle over the pace of work, working conditions, and wages encompasses the sum and substance of the perpetual antagonism between the capitalist quest for more surplus and the workers' avoidance of further alienation or their efforts to overcome present alienation at the point of production. Put differently, the capitalist devises control mechanisms within the enterprise to keep the worker powerless, and the worker counters with efforts to overcome his or her fate in this context.[17]

It should be further noted that changes in labor productivity are closely related to changes in the distribution of income arising from technological progress. Do the workers receive more than their socially determined minimum income as output expands? The Marxian answer is not axiomatic. It depends upon the way in which the class struggle unfolds. The workers' acquisition of more leisure as productivity increases is determined by strikes, demonstrations, and political activism. It is determined on the battlefield of the factory, where capitalists and workers make direct contact, and in the political arena, where the government mediates to prevent the possibility of civil war.

ORGANIC COMPOSITION OF CAPITAL

The ratio of the value of capital stock (means of production, or c) to variable capital (wages used to purchase labor power, v) is the organic composition of capital. It can be written $q = c/v$. This equation measures the extent to which labor is furnished with machinery and materials in the production process. The larger the value of c/v, the greater the productivity of labor. The ratio rests on the assumption that the growth of technology also means an increase in the value of augmented capital stock in the *long run*.[18] The ratio c/v thus also becomes greater as competitive capitalism evolves inevitably toward its noncompetitive stage. This has important implications, which we shall discuss momentarily.

THE RATE OF PROFIT

The profit rate is defined as the ratio of surplus value (s) to the sum of capital (c) advanced to replenish and expand capital stock and to pay wages (v). It can be written $p = s/c + v$. In a capitalist economy that is in motion the capital outlays are of three types: money to reproduce the given capital stock as it depreciates, or wears out, in the production process and to purchase raw materials; money to increase the absolute size of the capital stock; and money to pay workers their reproduction wages.[19]

In the long run the profit rate was assumed to move in the downward direction, a tendency identified as the "law of the falling rate of profit." This tendency was said to be interrupted periodically by counterforces and short-run cyclical movements. Although this tendency was difficult to document empirically, it was *assumed* to be likely, and this assumption led Marx to conclude that capitalism will ultimately have to face profound internal strife.

To appreciate the explanatory power of this model's main elements, it is necessary to understand the interaction of the three ratios introduced here: the rate of exploitation ($s' = s/v$), the organic composition of capital ($q = c/v$), and the rate of profit ($p = s/c + v$). They can be used to explain the behavior of capitalists and the actual ways in which the system is expected to unfold over time.

The rate of profit, $p = \dfrac{s}{c + v}$, can be restated so that it incorporates the other two ratios. By dividing the numerator and the denominator by v, we arrive at

$$p = \frac{s/v}{c + v/v} = \frac{s/v}{c/v + v/v} = \frac{s/v}{c/v + 1}$$

In this version the profit rate has the rate of exploitation ($s' = s/v$) in the numerator and the organic composition of capital ($q = c/v$) in the denominator. The profit rate p thus varies with changes in q, v, and s. If the capital stock (c) in the denominator should increase relative to the rate of exploitation (s/v) in the numerator, the profit rate will decline. If the size of the surplus (s) extracted from labor should increase relative to either variable capital (v) or constant capital (c), the profit rate will rise. If they all change proportionally, the profit rate will remain constant.

Although the formal expression of the forces determining the profit rate indicates that it may increase, remain constant, or decline over time, Marx expected that it would decline. In order to view this possibility, let us look into other interrelated strands important to an understanding of capitalism: the relation between employed and unemployed labor and the reason why the rate of production in the capital-goods sector tends to expand faster than the rate of production of consumption goods. The latter imbalance explains why the capitalist system as a whole cannot be coordinated to function smoothly and why the capacity to produce tends to outstrip the capacity to consume, thus producing crises and depressions.[20]

THE RESERVE ARMY OF LABOR

Critical to the whole Marxian model is the notion of extraction of the surplus in the process of production. By definition it involves the exploitation of labor. The main sources of such surplus during the early stages of capitalist development are, first, workers dislodged from the noncapitalist sector—peasants, landless agricultural laborers, and craftspeople—and, second, the intensification of work among workers already connected with capitalist enterprises.

Marx's notion of the absolute impoverishment of the working class, which has been severely questioned by mainstream critics, applies mainly to this transition period. The displacement of workers from their precapitalist work environments involved destroying the whole fabric of their lives. Herded into cities that were ill prepared to absorb them due to inadequate housing, transportation, sanitation, and recreation facilities, these workers' real incomes slipped downward. They were, moreover, forced into severe competition with one another and with those workers who were already involved in capitalist production. This continual influx of new laborers to compete with those who were already part of the capitalist vortex kept wages at a minimum. Capitalist expansion at that early juncture therefore proceeded rapidly without excessively rising wages and therefore without cuts in the surplus. Once this seemingly unlimited supply of rural labor dried up, that is, once it was fully absorbed into the capitalist system, absolute impoverishment associated with the dislodging of the worker from his or her previous habitat disappeared and relative economic exploitation became the common condition of the working class. Now the reserve army becomes internal to capitalism; its size and role fluctuate over the business cycle.

At that point capitalism became a fully competitive system. The precapitalist social order had been demolished, and the capitalist class had acquired uncontested power over the means of production. The government reflected this dominance and did whatever was necessary to reproduce capitalist relations, the essence of the Marxian notion of what capital accumulation is about.

How does such a system behave and develop through time?

What is its destiny? To answer these questions in the form of a theoretical model, Marx developed a reproduction schema. As our point of departure, and to provide a sense of the kind of reasoning that went into Marx's analytical efforts, we shall discuss this schema in the simplest possible terms.

MEANS OF PRODUCTION AND MEANS OF CONSUMPTION

Marx divided the whole economy into two sectors. In sector I capital goods are produced, in sector II consumer goods. Some friendly critics of Marx have argued that this distinction has been his most important and lasting contribution. In the words of well-known mathematical economist William Baumol:

> The model offers all the advantages of recognition of interdependence, and avoids the fallacies into which one can be entrapped by studying some one industry in isolation, without considering from where it draws its resources. Yet it is sufficiently compact to enable the analyst to understand its properties and to determine their implications for reality. [The profound contribution of the model is the light it shed on] simple and expanded reproduction.[21]

For capitalism to function smoothly, without booms and busts, sectors I and II must function in harmony; the supply of capital goods (means of production) produced in sector I must be equal to the demand for capital goods used in the production of consumer goods in sector II. Moreover, consumption by productive workers and by unproductive property owners must be equal to the value of consumer goods produced in sector II. If these conditions can be met, the capitalist economy can reproduce itself in a stable manner indefinitely. But for several reasons, even under the most ideal conditions of a nonexpanding economy, the necessary balance among all the parts of sectors I and II is highly unlikely, as Marx has demonstrated. Competition among very large numbers of uncoordinated units—which Marx viewed as anarchy in the production process—simply makes it extremely improbable that sectors I and II can achieve any kind of balance. The proper proportions between sectors, which are essential to prevent excessive production of constant capital and insufficient demand for consumer goods (requiring the production of constant capital), are nevertheless unlikely to occur. Marx expected such proportional imbalances arising from systemic planlessness to produce "technical" cycles of boom and bust.

More important, capitalists are periodically confronted with what Marx called a "realization crisis," the inability to transform appropriated surplus value into real profits. The reasons for these crises are varied. Perhaps the most critical one is that the demand for capital goods in sector I tends to rise and fall relative to the demand for consumer goods in sector II. The continuous cycle of expansion and contraction is intimately associated with "growing contractions and expansions in the industrial reserve army, which constitute the mechanism of the breakdown of the capitalist economy."[22] Unbalanced expansions in sector I accelerate rises in real wages, which function to squeeze the profit rate and to halt the expansion of capital in sector I. This process in turn sets in motion technological changes and short-run intervals of capital shrinkage, causing an increase in the reserve army of unemployed labor and a decrease in real wages. The demand for goods in sector II is then adversely affected, producing a "glut," which leads to price decreases more rapid than the decline in real wages. Sooner or later adjustments between the two sectors occur, and expansion begins again. Marx expected these swings in output, associated with regular imbalances in the rates of change between sectors I and II, to become greater and greater with time because of the secular rise in the organic composition of capital, which tends to cause the profit rate to fall.

This inherent instability can be characterized somewhat differently. Because capitalism, as a self-expanding system, seeks continually to enlarge its capital base, the means of production tend to expand more rapidly than the means of consumption necessary to absorb full-capacity output. This imbalance was described by Marx as follows:

> The creation of . . . surplus value is the object of the direct process of production. . . . But this production of surplus value is but the first act of the capitalist process. . . . Now comes the second act. . . . The entire mass of commodities . . . must be sold. If this is not done, or only partly accomplished . . . the laborer has been nonetheless exploited, but his exploitation does not realize as much for the capitalist. . . . The realization of surplus value . . . is . . . based on antagonistic conditions of distribution, which reduces the consuming power . . . [relative to the realization requirement of the capitalist].[23]

In essence, capital expansion increases costs while simultaneously leading capitalists to limit consumer demand by restricting the size of the wage bill. Both tendencies affect the realization of profits.

This perennial disparity undermines the rationale for expanding capital, a process that leads to contraction and unemployment until a balance between the capacity to produce and the means to consume is again restored. But this restoration involves tremendous social costs in wasted resources and unemployment. It should be emphasized that this process is not something that capitalists can control; it is built into the competitive struggle for survival. That is, the necessity for each capitalist to accumulate capital tends inevitably to increase the capacity to produce (sector I) at an accelerated rate. But, because accelerated expansion depends upon minimizing the capacity to consume (sector II), sector II must necessarily lag behind sector I. The lagging demand for capital goods from sector II undermines the expansion of sector I; there is little point in forever enlarging the capacity to produce if the demand for such capacity periodically disappears. The contradictory implications of the self-expanding impulse of capital have been described by Paul M. Sweezy, a leading American Marxist: "Capitalism's utopia in a sense is a situation in which workers live on air, allowing their entire product to take the form of surplus value; and in which capitalists accumulate all their surplus value. This would represent the maximum conceivable rate expansion of capital."[24]

However important this contradiction, it would be misleading to state Marx's views about the contradictions of capitalism in purely economic form. For purposes of clarity and simplification, we shall complete our exposition by bringing together the various parts of the Marxian system already introduced.

A GRAND SYNTHESIS: FROM DOMESTIC TO INTERNATIONAL ECONOMY[25]

The capitalist system drives individual capitalists to engage in a never-ending quest for profits. But, as all capitalists in the system are driven toward this same end, profitable opportunities tend to diminish, and the rate of profit tends to decline.

Capitalists try to arrest these declining tendencies in two ways:

in the short run, by increasing the size of the surplus through direct exploitation of labor, that is, by intensifying work; and, in the long run, by introducing labor-saving machinery.

As the dust settles, both methods employed to arrest declines in the profit rate turn out to have limited effects. Exploitation of labor means increasing the stock of capital without technological change, an accumulative process that sooner or later will lead to costs greater than consumer demand for final output. There is simply a limit to how much the pace of work can be accelerated or the working day lengthened. Introducing labor-saving machinery means changing the composition and enlarging the scale of capital stock; such moves depend upon technological change. The profit-realization problem is solved temporarily because both labor and other factors of production become cheaper. But, as the scale of production increases, so does the organic composition of capital; the profit rate is pushed into a decline. Moreover, the periodic fits of unemployment associated with new labor-saving machinery undermines demand for consumer goods relative to the economy's growing capacity to produce.

The sequence described suggests a critical feature of the capitalist process: recurring imbalance associated with capital booms in sector I and lagging demand in sector II for capital goods used to produce consumer goods. These twin developments of overexpansion and underconsumption lead to periodic crises and depressions, creating a rhythm of instability that is, in Marx's view, inherent in capitalism.

Each of these cycles of capital accumulation and shifts to capital-intensive machinery brings successive increases in the concentration of capital and the necessity for more centralized means of financing expansion. The competitive system is thus moving irreversibly toward a noncompetitive stage.

As concentration and centralization proceed, two major developments appear, one in the domestic and the other in the international sphere. In the former, concentration automatically brings together larger aggregates of labor, which, as a result of changes in the composition of capital, become less and less differentiated by skills than in the earlier, semimechanized era. Internationally, the tendency toward declining profits associated with a rising organic composition of capital impels capitalists to seek investment outlets in less developed countries, where cheap labor can be exploited because such countries lack mechanization and possess less capital. With this search for new outlets goes the export of capital and consumer goods, a process that temporarily postpones the decline in profits at home. Both the aggregation of labor and the export of capital increase the role of the state, or superstructure, in sustaining capitalist relations.

The consolidation of the working class, crudely correlated with the consolidation of capital, stimulates and even makes possible the organization of a mass union movement. This movement, Marx assumed, will eventually be forced by circumstances to develop its own political arm, in the form of a revolutionary socialist party that will seize state power in the midst of one of the system's colossal economic breakdowns. Workers will be moved to undertake this task because of the nature of their alienation, derived, as we have indicated, from their relation with capitalists in the production process. Workers will have to take control of the superstructure if they are to change the mode of production, for the superstructure is dominated by the business class or at least functions to reproduce, facilitate, and enforce capitalist relations, the immediate source of the workers' alienation.

On one level, the workers' alienation, and therefore their conflict with capitalists, derives from the production relations over wages, length of the working day, working conditions, employability, and so on. The organization of workers into unions is a natural means of dealing with some of these issues. But the task of altering the basic relationship between capital and labor, of destroying the political privileges and legal power associated with owning the means of production, is another matter; it cannot be understood in the way that the need for unions is understood. Eliminating the capitalist system by abolishing its superstructure requires individuals and unions to think and act consciously as part of a class for itself that manifests its interests politically. *Consciousness* must be cultivated by revolutionary ideologues and leaders of the working class. In the Marxian schema, revolutions are viewed as an outgrowth of objective conditions that converge with the working class's awareness of its own power to transform society. In this sense, Marx was a "conservative"; he did not believe in premature revolutions.

The role of the superstructure comes increasingly into play as the mode of production evolves. As economic dislocations increase in duration and magnitude, the superstructure is increasingly called upon by the dominant class to maintain and enforce capitalist relations. The ideology of the superstructure increasingly reveals class bias, which eventually shifts the arena of the struggle from the economic sphere (from trade-union struggles and the like) to the political one, from incremental changes to revolutionary ones.

Exporting the system's domestic stagnation leads to colonization by the capitalist class. There are at least two reasons for this. First, investments must be safeguarded against hostile reactions in the foreign country that has cheap labor to exploit, and, second, they must be safeguarded against competition from other capitalist countries also seeking markets beyond their national boundaries. For these reasons, nationally based capitalists, as they expand abroad, call their governments into action; one result is wars between major capitalist countries and between the capitalist countries and less developed ones that may resist colonization. War often stimulates supernationalistic and chauvinistic impulses in capitalist nations, which serve to justify imperial penetration. The process of expansion, it should be further noted, is accelerated as the market structure of capitalist countries becomes increasingly less competitive. External expansion is thus related to a particular stage of the internal development of capitalism.

Finally, the total unfolding of the capitalist process has both limitations and contradictions. The very success of capitalist countries breeds a reaction in colonized countries that causes business bankruptcies and the shrinking of international opportunities for investment. It also stimulates revolutionary action in a working class that has already organized itself on a mass basis.

CONCLUSION

The validity of the Marxian vision is not our present concern. There is no doubt that it can be attacked in specific areas. No schema that aims to explain so much can be devoid of errors. What is critical for our purpose is its intellectual power, its scope, its capacity to bring together a broad range of apparently unrelated phenomena, economic and noneconomic, into a unified framework. As we have indicated earlier, the

> categories of Marxian political economy are at once economic, sociological and political. Consider, for example, the conept of labour power as a commodity. It involves the existence of separate "sociological" classes between which purchase and sale can take place, a *legal* framework within which a labour contract can exist, and an existence of a *state* which can protect capitalist

social relations, as well as the more obvious "economic" connotations. It is only within this *unity* of the "political," the "economic," and the "sociological" that we can recognize the significance and prominence of *production* in Marxism.[26]

This integrated, interdisciplinary approach is what gives the Marxian perspective power and makes it attractive to younger radical economists, whose sense of truth requires synthesizing diversity and seeing the system whole. It is this legacy from Marx that has had a lasting influence on contemporary radical economists, even though many of them are only partially committed to Marxism in the sense of wanting to write and do research in the tradition arising from Marx's initial contribution.

Having developed a relatively orthodox statement of the Marxian schema that analyzed the conditions of nineteenth-century capitalism, we shall now proceed to discuss a modified Marxian framework that is used to analyze contemporary American capitalism. This neo-Marxian schema, as we have chosen to call it, will set the stage for a more thorough exploration of the way in which radical political economists examine specific problems of the American capitalist system.

NOTES

1. Joseph Schumpeter, *Capitalism, Socialism, and Democracy*, 3rd ed. (New York: Harper Torchbooks, 1950), p. 9.

2. When mainstream economists argue that many of Marx's predictions have not been borne out, they often neglect this aspect of his reasoning.

3. Schumpeter, *Capitalism, Socialism, and Democracy*, pp. 45–46.

4. Quoted by Z. A. Jordan, ed., *Karl Marx: Economy, Class and Social Revolution* (New York: Scribner's, 1971), p. 59.

5. This point was made by S. Resnik in a conversation at Queens College, 1975.

6. Alice Kessler Harris, "Stratifying by Sex: Understanding the History of Working Women," in *Labor Market Segmentation*, eds. Richard Edwards, Michael Reich, and David Gordon (Lexington, Mass.: Lexington, 1975), p. 219.

7. Karl Marx, *German Ideology*, cited by Richard Lichtman, "Marx's Theory of Ideology," *Socialist Revolution* 5 (April 1975): 49.

8. It should be pointed out that the capitalist class can oppose

threatening ideas by using the superstructure to distort them or to repress those responsible for their promulgation.

9. A third aspect, which we shall discuss briefly later in connection with alienation, is competitive relations among workers themselves.

10. For a discussion of Marx's conception of class, see Ralf Dahrendorf, *Class and Class Conflict in Industrial Society* (Stanford: Stanford University Press, 1959).

11. See Karl Marx, "The Class Struggles in France: 1848–50," and "The Eighteenth Brumaire of Louis Bonaparte," in *Selected Works* (New York: International Publishers, 1951), pp. 169–310, 311–426.

12. For a provocative discussion and development of this idea, see Thomas Vietorisz, "From Class to Hierarchy: Non-Price Aspects of the Transformation Problem" (Unpublished paper, February 1975).

13. Karl Polanyi, *The Great Transformation* (New York: Rinehart, 1944), Chapter 6.

14. Quoted in Jordan, ed., *Karl Marx*, p. 226.

15. See Geoff Hodgson, "The Falling Rate of Profit," *New Left Review* 84 (March–April 1974): 55–84; see also, Roger Alcaly, "What Is Marxian Economics?" (Paper delivered at the Columbia University Seminar on the Political Economy of War and Peace, New York, February 1975).

16. There is a problem of the independence between intensity of work and length of the working day, on the one hand, and the quantity of output necessary to reproduce the worker, on the other. If the first two increase, most likely the socially required minimum output to reproduce the worker will also increase. Then s/v will tend not to change, unless intensity of work and length of the working day increase more rapidly than the required rise in output necessary for the reproduction of the labor force. In the absence of population increases, the labor supply would decline from possible impoverishment.

17. See Stephen A. Marglin, "What Do Bosses Do? The Origins and Functions of Hierarchy," *Review of Radical Political Economics* 6 (Summer 1974): 60–112.

18. This definition of the organic composition of capital ignores some very critical problems involving the stock of capital relative to its augmented value, the problem of its age structure, and the index of estimated value of the diverse items that make up the means of production. See Hodgson, "The Falling Rate."

19. Money is also required to maintain the consumption habits of the capitalist class. This type of outlay is more important in neo-Marxian analysis; see Chapter 10.

20. Joan Robinson, *An Essay on Marxian Economics* (London: Macmillan, 1942), p. 4.

21. William J. Baumol, "A New Critique of Marx's Economics," *Monthly Review* 26 (February 1975): 60. Copyright © 1975 by Monthly Review, Inc. Reprinted by permission of Monthly Review Press.

22. *Ibid.*, p. 61.

23. Karl Marx, *Capital*, ed. Charles H. Kerr (Chicago: Kerr), Vol. 3, p. 286; quoted by Howard

Sherman, "Inflation, Unemployment, and Monopoly Capital," *Monthly Review* 27 (March 1976): 27.

24. Paul M. Sweezy, "Some Problems in the Theory of Capital Accumulation," *Monthly Review* 26 (May 1974): 54.

25. A considerable part of this section has been drawn from Schumpeter, *Capitalism, Socialism, and Democracy*.

26. Hodgson, "The Falling Rate," p. 78.

THE NEO-MARXIAN ANALYSIS
OF AMERICAN CAPITALISM

As we pointed out in Chapter 9, the extraction of surplus and its transformation into profits are the preoccupations of classical Marxism. They occur, moreover, under reasonably competitive conditions. Marx's original analysis was not intended to apply to a noncompetitive or monopolistic system, and until recently there has not been a serious attempt to adapt or to develop his scheme to fit contemporary American capitalism. The first and most influential effort in this direction has been the book *Monopoly Capital* by Paul A. Baran and Paul M. Sweezy.[1] For this reason, we have chosen to discuss their specific contribution. We have taken a few liberties with the language used to discuss some concepts, without, we hope, altering the thrust of their arguments.

The authors of *Monopoly Capital* have sought to explore the strategic forces that shape the American economy and thus also the broad contours of American society. Occupying the center of the stage is the giant multinational corporation. The market situation in which the giants act out their inevitable roles is that of oligopoly, competition among a few large firms. The basic economic problem is how the system generates (produces) and absorbs (consumes) surplus output, which, if not absorbed, will manifest itself in idle resources like unemployed labor and redundant capital. Although this terminology could easily be recast in Keynesian terms of aggregate supply and demand, Baran and Sweezy base their thesis on a single concept: surplus. Their reason for doing so is that it sheds light on the central paradoxes and irrationalities of the system.

In contrast to mainstream economics, which is primarily preoccupied with scarce resources and how they can be channeled to achieve efficient results, neo-Marxian economics concerns itself with the size of the *surplus* and its composition. The size of the surplus "is the difference between what a society produces and the costs of producing it. . . . [It] is an index of productivity and wealth."[2] It reveals the extent to which society as a whole produces more than the minimum, more than some specific quantity of goods and services (food, clothing, shelter, education, and so on) essential to the average individual's functioning. It is thus indicative of the extent to which the forces of production are developed. The larger the surplus, the greater is society's *potential* discretionary capacity to live according to its inclinations (freedom of its members from the necessity to work to reproduce some socially necessary minimum and therefore freedom to develop personal talents in a noncoercive context).

The composition of the surplus reveals to us the substantive character of the community's uses of discretionary time—the time in excess of that required to produce the necessities of life. It suggests "how much [the community] invests in expanding its productive capacity, how much it consumes in various forms, how much it wastes and in what ways."[3] For example, members of a society with a large surplus may have to devote only an average of thirty hours a week to reproduce the basic necessities. If the average work week is forty hours, the society produces a surplus that can be used in a variety of ways. If it chooses to use the surplus to build cathedrals, the choice suggests something about the religious feeling prevailing in the community and the nature of the rulers who appropriate the surplus. If it chooses to produce a whole battery of military hardware, the choice reveals aggressive or imperialist qualities of the society and its rulers' needs. Finally, if it chooses to develop musical and artistic sensitivities and capacities, another interpretation would be necessary. Clearly, the composition of the surplus reveals something about the nature of the society's cultural, social, and political life, about the superstructure. But, because the superstructure, in the Marxian sense, is intimately related to the mode of production, it follows that alternative modes of production allegedly determine alternative compositions of output.

SURPLUS: ITS MULTIPLE DIMENSIONS

Surplus has four general dimensions; it is necessary to understand each in order to avoid both empirical and theoretical misunderstandings. First, there is a notion of *optimal*, or planned, surplus. This surplus is not available under capitalism. Given the present state of technology and known resources, it could exist only if the economy were rearranged on rational principles. Such principles would have to reflect the collective wisdom of a population consciously involved in planning the production and distribution of society's wealth and income. They would involve notions of *essential* production and consumption, implying that under capitalism a consequential portion of both is not essential to the achievement of a healthy and humane life. This optimum surplus does "not reflect a configuration of production and consumption determined by profit considerations of individual firms, by the income distribution, tastes, and social pressures of a capitalist order."[4] The achievement of the optimum surplus involves the "liquidation of inefficient units of production . . . elimination of redundant product differentiation, abolition of unproductive labor" and other forms of waste.[5]

On the one hand, the optimum surplus has little practical relevance, for to realize it requires revolutionary change. On the other hand, the concept, ultimately derived from rational thought and knowledge of the world acquired through science, is used by radical economists as a template to highlight the capitalist system's quantitative and qualitative deficiencies. In a sense, then, the concept of an optimum surplus is a functional alternative to the notion of "pure competition" in mainstream thinking, and it is used in a similar fashion.

Second is the notion of the *maximum* surplus that is theoretically possible in a capitalist society. In any period of time there is an output over and above socially necessary costs. This is an output that maximizes profit and ensures the full and efficient use of all resources of the economy for any given technological mix. The problem, of course, is that this output level has been achieved only rarely in the history of capitalism.

Third, there is the notion of *actual* surplus, defined as equal to the actual output beyond the socially necessary costs to produce it. Actual profit is a crude empirical measure of actual surplus.

Finally, there is the idea of an *underutilized* surplus, the difference between actual output and the maximum obtainable output in any given capitalist system. The underutilization of surplus is apparent in excess plant capacity and unemployment, rather than in output, for output not produced cannot be recognized. If there is a maximum output that can be achieved with existing resources operating at normal capacity and if this maximum is not produced, it means that some existing resources are not being employed; that is, the economy is operating below normal capacity.

SOCIALLY NECESSARY COSTS

Because the notion of socially necessary costs is so critical to understanding the size of the surplus, we must devote more attention to it. Suppose, for example, that GNP is currently running at $900 billion a year and consists only of loaves of bread and baking equipment to make the bread. Assume also that the socially necessary costs of producing the $900 billion worth of output are $500 billion; that is, it costs $500 billion to produce $900 billion worth of bread. The items included in these costs are

1. Replacement investment: $50 billion
2. Wage payments to productive labor: $400 billion
3. Minimum necessary costs of government: $50 billion.[6]

Replacement investment is that portion of total output that is employed "to make good the wear and tear which the capital stock suffers through use and the passage of time."[7] Productive labor is labor that produces socially necessary or useful output. This notion implies that there can be output, or ingredients related to it, that is useless and thus uses labor unproductively. Finally, some government expenditures, like those for essential roads and education, are necessary to socially useful production, but not all government expenditures are necessarily useful.

The difference between the costs of production ($500 billion) and the value of total output ($900 billion) is the surplus appropriated by capitalists in the form of profits, interest, and rents. Labor's share of net output or income is 50 percent ($900 billion minus the sum of government expenditures and depreciation costs); the capitalists' proportion is, of course, the same.

How do useless output and unproductive labor enter into these economic processes? The following illustration was developed by Baran.[8] Let us envision a bread economy that has evolved from a competitive or premonopolistic phase into a monopolistic one. In the course of this transformation, bread output has increased and the composition of the labor force that produces bread has changed. As the total number of workers has remained the same, the increase in output is necessarily due to dramatic improvements in bread-making technology. The two stages of the bread economy are shown in Table 10.1.

In examining the two stages, we can readily see that the productivity of the average baker increases from 2 loaves to 12.5 loaves, or by 525 percent. Moreover, the average wage per worker increases from one loaf to five loaves. In stage II, the workers have also increased their per capita consumption of bread. Finally, the relative distribution of income between capital and labor has not changed; it remains 50 percent for each group. What has been the critical change? According to Baran:

> What has happened is that a share of the surplus, all of which was available to the capitalist as profit and as payment of land rent and interest, is now used to support costs of [socially unnecessary inputs which in stage II are an outgrowth of noncompetitive market structures associated with the development of monopoly dominated capitalism].[9]

For our present purpose, the main point of this illustration is to show how Baran and Sweezy have defined unproductive labor and useless output. It should be emphasized, moreover, that waste is estimated from society's point of view, not in relation to the survival needs of any individual enterprise. In fact, that is the main point: The system requires each separate unit to employ resources irrationally. Costs necessary to the capitalist system at this historical point serve no socially necessary or useful purpose. The optimum surplus, in the radical view, can be achieved only by eliminating the necessary micro and macro costs inherent in the monopolistic system. This necessarily entails overhauling the system by eliminating the host of unproductive workers (gimmick employees and tax lawyers and so forth) who have become central to the system's functioning under monopolistic conditions.

Table 10.1 • Two Stages of the Bread Economy

STAGE I. PREMONOPOLY
Total Output: 200 Loaves

Workers' Situation

Number of bakers	100
Total wage bill	100 loaves
Average wage	1 loaf per worker
Productivity	2 loaves per worker
Labor share of income	50% (100/200)

Capitalists' Situation

Profit or surplus	100 loaves
Capitalist share of income	50% (100/200)

STAGE II. MONOPOLY
Total Output: 1,000 Loaves

Workers' Situation

Number of bakers	80
Productivity per baker	12.5 loaves
Additional workers	
Bread-shaping gimmick workers	
Chemical-additive makers	
New wrapping-design specialists	
Advertising workers	
Tax-avoidance lawyers	
Total	20
Total wage bill	500 loaves
Average wage bill	5 loaves per worker
Labor share of income	50% (500/1,000)

Capitalists' Situation

Profit or surplus	500 loaves
Capitalist share of income	50% (500/1,000)

THE GIANT CORPORATION

The *modus operandi* of the system can be understood if we follow the behavior of the giant corporation in an oligopolistic market context. We see how it is driven by its needs and rationality to increase the gap between maximum output and socially necessary costs, that is, to increase the size of the capitalist society's potential surplus. Why corporate giants have a propensity to increase this gap is one matter; the particular means by which the system absorbs the surplus and avoids the social instability associated with underuse of resources are another. The former requires understanding of the prevailing price-cost relations among giant corporations. The latter casts critical light on the *content* of capitalist society: the composition of its output, its essential qualities, its limitations, and its basic tendency to distort the individual's humane capacities.

The giant corporation is a price maker, with a long-run profit horizon. Because the giants realize that direct price competition in oligopolistic markets tends to cause mutually destructive conflicts, they interpret their own interests in terms of the interests of the whole group. Price competition then fades away, and other competitive tactics emerge in its place. The other kinds of competition (in advertising, special credit arrangements, service, fictional differences in product, and so on) propel giants to cut costs and rationalize methods of production in order to accumulate capital ad infinitum. This strong propensity to accumulate capital, as in the nineteenth century when competition was more rigorous, is still considered the prime mover of the system. Each giant, no matter how large and how powerful, still accounts for a relatively small fraction of total national output. Each is perpetually driven to accumulate in order to maintain (if not to enhance) its share of the total surplus pie; it does so by way of wasteful employment of resources.

The outcome of this blunting of price competition has four main consequences. First, it produces price "stickiness," downward but not upward. Second, it leads to joint-profit maximization of the whole group. Third, it slows the introduction of innovations. Finally, it stimulates the use of selling instruments on a grand scale in order to maintain or increase the individual giant's share of the surplus (profit) that has been jointly maximized cooperatively.

THE TENDENCY TOWARD STAGNATION

The giant corporation is seen in more dynamic terms as generating a growing relative gap between prices (a component of revenue) that "irreversibly" increase at a faster rate than average costs. The latter tend to change more slowly for two reasons. First, short-run costs associated with the employment of labor and use of natural resources are assumed to be constant and overhead or fixed costs to decline as output increases; total average costs thus decrease. Second, capital-goods industries make their profits by producing and introducing cost-reducing machinery in order to induce other giants to purchase it. As the difference between prices (revenue) and costs is profit, the most important component of measurable surplus, the system will tend to generate larger and larger surpluses as output increases. In the affluent society of monopoly capitalism, this tendency is called the "law of rising surplus"; it replaces Marx's "falling rate of profit." It has been estimated that the surplus, as a percentage of GNP, rose from approximately 46 percent in 1929 to about 53 percent in 1963. The major components in this rise were total property income, waste in distribution, corporate advertising, finance, insurance and real-estate compensation to employees, legal services, and surplus absorbed by government.[10] A revised estimate of the economic surplus, based on different measures, was made for a more extended period (1929–1970). Using the notions of potential GNP and of essential personal and social consumption, researchers found that the surplus rose from about 39 percent of total GNP in 1929 to 58 percent in 1970.[11] The law of rising surplus is at the heart of a systemic tendency to stagnate.

In the system's normal operations, especially during the upswing of the business cycle when output is increasing, monopoly capitalism inevitably develops an imbalance between the capacity to produce and the rate of effective absorption of output. There are numerous reasons why (for example, the fact that not all corporate earnings are distributed to stockholders). Private capitalists' consumption and investment demand, left alone, are simply insufficient to absorb all the surplus that the system can generate. As a result, a further imbalance, between changes in the investment-seeking portion of the surplus and investment outlets, develops. Investment opportunities decline because of the growth in productive capacity relative to effective demand. When this differential reaches its critical limit, the upward swing of the business cycle (which tends not to reach a full-employment peak) turns downward. Investment, output, and income decline. The underutilized portion of the surplus manifests itself in increased unemployment and more unused capital. With this model the historic tendency toward stagnation can be explained. The system would, if left to itself, come to rest at a level far below what is necessary to maintain full employment, and thus it would tend to generate a social instability incompatible with economic viability.

It must be noted that the tendency toward stagnation is not always apparent, because it can be held in check by counteracting forces. It does, however, become apparent at intervals, when counteracting forces have subsided or when the influence of military spending has been subtracted from the system. Discovering the evidence of this process thus requires historical imagination, as well as the ability to look beyond short-term deviations from the permanent tendencies of monopoly capitalism. It requires imagination because the effects of wars and unique historic innovations* must be discounted if we are to see the "permanent" direction of the economy. For example, by the 1890s monopolization had developed sufficiently to produce stagnation in the economy, but stagnation was not apparent because the railroad boom provided outlets sufficient to maintain investment plans. By 1907 investment in rails had been normalized without being replaced by such additional external factors as wars. Between 1907 and 1915 conditions thus prevailed for a "test" in the laboratory of history of the association between monopolization of the economy and stagnation. The data for this period show that the average unemployment rate was 6.7 percent, a rate 2.3 times greater than that of the preceding period. In general, the period 1907–1915 was characterized by "mounting surplus absorption difficulties, and the kind of 'creeping stagnation' with which we have become familiar in the later 1950's and early 1960's."[12]

An example of perceiving beyond the data in order to observe

---

* Such innovations differ from normal innovations in two ways. First, they tend to increase the rate of investment outlets more rapidly than investment plans, thus narrowing the gap between the actual and theoretical surplus and temporarily bringing about the full utilization of resources. Second, they alter the composition of output, change the locations of industry, stimulate shifts in the population, and so on. They are the kinds of innovations that alter the contours of the whole society.

the underlying stagnation is embodied in the argument that the American economy has been stagnant from 1939 to the present. Except for the World War II period and the immediate postwar years (1947–1949), in which the performance of the economy reflected the backlog of demand and the high level of savings unspent during the war (see Chapter 6), the American economy has revealed, according to Baran and Sweezy, an unemployment rate equal to the one that prevailed in 1939, that is, 15 percent. Is the economy currently operating at a 15 percent "unemployment equilibrium"? The answer is "yes," if the portion of the employed labor force absorbed by the military sector is added to the actual rate of unemployment that has prevailed for the past few years. The immediate objection, of course, is that there are nondefense alternatives to military spending. The neo-Marxist answer is that these alternatives exist only in the textbooks of Keynesian economists. In reality, as the seven-year New Deal effort demonstrated, a coalition of property interests limits the nature and level of nondefense expenditures that can be mobilized to buoy the economy to a full-employment level.

MODES OF UTILIZING THE SURPLUS

Once having established the logic of and evidence for a tendency toward stagnation when private investment and consumption propensities prevail without props, Baran and Sweezy have proceeded to discuss the adaptation of the system to other means of using surplus, all of which are efforts to increase aggregate demand relative to potential output, or to the unproduced output that manifests itself in the form of unemployed resources. The three main means, other than private consumption and investment, are sales efforts, nondefense government spending related to the irrational needs of capitalism, and imperialism and militarism.

SALES EFFORTS

The immediate and apparent purpose behind sales efforts is to create new tastes or to intensify old ones in order either to increase demand or to make consumers more insensitive to price changes, thus making it possible to shift the costs of advertising onto consumers in the form of higher prices. The real income of productive workers is, of course, less than its potential. More important, sales efforts serve to provide increments of income to unproductive portions of the labor force (defined as those working directly or indirectly because of the existence of the advertising complex) at a rate greater than the costs of the sales efforts. Speaking more technically, Baran and Sweezy have argued that advertising outlays have effects on aggregate demand similar to those of the balanced-budget multiplier. Increments in income associated with increments in advertising outlays are greater than the increments in cost by a factor of one.

Sales efforts indirectly affect the availability and nature of investment opportunities and the division of the social product between saving and consumption. They create demand for plant and equipment that otherwise would not occur, and they encourage spending to the detriment of saving.

The most important observation made in the discussion of sales efforts is that selling is not peripheral to production, that is, it is not simply related to the circulation of goods, but is imbedded in the production process itself. The engineer, whose alleged preoccupation is with technological efficiency, takes orders based on market "research" from the sales division. Of course, many so-called production workers may essentially be part of the advertising complex, in that they make gadgets, parts, and designs primarily related to sales efforts. Not only are the labor and resources used unrelated to the commodity's function, they may even be detrimental to its technical efficiency. The latter point can be illustrated by the notion of "obsolescence" in the motor-vehicle industry. Here we have an instance in which the car's functional efficiency (gas usage, maintenance costs, and so on) has actually declined over the years, at great cost in human and other resources.

NONDEFENSE EXPENDITURES

It has been observed that government participation and activities have widened in scope. This process has been permitted by giant corporations because of chronic excess capacity in a monopolistic economy. Government activity, in contrast to what neoclassical economists of the nineteenth century assumed, is not financed out of actual surpluses; instead, it is paid for in real terms by some portion of the potential surplus in the form of unused resources. For example, unemployed workers mobilized by government expenditures generate the revenues to meet the costs of added output. Public expenditures are not at the expense of private ones.

Certain kinds of resistance to government activity that prevailed among property owners in the past have thus disappeared.

It should be noted as well that some portion of nondefense expenditures is essential to productive private investment or the reproduction of the working class and must, technically speaking, be distinguished from nonessential government expenses related to the wasteful propensities of capitalism. Expenditures on higher education, for example, are an example. Some portion of these expenses are necessary to develop the skills necessary to the productive part of the private sector. However, some portion is also required in order to postpone students' entrance into the labor force, for a great influx into the labor market increases the rate of unemployment and general social unrest. Much of what passes for higher education thus involves make-work, designed to pass the time. "Killing" time in college is thus a necessary but wasteful means of absorbing surplus output.

The net effect of the expansion of governmental activities is to increase aggregate demand, a function of both the absolute level of demand and the size of the deficit (government spending in excess of government revenues). Deficits, if they are perpetually to absorb the surplus (unemployed labor), must not only be permanent, but they must also continually grow larger. The necessity to increase the absolute size of the deficit arises from the fact that government spending pushes the economy to capacity output levels, at which the potential and actual surplus grows faster than effective demand. This achievement requires a larger deficit in the next round if total demand is to equal total supply at full employment.

The paradox is, on the one hand, that the rhythm of government spending creates ever-larger surpluses that require increases in government spending to absorb them, and, on the other, that the system of private enterprise generates vested interests (singly or in coalition) against increases in *productive* participation by government in any period of time. Civilian government spending thus provides a limited means of absorbing underused surplus.

IMPERIALISM AND MILITARISM

The final way of absorbing surplus output is through militarism and imperialism. Corporate monopolists want

> control over foreign sources of supply and foreign markets, enabling them to buy and sell on specially privileged terms, to

shift orders from one subsidiary to another, to favor this country or that depending on which has the most advantageous tax, labor, and other policies. . . . And for this they need "allies" and clients who are willing to adjust their laws and policies to the requirements of American Big Business.[13]

The preservation of giant multinational corporate interests abroad requires military and economic aid, the former to maintain the domestic tranquillity of the underdeveloped world and the latter to maintain the allegiance of its corrupt oligarchies.

In any event, the building of the American military juggernaut is unrelated to the military posture of the socialist nations, for (as Baran and Sweezy have documented) many members of the American establishment have explicitly declared that the threat of the socialist bloc is not of a military nature; it is economic, social, cultural, and ideological.

Be that as it may, militarism and imperialism are limited in their capacity to absorb surplus output. Militarism is limited for three reasons: First, science and technology are giving us more killing power per unit of investment; second, the logic of military strategy itself is becoming increasingly irrational in that it borders on destruction of all parties locked in the game of military emulation; and, third, bottlenecks in the supply of skilled manpower tend to increase costs before the full use of resources is attained. Military outlays may in fact abate because they cause problems that can be even more difficult for capitalism to solve than that of absorbing surplus output.

Imperialism is also limited, because it increases, rather than decreases, the problem of absorbing the surplus. Here, in a departure from the traditional Leninist treatment of imperialism (see Chapter 14 for a more detailed discussion), Baran and Sweezy do not view underdeveloped countries simply as receptacles for unabsorbed surpluses from the capitalist world. On the contrary, the "have not" nations are sources of accumulation and growth in productive capacity for the capitalist world and therefore function ultimately to accentuate the problem of absorption of surpluses while simultaneously draining themselves of their own capital.

All the system's mechanisms for counteracting stagnation are either limited in scope over the long run, are contradictory, or are capable of generating ruinous inflationary spirals of uncontrollable dimensions. To the extent that together they make it possible to maintain a "tolerable," or stable, level of surplus absorption (total demand), they produce a social, psychological, and cultural climate inimical to the essential needs of individuals to realize their potential. In a society dominated by monopoly capital there is thus more potential leisure, but there are not and cannot be social and psychological avenues to freedom and self-realization.

The conclusions of Baran and Sweezy's neo-Marxist argument are grim, not only because of the authors' belief that the capitalist system is incurably sick, but also because they think it futile to expect domestic agencies to mobilize forces to alter the system.

> Industrial workers are a diminishing minority of the American working class, and their organized cores in the basic industries have to a large extent been integrated into the system as consumers and ideologically conditioned members of the society. . . . The system of course has its special victims . . . the unemployed and the unemployable, the migrant farm workers, the aged subsisting on meager pensions . . . but these . . . are too heterogeneous, too scattered and fragmented, to constitute a coherent force in society. And the oligarchy knows how, through doles and handouts, to keep them divided and to prevent their becoming a lumpenproletariat of desperate starvelings. . . . It is hard to avoid the conclusion that the prospect of effective revolutionary action to overthrow the system is slim.[14]

To the extent that there is hope, it arises from the role of the working class in underdeveloped countries. As national capital becomes multinational, it penetrates and further upsets the stability of Third World countries. It destroys whatever remnants of the traditional order exist without encouraging viable capitalist alternatives in such areas. It thus produces an enormous anti-imperial and anticapitalist backlash among peasants and workers. Sooner or later, according to Baran and Sweezy, the establishment of Third World socialist states will turn American capitalism on itself, destroy its expanding opportunities, and stimulate American workers to action. At that juncture, the choice before the American public will either be some kind of garrison society or the development of a humane socialist one. A benign mixed democratic-capitalist system of the kind generally projected by mainstream economists is not possible.

CONCLUSION

In these pages we have concerned ourselves with generation of surplus output by the giant corporations and its absorption by the superstructure. Baran and Sweezy, in their efforts to develop a comprehensive neo-Marxist view of American capitalism, have rightly warned that their analysis is seriously incomplete because of their almost total neglect of a "subject that occupies a central place in Marx's study of capitalism: the labor process."[15] No attempt has been made to "inquire systematically into the consequences . . . of technological change, [into the consequences] . . . of the monopoly capitalist period [for] the nature of work, the composition (and differentiation) of the working class, the psychology of workers, the forms of working-class organization and struggle, and so on."[16] For this reason our next concern will be specifically with the radical view of the labor process.

NOTES

1. Paul A. Baran and Paul M. Sweezy, *Monopoly Capital: An Essay on the American Economic and Social Order* (New York: Monthly Review Press, 1966). Copyright © 1966 by Paul M. Sweezy. Reprinted by permission of Monthly Review Press.

2. *Ibid.*, p. 9. The reason for using the notion of surplus, rather than the orthodox Marxian concept of "surplus value," is explained by the authors: "[The concept of surplus value is] equal to the sum of profits + interest + rent," whereas the concept of surplus comprises "other items such as the revenues of state and church, expenses of transforming commodities into money, and the wages of unproductive workers." *Ibid.*, p. 10, footnote 6.

3. *Ibid.*, pp. 9–10.

4. Paul A. Baran, *The Political Economy of Growth* (New York: Monthly Review Press, 1957), p. 42.

5. *Ibid.*, p. 42.

6. This illustration was developed by Louis A. Dow, *Economics: Analysis, Issues and Policies* (Columbus, Ohio: Bell and Howell, 1974), pp. 579–581.

7. Baran and Sweezy, *Monopoly Capital*, p. 99.

8. Paul A. Baran, *The Longer View* (New York: Monthly Review Press, 1969), pp. 327–328.

9. *Ibid.*

10. The statistics were computed by J. D. Phillips, "Estimating the Economic Surplus," in Baran and Sweezy, *Monopoly Capital*, Appendix.

11. For the details and procedures of this estimate, see Ron Stanfield, "A Revision of the Economic Surplus Concept," *The Review of Radical Political Economics* 6 (Fall 1974): 69–74.

12. Baran and Sweezy, *Monopoly Capital*, p. 234.

13. *Ibid.*, p. 208.

14. *Ibid.*, pp. 363–364.

15. *Ibid.*, p. 8.

16. *Ibid.*, p. 9.

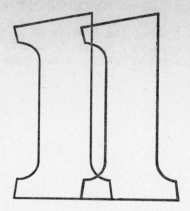

THE LABOR PROCESS

In discussions of the labor process, differentiating the radical analysis from the mainstream analysis is complicated by the fact that the mainstream itself is split between two separate views. One group, consisting of traditional labor-relations and manpower economists who have devoted their time to examination of specific labor markets, is weak on theory and strong on description. Although some of their findings are accepted by radical economists, for example, data on differences among industries in bargaining power to determine wage variations among groups of laborers, the major empirical work of this group is rarely integrated into a general vision of the capitalist process. To the extent that there is a larger theoretical edifice in the background, it is the pluralistic power-bloc thesis of the mixed capitalist system as propounded by welfare liberals (see Chapter 3).

The other mainstream group consists of the "human-capital" economists. The proponents of this school argue that each individual's lifetime income and position in society are related to his or her abilities, that altering income and social position is a matter of acquiring better education or more skills through work experience.[1] The worker is viewed as similar to an ordinary commodity or capital asset, the value of which "is the maximization of discounted earnings."[2] From the radical perspective, the human-capital economists seem to ignore the social structure (and therefore the character of class) and the fact that the individual's work arrangements are *independent* of his or her volition. In the hands of human-capital theorists, the individual worker, lamented R. A. Gordon (a former president of the American Economic Association),

> becomes a caricature . . . [of a computor] who continuously and consciously balance[s] costs and benefits at the margin, whether in deciding on another year of schooling, whether and when to marry or be divorced, how many children to have and when, or whether and when to commit a crime. And after a substantial amount of intensive research, the human capital approach still leaves unexplained a significant part of the differences in personal income.[3]

At times it is often difficult, in human-capital terms, to know whether the human being is an output or another input.[4] The human-capital approach, moreover, is ideologically "safe," for it belongs to the family of individual-choice models that characterize mainstream thought in general; that is, the focus is on how individuals "choose" to invest in themselves or "choose" the rate at which to accumulate "stocks" of educational capital. As the social parameters are given, the individual becomes responsible for his or her own failure or success.

To the extent that stocks of capital, education, and work experience are not related to income, "imperfections" in the market (on either the demand and/or the supply side) are acknowledged; supposedly they can be corrected through proper social policies. There is nothing in capitalist relations per se that prevents individuals from receiving incomes related to their productivity.

Radical economists believe that the human-capital explanation is so gross an oversimplification as to be basically erroneous or misleading. Far more goes into determining income and position in the economy than education, work experience, or native endowment (IQ). A worker sweeping the floors of an auto plant in Detroit earns much more than a worker sweeping the floors of a New York bank. These workers are not fundamentally different, and therefore the observed income differences between them have little to do with human capital. Even so, the problem does not revolve around simply the question of evidence.

The main thrust of the radical critique is less toward *what* is being observed than toward *why* it is taking place. Radicals suggest that what the human-capital economists are observing may be empirically demonstrable in market exchanges but that their explanation is superficial. Radicals themselves furnish an alternative framework leading to a different set of questions, different explanatory variables, and, of course, different solutions to the alleged imperfections in the system. This framework is diagrammed in Figure 11.1. The figure represents the total structure of the radical argument. The flow chart will serve, we hope, to keep our discussion organized.

Operating beneath the surface of income differences reflecting market-exchange relations is the accumulation drive of business enterprises to determine the rate and form of technological change ($II \rightarrow IV$, Figure 11.1). On the other hand, there are the labor needs of giant corporations (see II, "big capital"), whose power and influence are both national and international. The capital-accumulation process in this part of the system embraces capital-intensive technologies (see IV). On the other hand, there are the labor needs of the more numerous but less powerful competitive firms (see II, "small capital"), which operate in the local and regional markets of the system's periphery. This duality, or uneven development, generates a dual labor market (see III), which nurtures or sustains racial, ethnic, and sexual criteria used to employ, promote, allocate, and dismiss workers. Together, II, III, and IV constitute the mode of production that directly generates a hierarchy of occupational roles ($f \rightarrow B$). To fill these roles, workers are recruited and screened through an educational system ($C \rightarrow i \rightarrow B$). They are also "screened" by means of differences in inherited wealth, that is, by means of the intergenerational process associated with family background and social status ($A \rightarrow g \rightarrow B$; $A \rightarrow h \rightarrow C$). The educational system is the product of the superstructure ($I \rightarrow l \rightarrow C$), itself dependent upon changes in the mode of production. In this way, the differences in human capital are determined ($C \rightarrow j \rightarrow D$); these, in turn, are related to income differences ($D \rightarrow K \rightarrow E$), a surface market outcome that reflects the more deeply rooted processes identified. Finally, we note in passing that the broken arrows (i', j', k') represent the feedback process. Income differences, once determined from one direction, reinforce inequities and other differences in the chain. Although the system is not as nearly closed as it seems in the flow chart, we should have no illusions about the difficulties of achieving funda-

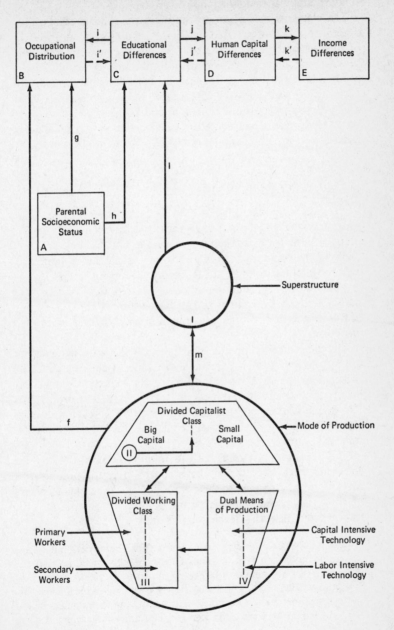

Figure 11.1 • Mode of Production, Market Segmentation, Occupational Distribution, and Income Differences

179

mental changes in the distribution of income and wealth without fundamentally altering the mode of production.

The elements that make up the radical argument can be classified into three interrelated parts: the accumulation propensities of the corporation as related to hierarchical control of the work process, the homogenization of job routines as established by production techniques determined by capitalist relations, and the necessity of market stratification according to such ascribed characteristics as race, ethnic affiliation, and sex. Each of these categories will now be considered in more detail. In our concluding remarks, we shall discuss their interrelations and implications.

CAPITAL ACCUMULATION AND HIERARCHY[5]

In mainstream thinking it has been assumed, at least since Adam Smith's discussion of the pin factory, that division of labor and economic efficiency are synonymous. That is, dividing and subdividing the process of making pins into trivial and monotonous tasks (stretching the pin, straightening it, cutting it, and so on) make possible the production of more pins with the same inputs or the same number of pins with smaller inputs.[6] A close inspection of the early history of modern capitalism has, however, stimulated challenges to this view.

It is the radical contention that both the early development of the putting-out system dominated by commercial capitalists and the subsequent development of the early factory system were based on primarily hierarchical modes of organizing production. The focus was on control and accumulation of capital, not on more efficient production that would lead to a higher material standard of living.

The putting-out system, with its minute division of labor, led to the destruction of the worker's control over the product; the early factory system led to the destruction of the worker's control of the work process. In the words of Stephen A. Marglin, the radical economist who developed this thesis:

> Rather than providing more output for the same inputs, these innovations in work organization were introduced so that the capitalist got himself a larger share of the pie at the expense of the worker. . . . The social function of hierarchical work organization is not technical efficiency, but accumulation. By mediating between producer and consumer, the capitalistic or-

ganization sets aside much more for expanding and improving plant and equipment than individuals would if they could control the pace of capital accumulation. . . . [That is to say], in the absence of hierarchical control of production, society would either have to fashion egalitarian institutions for accumulating capital or content itself with the level of capital already accumulated.[7]

It is important to understand that this argument does *not* imply that hierarchical organization is unique to capitalism. Mainstream economists generally argue that hierarchy, because it is universal and predates capitalism, requires no special investigation in relation to capitalist enterprise. In their view, the issue is settled simply by raising a "self-evident" hypothesis: Is there not an "iron law" of hierarchy? Radicals greet this reasoning as simply a device for avoiding concrete inquiry into the specific role of hierarchy in capitalist enterprises. Not only is this evasion characteristic of ahistorical and formalistic economic theorizing; it also enables mainstream economists to justify profit and accumulation ideologically by criteria other than the capitalist's drive to control work and his or her desire to distribute society's surplus according to the privileges of property. In the radical mind there are different kinds of hierarchy, and not all function toward the same ends. Again in the words of Marglin:

Hierarchy was . . . not invented by capitalists. . . . In precapitalist societies, industrial production was organized according to a rigid master-journeyman-apprentice hierarchy, which survives today in anything like its pure form only in the graduate departments of our universities. What distinguished precapitalist from capitalist hierarchy was first that the man at the top was, like the man at the bottom, a producer. The master worked along with his apprentice rather than simply telling him what to do. Second, the hierarchy was linear rather than pyramidal. The apprentice would one day become a journeyman and likely a master. Under capitalism it is a rare worker who becomes even a foreman, not to mention independent entrepreneur or corporate president. Third, and perhaps most important, the guild workman had no intermediary between himself and the market. He generally sold a product, not his labor, and therefore controlled both product and work process.[8]

This thesis has been extended by Marglin to include the use by the modern giant corporation of its hierarchical powers in the control of corporate dividends to prevent individuals from disposing of their own savings, which would interfere with the corporation's capacity to accumulate capital in accordance with its owners' needs and preferences. The argument suggests that, if saving decisions were left to individuals rather than to a small elite group of corporate representatives, "accumulation of productive capital, at least in plant and equipment, on which workers depend for increases in wages, would come to a virtual standstill."[9] This point is not beyond the understanding of capitalists themselves. According to one highly reputable study of business, "the dominant business opinion is that earnings have to be retained because it is impossible to obtain capital otherwise."[10] To use the actual words of one business leader, who was questioned by a congressional committee:

> . . . if you give it [earnings] all to the stockholders, by what rhyme or reason do we assume that they are going to save enough and have it ready for you when you want it? [The answer was quickly supplied:] . . . We have to take calculated risks in business, but as an administrator, I would not care to take that risk.[11]

One further point should be emphasized: The argument against capitalist forms of hierarchy associated with minute division of labor in manufacturing specific commodities is not an argument against the social division of labor, against individuals' and groups' working in different occupations. The capitalist division of labor, in its most elaborate form, arises from the need to control the work process in order to accumulate capital. The social division of labor is characteristic of all but the simplest hunting and food-gathering societies.[12] The capitalist division leads to mindless fragmentation of work routines, which brings us to the second major element of radical thinking about the labor process: the relationship between standardized work roles, associated with the division of labor, and specialization, on the one hand, and capitalist forms of technical innovation, on the other.

WORK ROUTINES
AND TECHNOLOGICAL CHANGE[13]

If controlling both the workers' ability to dispose of their own products and their ability to control their own work processes is necessary for capitalists to acquire power to function as accumulators of society's wealth, it follows that the technology harnessed by the capitalist will be shaped to further control of the details of the work process (Figure 11.1, M-n-O-p-Q). Radicals think that the efficiency of modern technology may therefore be overemphasized, less for the assumed purpose of achieving more output for the same magnitude of input than for the purpose of maintaining control of the work process in the modern corporation. It is possible, of course, that the two tendencies proceed simultaneously. In any event, the capitalists' focus on technological options that fragment and routinize the work process necessarily degrades work itself.

In the history of capitalism, from the period when rigorous competition prevailed to the present, when giant corporate oligopolies and monopolies reign, one secular trend has been apparent in the evolution of work routines for the vast majority of people: They have become simpler, more repetitive, and devoid of any requirement for knowledge of the whole work process. Increasingly, therefore, masses of workers have become interchangeable and even, from the point of the owners and controllers of capital, indistinguishable.[14] The history of this trend is fundamental; we have already touched upon it in discussion of the appearance and development of competitive capitalism. For this reason we shall devote our attention here to the work processes that have been initiated under the direction of the modern giant corporation. Our discussion will be divided into two parts: the rise of "scientific" management and the perpetual proletarianization of the labor force.

SCIENTIFIC MANAGEMENT

As the corporation became more complex, as larger aggregates of capital fell into the hands of corporate managers, competitive capitalism was replaced by monopolistic capitalism, a transformation that reached its peak between 1890 and 1910. Concomitant with this development there emerged a new school of management called "Taylorism" (after its founder, Frederick Winslow

Taylor) or "scientific management." The essence of Taylorism was a series of managerial control techniques that specified in extreme detail the way in which work should proceed. Every process was broken down into activity units that could be timed: the beginning of time-motion studies of the work process. There were three basic principles of "scientific management":

1. "The dissociation of the labor process from the skills of the workers"[15]
2. The separation of the conception of work from its execution, the former falling under the monopoly control of management[16]
3. "The use of this monopoly over knowledge to control each step of the labor process and its mode of execution."[17]

One general consequence of this development was the appearance of a wide chasm separating manual work from mental work, physical functioning from brain functioning. This chasm did not go unnoticed by the craft workers of the day. In an editorial that appeared in the *International Molders Journal*, we can see how workers greeted some of these new ideas:

> The one great asset of the wage worker has been his craftsmanship . . . the ability to manipulate skillfully the tools and materials of a craft or trade. But true craftsmanship is much more than this. The really essential element in it is not manual skill and dexterity but something stored up in the mind of the worker. . . . [But this disappears by] the gathering up of all this scattered craft knowledge, systematizing it and concentrating it in the hands of the employer and then doling it out again only in the form of minute instructions, giving to each worker only the knowledge needed for the performance of a particular relatively minute task. The process, it is evident, separates skill and knowledge even in their narrow relationship. When it is completed, the worker is no longer a craftsman in any sense, but is an animated tool of the management.[18]

In the radical view, this growing separation between those who execute the work and those who conceive it is simply the concrete counterpart of the general institutional separation between those who work (but do not own) and those who own and control the means of production (but do not work). This separation propels capitalism in a single direction. Whatever the initial relation between the execution of work and its conception in any specific industry or sector of the economy, the harnessing of technology by capitalists in the process of accumulating capital necessarily leads to the breakdown of crafts and skills and to the private confiscation of knowledge related to the work process. When we look at the modern white-collar worker, we see that he or she is being "proletarianized" in ways very similar to those that have already been applied to blue-collar workers. The factory has come to office and service industries. The need for a new reserve army of cheap labor has recently pushed corporate accumulators into the home, where females have labored to produce nonmarket goods and services. The success of this recruitment process is partly related to inadequate incomes for male factory workers; the necessity for it, however, was related to corporate needs to expand sales and distribution of goods and services in order to realize and maintain profits.[19]

PROLETARIANIZING TENDENCY

For the longest time, mainstream criticism of Marx revolved around his failure to anticipate the rise of the "new" middle class, a segment of the population that was considered fundamentally different from both wage earners and capitalists. This new class, often inappropriately used as a synonym for white-collar workers in general, was said to have incomes significantly higher than those of the average factory worker, which meant also a lifestyle and work routine very different from those of the proletariat. This allegedly growing class (hedged between the foreman overseeing blue-collar workers and the general manager) consisted of technicians, engineers, chief engineers, production managers, planners, salesmen, market researchers, teachers, social workers, lawyers, doctors, and the like; their numbers were expected to become sufficiently large to dominate the social and political scene. The old-fashioned production workers and the small elite who owned the means of production were considered disappearing breeds.

It cannot be denied that an upper middle stratum, consisting of functionaries serving a much smaller elite that directly owns the largest portions of the means of production, has developed. But the magnitude of this class has been exaggerated in the popular media; it probably does not include more than 20 percent of the total labor force. The reason for this exaggeration, ideology aside, is that the growing numbers of this class are frequently compared with the shrinking numbers of blue-collar workers. But between this upper middle stratum and the traditional working class there has emerged, *not* a new white-collar middle class, but a new white-collar proletariat, consisting mainly of women working in service and office industries. "White-collar industries," it should be noted, pay their workers less on the average than the older, more stagnant industries pay blue-collar proletarians. The differences in earnings between industries absorbing the growing number of women entering the labor force and the older industries are shown in Table 11.1.

Aside from lower incomes, the work routines of this new group of white-collar workers increasingly resemble those found in factories.[20] The whole batch of service, sales, and clerical workers that have sprung up in the past twenty years is employed at jobs that require minimal skills and no knowledge of the general work process. For example, let us glance at the new-product goals specified for IBM's "system Q":

> The system must be usable by people who are not programmers, not professional, not college graduates, and not necessarily high school graduates. . . .
>
> The casual user needs no knowledge of what computer is running his program, how many and what kind of storage devices contain this data, how much (main) memory is available, or any other hardware characteristic. . . .[21]

Table 11.1 • *Gross Average Weekly Earnings of Production or Nonsupervisory Workers on Private Nonagricultural Payrolls, 1971*

RELATIVELY STAGNANT INDUSTRIES		RAPIDLY GROWING INDUSTRIES	
Mining	$171.74	Wholesale and retail trade	$100.74
Contract construction	212.24	Finance, insurance, and	
Manufacturing	142.04	real estate	121.36
Transportation and public		Service industries	102.94
utilities	168.84		

SOURCE: *Monthly Labor Review* (December 1972): 96, Table 22. Quoted in Harry Braverman, *Labor and Monopoly Capital* (New York: Monthly Review Press, 1974), p. 393.

Although contemporary radicals do not claim that current developments in the labor force match Marx's original expectations, they do believe that the mainstream image of a vast middle class is well off the mark. More generally, they see current trends in work routines as evidence of a growing tendency toward homogenization, or proletarianization, of the labor force, a pattern that accompanies changes in the industrial structure and in the composition of the labor force. Such changes in structure, composition, and work pose a problem: They appear initially to be somewhat inconsistent with the third element of radical analysis, market stratification along the lines of ascribed characteristics (Figure 11.1, Q-r-C). We shall now turn to this question.

INDUSTRIAL STRUCTURE AND MARKET STRATIFICATION

The labor process is, in the most concrete sense, the means by which the capitalist class, functioning within its own factories or corporate units, transforms labor power into marketable goods and services. The market is the pool from which labor is recruited and in which labor is disposed of when it is no longer needed. Capitalist markets are shaped by these recruiting and dumping processes, exhibiting patterns appropriate to the organizational needs of the separate capitalist enterprises. The aggregation of decisions made within different industries with varying structures shapes the general contours of the market. While the market and the organizational needs of enterprises are not identical, they are related and function as parts in a feedback system. Market stratification suits the respective needs of firms or industries, which, deliberately or not, reproduce the market stratification. As the first step in our analysis it is necessary to focus on the connection between a dual industrial structure and a segmented labor market.

DUALITY AND SEGMENTATION

As division of labor and specialization were pushed to the point of absurdity, as the possibility of any intrinsic job satisfaction vanished for the vast majority of workers, small differences in job routine within the working class were magnified in importance by the managers of capital. To the extent that some of these differences reflected preexisting differences in ethnic groups, race, and sex, such ascriptive traits became important in the recruiting of business enterprises.

Managers of capitalist enterprises, as we have argued, have a general need to control the work process, which necessarily involves preventing or undermining class solidarity and class consciousness. Orchestrating control, in the absence of more costly coercion, often entails generating or adapting to various divisions within the working class (Figure 11.1, Q). This is not to argue that businesspeople necessarily *create* ascriptive differences, but they can *use* such differences in a variety of ways: as symbols to preserve meaningful aspects of a group's heritage and bring about continuity or chauvinistically to protect narrow economic interests at the expense of others. In the radical view, the insecurities of a competitive labor market periodically nurtured by the existence or threat of unemployment operate to accentuate aggressive use of ascribed differences within the working class and thus to weaken class consciousness and solidarity and ultimately to serve the interests of the business system. In this sense, ascribed traits, as criteria for recruiting, promoting, and discharging workers, are "functional" for the business system.

As radicals see it, the evolution of capitalism is marked by uneven development, by convulsive movement of capital from one area or industry to another, by dislodging some portions of the population and absorbing others. The broad contours of the economy can be described initially as consisting of a dual industrial structure that has generated a fragmented labor market to fit its needs.[22] The oligopolistically structured industries are capital-intensive and relatively profitable; they invest to some degree in training their workers, and they pay wages above the subsistence level. They tend to employ the "responsible" portion of the white working class, with some inferior jobs "reserved" for minority workers. To the extent that such industries need large administrative hierarchies, involving mechanized office jobs, they recruit women; some of these jobs are stable, and others are not.

The periphery of the dual industrial structure encompasses a number of labor-intensive firms, frequently unstable and unprofitable, which generate many dead-end jobs at poverty wages. Such industries breed a secondary labor market of workers whose "traits" are susceptible to the "yo-yo treatment," a rhythm calling for more transient workers who can be employed, laid off, and reemployed without additional costs. Perhaps a more graphic description of the segmentation of the labor market owing to the dual industrial structure will highlight the radical analysis in this sphere.

At the bottom of the labor market are those who do the "dirty work" of society: the lettuce pickers, chambermaids, dishwashers, janitors, messengers, car washers. For the most part, their jobs are dead ends, bringing low pay and alienation. There is an extremely high turnover rate in these jobs: People work at them for a while, quit or are fired, and then look for similar jobs. Most of these "secondary" workers are black, Puerto Rican, chicano, female, or teenaged.

On the next rung are workers who do routine "primary" work, such tedious manual labor as assembly-line, construction, and retail sales or clerical work. Some of these jobs offer chances for promotion, union protection, and better pay; they are mostly held by ethnic whites.

The line between primary and secondary jobs is not always distinct; a typist in a pool or a keypunch operator is clearly in the secondary job market, whereas a personal secretary may be in the primary one.

Below the secondary work force is the welfare population; above the primary work force are creative workers: professionals, media people, managers, and the like. At the very top are those who receive their incomes from ownership, rather than from participation in the labor market.[23]

Although not immutable, this stratification shows a strong propensity to perpetuate itself; it cannot be altered without profound changes in the rules of the game. If, for example, welfare payments were to rise to levels that people could live on, then poorly paid, low-status jobs would lose their appeal altogether. Welfare payments (or any scheme for income maintenance or minimum incomes) cannot be adequate, or secondary workers will lose the incentive to work.[24] Nor is it clear that a family-assistance or negative income-tax plan would overcome this incentive problem. If adequate incomes or decent housing were offered to the very poor, then the *working poor*, who would perceive themselves as bearing the tax burden of these programs, would become upset. The basic line for a negative income tax cannot therefore be set at livable levels. Furthermore, when unionized primary workers see government programs aimed at training secondary workers to compete for their jobs, they often turn to political demagogues or at least reassert their ethnic "superiority" over those beneath them.

HOMOGENEITY AND ASCRIBED TRAITS

Because capitalism is viewed by mainstream economists as rational and impersonal, it is assumed also to be oblivious to ascribed traits (ethnic, race, and sex differences). To the extent that these differences determine occupational opportunities in the market, they are considered noneconomic atavisms, which are likely to vanish with time.[25] This argument is not totally alien to Marx's notion of the commodity fetish of the capitalist system, the conversion of social relations into relations of exchange.[26] It is partially true that capitalism, in transforming all aspects of life into commodities for exchange and profit, has tended to destroy the social and ethnic differences once associated with craft divisions. In fact, capitalism has tended to destroy the whole social fabric that once complemented human economic existence.[27] And, as we have already argued, the nature of technological innovation under capitalism tends to level job routines, obviate the need for skills, and eliminate even the need for any knowledge about the work process. This homogenizing process tends to breed the objective conditions for *potential* development of class solidarity. The movement of capital and the corresponding revolutionizing of the means of production throw masses of workers into a single market, at least in the long run. Through the system's perennial cheapening of skills, workers become interchangeable commodities, which can be manipulated without regard for their larger social context.[28]

In fact, the divorce of the social habitat from the private motivations that propel the economy defines the institutional context in which the mainstream notion of "economic man" emerged. This individual is entirely one-dimensional, driven to accumulate wealth and become oblivious to all noneconomic distinctions. Marx deplored this development, which the bourgeois economists of his day extolled. Both underestimated the ways in which capitalists can make use of ascriptive distinctions within the working class, however weak in relation to precapitalist social formations. Subordination and destruction of social relations had created a communal vacuum, a sense of anomie; frequently this vacuum could be filled by resurrecting ascribed differences between segments of the working class—by the workers themselves or through the manipulations of capitalists. The consequence was a divided working class, which facilitated capitalist control of it.

Capitalism, with its competitive labor market and its unevenly developed industrial structure (which has differentiated short-run labor needs), cannot rely on wage differentials alone to ensure the necessary allocation of workers. Contrary to the natural tendency of capitalism to transform all aspects of society into commodities are the persistent needs of people who do not "live by bread alone." The noneconomic characteristics of the labor force must therefore be nurtured by the dominant class in order to place workers in the unplanned, convulsively changing, and unevenly structured parts of the system. But, because the system also encourages competitive personal traits, rather than cooperative ones, ascriptive traits, as they settled into the various crevices of the market, became invidious rather than diverse cultural formations for mutual respect and appreciation. In this way, the radical explains the apparently paradoxical trend toward homogeneity of the labor force, on the one hand, and market stratification along ascriptive lines, on the other.

CONCLUSION

As we suggested at the beginning of this chapter, hierarchy, labor homogeneity, industrial structure, and market stratification are the interrelated elements of the radical alternative to the human-capital approach to explaining lifetime income and wealth patterns among groups and individuals. In the radical view, the human-capital approach at best captures some of the empirical symptoms, rather than identifying causes. Differences in education and work experience reflect *previous* wealth and have an important impact on differences in lifetime earnings. Although differences in income can be partially explained by educational differences, the latter are not as closely related to IQ scores as is commonly assumed. Let us look, for example, at Figure 11.2, reported by the radical economists Samuel Bowles and Herbert Gintis.[29] Two points must be emphasized: First, in the unshaded left-hand bars, the figure shows that "the number of years of schooling attained by an individual is strongly associated with parental socioeconomic status."[30] Second, the shaded right-hand bars show "that even among children with identical IQ test scores at ages six and eight, those with rich, well-educated, high-status parents could expect a much higher level of schooling than those with less-favored origins."[31]

These longitudinal processes are shaped by class relations that are themselves determined by the imperatives of the capitalist

Figure 11.2 • *Educational Attainments Related to Social Background*

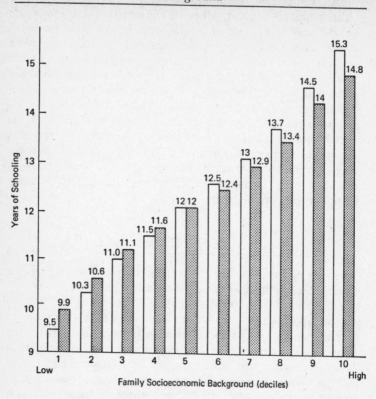

NOTES: For each socioeconomic group, the left-hand bar indicates the estimated average number of years of schooling attained by all men from that group. The right-hand bar indicates the estimated average number of years of schooling attained by men with IQ scores equal to the average for the entire sample. The sample refers to "non-Negro" men of "non-farm" backgrounds, aged 35–44 years in 1962.

SOURCE: Samuel Bowles and Valerie Nelson, "The 'Inheritance of IQ' and the Intergenerational Transmission of Economic Inequality," *The Review of Economics and Statistics*, LVI (February 1974). Reprinted by permission of the President and Fellows of Harvard College.

system. In the radical view, the educational system is part of the superstructure; that is, the educational system is a subsystem in which people are socialized to fit the economic slots associated with the given mode of production and structure of power. The system has needs, and it shapes people to fit them in particular ways. For this reason, radicals view the educational system as reflecting the contours of a stratified economy, as a screening process for maintaining economic privileges and social equilibrium.[32] Segmentation of the economy leads to the "freezing" of social distinctions. Career ladders are contrived to nurture status preoccupations among workers who have neither job satisfaction nor control over their work. Occupational statuses of the kind that we have been discussing are structured for control. In the absence of intrinsic motivation to work, control is necessary if "efficiency" and the appropriation of profit are to be achieved.

Complementary to the system's control mechanisms is their operation in a competitive labor market; the two factors interact to breed considerable social envy within the working class. Each segment of the total class views other segments as actual or potential enemies, as threats to its own security. Energies are diverted from the interclass struggle to the intraclass struggle. Broad class antagonisms derived from the general structure of capitalism are obscured by exaggeration of differences within the working class.

Mainstream economists, who tend to assume that the structure of preferences and the distribution of income and wealth are determined exogenously, generally ignore the class structure, its segmentation, and the obstacles to social mobility in their economic analyses. We do not claim that the class system is immutable or that its socializing institutions are perfectly geared to its structure. On the contrary, the system actually needs some fluidity between classes and strata, especially during periods of economic expansion. Indeed, one of the real sources of pressure for change is the contradictions and disparities between the economic and other components of the system. Unfortunately, because analysis of such matters lacks the tidiness necessary for the use of "pure" economic tools and methods of measurement, the dynamics of such processes are frequently ignored by mainstream economists. When establishment economists recommend policies to encourage upward occupational mobility, they usually tie them closely to cost-benefit analyses based on the cost-price structure of the system. This approach inevitably leads to recommendations for changes in mobility "on the margin," because the calculated costs of skipping too many rungs on the social ladder must necessarily be exorbitant. When "over education" for available jobs appears to be the problem, mainstream economists begin to ask whether everyone should really be encouraged to seek higher education. These short-run ebbs and flows can be illustrated in recent efforts by human-capital economists to justify moderate improvements in educational opportunities for minority groups, efforts that have now been tempered or even reversed because of changes in labor-market conditions and the problems of financing higher education. Now economists ask whether the benefits of higher education for so many disadvantaged youths are worth the costs. This zigzag pattern is simply one result of viewing education in narrow market terms, a common failing of mainstream economists.

What are the main implications of the radical analysis of class, industrial structure, and stratification, and what ideological presuppositions underlie them? First, radicals study the labor process as determined by the capitalist mode of production. "Work" is defined by technologies that are controlled by conflicting class relations. If the work process is to be altered, the worker must, in the words of Harry Braverman,

> regain mastery over collective and socialized production . . . by assuming the scientific, design, and operational prerogatives of modern engineering; short of this, there is no mastery over the labor process. The extension of the time of education which modern capitalism has brought about for its own reasons (postponing entrance into the labor force) provides the framework; the number of years spent in school has become generally adequate for the provision of a comprehensive polytechnical education for workers of most industries. But such an education can take effect only if it is combined with the practice of labor during the school years, and only if education continues throughout the life of the worker after the end of formal schooling. Such education can engage the interest and attention of workers only when they become masters of industry in the true sense, which is to say when the antagonisms in the labor process between controllers and workers, conception and execution, mental and manual labor are overthrown, and when the labor process is unified in the collective body which conducts it.[33]

The contemporary radical political economist is not a "back to nature" or an "arts and crafts" advocate. He or she believes strongly in history, reason, science, and the potentials inherent in modern technology. It is a tenet of the radical faith that integration of the total work process (both its mental and physical dimensions) with the broad needs of society is possible. What is required is more than workers' control of the factories or their participation in the election of management. In the radical view, it is a new, socialized person, who consciously understands his or her interests in relation to the organizational and cultural evolution of the larger society.

To mainstream economists, the radical view of work seems sheer utopian nonsense; as they see it, it violates human nature and certain oppressive organizational features required in modern societies. Radicals reply that it is easy to rationalize what already exists as "inevitable." As John Kenneth Galbraith has cleverly pointed out, in connection with the "virtues" of practical wisdom: "People who are concerned with being practical never urge anything that is new. . . . If you want to be practical, you should vehemently support what has already happened."[34] Such support, of course, is one task of mainstream economists. The radical's advocacy necessarily takes him or her beyond the boundaries of present institutions.

One important consequence of the radical analysis of the role of hierarchy in accumulating capital and the role of market stratification in undermining class solidarity is that it leads to rejection of the mainstream focus on economic growth. Growth, as we have suggested in Chapter 6, is considered a "solution" to both poverty and the class struggle over distribution of the income pie. The question of growth is therefore an appropriate topic to analyze from the radical perspective.

NOTES

1. J. Mincer, "The Distribution of Labor Incomes: A Survey with Special Reference to the Human Capital Approach," *Journal of Economic Literature* 8 (1970): 1–26.

2. Finis Welch, "The Human Capital Approach: An Appraisal," *The American Economic Review: Papers and Proceedings* 65 (May 1975): 63.

3. R. A. Gordon, "Rigor and Relevance in a Changing Institutional Setting," *The American Economic Review* 66 (March 1976): 3.

4. Samuel Bowles and Herbert Gintis, "The Problem with Human Capital Theory—A Marxian Critique," *The American Economic Review: Papers and Proceedings* 65 (May 1975): 74.

5. The argument in this section is largely based on the study by Stephen A. Marglin, "What Do Bosses Do? The Origins and Functions of Hierarchy in Capitalist Production," *The Review of Radical Political Economics* 6 (Summer 1974): 60–112.

6. Adam Smith, *An Inquiry Into the Nature and Causes of the*

Wealth of Nations (New York: Modern Library, 1937), p. 4.

7. Marglin, "What Do Bosses Do?" pp. 62–63.

8. *Ibid.*, p. 63.

9. Stephen A. Marglin, "What Do Bosses Do? Part II," *The Review of Radical Political Economics* 7 (Spring 1975): 20.

10. Francis Sutton, *et al.*, *The American Business Creed* (Cambridge, Mass.: Harvard University Press, 1956), p. 86; quoted by Marglin, "What Do Bosses Do? II," p. 23.

11. Quoted in Marglin, "What Do Bosses Do? II," p. 23.

12. *Ibid.*, p. 63. We should point out that Marglin argues that, insofar as the Soviet Union has repeated the history of capitalism in its accumulation propensities, the Soviet's hierarchical system has a function similar to that of the capitalist hierarchy.

13. In this section we rely heavily on the work of Harry Braverman, *Labor and Monopoly Capital* (New York: Monthly Review Press, 1974).

14. It is not without reason that mainstream economists frequently begin with the assumption that all workers are perfect substitutes, an assumption usually explained as a heuristic device permitting measurement of "frictions" or elasticity coefficients in the substitution of labor for labor.

15. Braverman, *Labor and Monopoly Capital*, p. 113.

16. *Ibid.*, p. 114.

17. *Ibid.*, p. 119.

18. This was a quote from an editorial in the *International Molders Journal* that appeared in *Scientific Management of Labor* (New York, 1918), pp. 131–132; quoted in Braverman, *Labor and Monopoly Capital*, p. 136.

19. Braverman, *Labor and Monopoly Capital*, Parts IV and V.

20. *Ibid.*, Chapters 16, 17.

21. Quoted by Maarten de Kadt, "A Review of Labor and Monopoly Capital: The Degradation of Work in the Twentieth Century," *The Review of Radical Political Economics* 7 (Spring 1975): 87.

22. Bennett Harrison, "The Theory of the Dual Economy," in *Post-Industrial Capitalism: Liberal and Radical Responses*, eds. Bertram Silverman and Murray Yanowitch (New York: Free Press, 1974), pp. 277–287.

23. For examinations of the labor force along these lines, see Barry Bluestone, "The Tri-Partite Economy: Labor Markets and the Working Poor," *Poverty and Human Resources* 5 (July–August 1970):15–36; and David H. Gordon, *Theories of Poverty and Underemployment* (Lexington, Mass.: Heath, 1972).

24. Frances Fox Piven and Richard A. Cloward, *Regulating the Poor: The Functions of Public Welfare* (New York: Vintage, 1971).

25. See Barbara Bergmann, "Can Racial Discrimination Be Ended Under Capitalism?" in *Economics: Mainstream Readings and Radical Critiques*, 2nd ed., ed. David Mermelstein (New York: Random House, 1973), pp. 305–308.

26. See Daniel D. Luria, "Trends in the Determinants Underlying the Process of Social Stratification: Boston, 1880–1920," *The Review of Radical Political Economics* 6 (Summer 1974): 174.

27. For a most lucid discussion of this theme, see Karl Polanyi, *The Great Transformation* (New York: Rinehart, 1944).

28. The very way in which mainstream economists separate notions of social costs or externalities from the central core of their theories illustrates the extent to which they ignore the social context. When such concepts *are* considered, they are often used to analyze problems viewed as marginal to a system that in other respects is functioning well.

29. Samuel Bowles and Herbert Gintis, *Schooling in Capitalist America* (New York: Basic Books, 1976), p. 31.

30. *Ibid.*, p. 30.

31. *Ibid.*, p. 32.

32. See Herbert Gintis, "Education, Technology and Characteristics of Worker Productivity," *The American Economic Review: Papers and Proceedings* 65 (May 1971): 266–279; Samuel S. Bowles, "Unequal Education and the Reproduction of the Social Division of Labor," *The Review of Radical Political Economics* 3 (Fall 1971): 1–30; and Christopher Jencks, *et al.*, *Inequality* (New York: Basic Books, 1972).

33. Braverman, *Labor and Monopoly Capital*, p. 445.

34. John Kenneth Galbraith, "Eleanor and Franklin Revisited," *The New York Times Book Review,* March 19, 1972, p. 2.

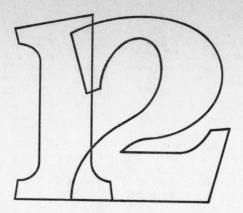

GROWTH:
BANE, BOON, OR WHAT?

Few mainstream economists have ever doubted that producing more goods and services is good—at least until very recently. John F. Kennedy's 1960 campaign was built around this unquestioned fixation on growth. Behind him, lending intellectual credibility to his rhetoric, stood the country's most prominent welfare-liberal economists. A large GNP was viewed as a panacea for all the nation's problems. Aside from the assumption that happiness equals more, there was also a belief that growth would "solve" the problem of distributing income, as well as providing additional resources for the public sector. If the economy can be stimulated to grow at some optimum, mainstream economists reasoned, part of the increment in goods can be distributed to the poor and absorbed by the public sector without the middle and upper classes feeling the pinch. In fact, the upper echelons may also experience an increment from year to year, though a smaller one (in percentage terms) than that which the poor and public sector will receive. The process of achieving "equity" and more public goods will reduce the class struggle over the allocation of given resources and distribution of the given product, because growth means that no one is required to become worse off as others become better off. In fact, the whole concern with efficient allocation can be swept under the rug if growth is sustained, because the additional goods and services derived from such growth tend to swamp those gained from reallocating the given stock of resources under constant technical conditions.

Mainstream policy recommendations aimed at facilitating growth thus seem "practical," in that they are to meet the needs of the corporate power structure, on the one hand, and to supply dominant segments of the political system with programs for bringing hope of betterment to the underprivileged classes, on the other. Mainstream economists (not excluding conservatives) thus have a strong ideological vested interest in growth, and this interest is not going to be readily shaken by alternative considerations—even when alternatives are persuasively argued by well-respected mavericks of their fraternity.[1]

The penchant for growth is matched, as we might expect, by business captains' view of their own life-and-death needs. One study of top multinational corporate executives has revealed that

> the desire to survive [in a competitive world] is what motivates companies to grow. Profit is important . . . but to ensure a continuous flow of reasonable profits over the long run, they must grow. And if they are to grow, expansion of manufacturing and sales abroad is a must, because either the home market is not big enough or the domestic economy is not growing fast enough to sustain the company's desired growth.[2]

Along the same lines, the vice-president of a large American drug company has remarked: "The desire of this company is to be a growth company. The responsibility of this management is to make the company grow both here and abroad, to be a growth company. Otherwise we are not doing our job."[3]

This faith in growth, it should be noted, is strongly shared by large stockholders, who seek to avoid taxes on stock dividends. Finally, growth requires, as statements from business leaders suggest, preoccupation with a predetermined magnitude of profit as a proportion of investment. Whether or not corporations seek to maximize profits in the technical sense is not relevant; the point is that they have profit targets that must continually rise as they succeed in their compulsive drive to expand.[4] It was not without reason that Marx compared the guiding principle of capitalist-owned enterprises to the miser's passion for wealth for its own sake. But, he went on to observe, that which in the miser is a mere idiosyncrasy is, in the capitalist, the effect of the social mechanism of which he is but one of the wheels. Moreover, the development of capitalist production makes it constantly necessary to keep increasing the amount of the capital laid out in a given industrial undertaking, and competition makes immanent laws of capitalist production to be felt by each individual capitalist, as external coercive laws. It compels him to keep constantly extending his capital, in order to preserve it . . . by means of progressive accumulation.[5]

A consequence of this propensity to accumulate is, as Marx pointed out in *The Communist Manifesto*, that capitalists cannot exist without "constantly revolutionizing the instruments of production, and thereby the relations of production, and with them the whole relations of society."[6] As a result, technological change, driven by the quest for profit, has destroyed the older social and political framework and modes of thought that once operated to check the wanton application of technologies destructive to the human habitat in the larger sense. It appears that conservative and welfare-liberal economists, American business executives, corporate stockholders, government policy makers, and Karl Marx are in complete agreement on the matter of capitalism's obsessive need to grow.

Given this almost universal consensus, it is understandable why the celebrated Club of Rome study *The Limits of Growth*[7] shocked the "growthophiles" of the capitalist system. Echoing the concerns of ecologists, the Club of Rome—consisting of scientists, educators, economists, industrialists, humanists, and civil servants from ten countries—"proved," through its statistical model, that continuing the present rate of growth, especially among the industrial nations, is likely to bring the world to a dramatic end in the next 100 years or so. The prevention of such an outcome is said to require termination of growth now, a position that is in direct conflict with that of the growth advocates. Much of the public controversy revolves around the question of growth versus no growth. Is growth necessary? Is continued growth desirable?

Although radicals are unequivocally antagonistic to the growth advocates, they have also refused to go along with the no-growth position of the ecology-minded Club of Rome professionals. In a basic sense radicals focus outside this debate, which they see as ahistorical and devoid of concern about forces within the system that limit its options. The debate is between a purely formal dimension (abstract consideration of the pros and cons of growth) and a purely alarmist one (warnings that the end of the world is at hand). Radicals provide a third alternative. To understand it we must first develop a fuller understanding of the first two approaches.

THE CASE FOR NO GROWTH

The case for no growth can be put this way: Continued economic growth, especially among the industrial nations, is producing environmental chaos and disequilibrium destined to make the earth uninhabitable in the near future. World civilization as we know it will end. This projection is based on interrelated factors in four categories: scarce resources, population oversupply, pollution and contamination, and atmospheric overheating.[8]

SCARCITIES

Industrial growth requires large quantities of nonrenewable sources of energy and raw materials, as well as water reserves, that can no longer be satisfied by natural circulation. It is argued that fossil fuels will soon be exhausted and that practical alternatives are not likely to be developed soon enough. We are admonished that "at current rates of usage, all known reserves of silver, gold, copper, lead, platinum, tin, and zinc will be used up within twenty years."[9] Meeting the water-reserve problem, though clearly possible by means of desalination of sea water, will require greater quantities of energy, which will exacerbate the fuel shortage.

POPULATION OVERSUPPLY

Needless to say, the problem of overpopulation has a long history; basically, population growth is outrunning food production. "Neither the area of land suitable for cultivation nor the yield per acre can be arbitrarily increased."[10] Moreover, some of the very techniques employed to expand food supplies tend to create greater ecological disturbances than they resolve; for example, pesticides and nitrate fertilizers useful in agriculture poison the water table.

POLLUTION

The critical pollution issue is not whether a "clean" world is possible; the world never has been "clean." What is at stake is a profound disruption in the

> metabolism between nature and human society [stemming from accelerated and unabsorbed industrial wastes causing physiological damage from] pesticides, radioactive isotopes, detergents, pharmaceutical preparations, food additives, artificial manures, trace quantities of lead and mercury fluorides, carcinogens, gene mutants, and a vast quantity of other substances. . . .[11]

To this material pollution, there must be added "psychic pollution," "increasing exposure to excessive noise and other irritants, the psychological effect of overpopulation (and overcrowding),"[12] and perhaps also the general tension associated with the pace of industrial urban societies as they undergo constant change in occupational structures and living patterns.

ATMOSPHERIC OVERHEATING

Finally, there is the ultimate catastrophe "presented by 'thermal pollution.' The laws of thermodynamics show that even in principle, this limit cannot be crossed. Heat [that] is emitted by all processes involving the conversion of energy" will reach, it is claimed, a critical threshold that will dramatically upset the total atmosphere, making the earth uninhabitable.[13]

Reduced to its barest essentials the no-growth argument assumes that

> stocks of things like . . . natural resources and waste-disposal capacity of the environment are finite, that the world economy tends to consume the stock at an increasing rate . . . and that there is no built-in mechanism by which approaching exhaustion tends to turn off consumption [in sufficient time to avoid catastrophe].[14]

In the ecological view, our voyage along the path of growth must be terminated. We shall either run into scarcities for which there are no readily available remedies or find that the substitutes that are available to "solve" one cluster of problems will create disequilibria elsewhere in the environment. Ecological considerations thus require us to view the earth as a spaceship with finite boundaries dictating that consumption and production activities be evaluated in the total context. Because the negative consequences of such activities accumulate exponentially, we must learn to recycle many aspects of our universe.

THE CASE FOR GROWTH

Two main aspects of the case for growth are articulated by mainstream economists: One is closely pegged to policy considerations, the other to theoretical ones.

We have already noted, however briefly, why practical people of affairs and practitioners of the economic art cling to the growth ethos. Policy instruments for achieving growth (for example, tax reductions, investment credits, deficit spending, loosening the money supply) are favorable to the existing institutions of welfare capitalism; the growth process itself is instrumental in "solving," or, at least theoretically, reducing a whole range of problems—discrimination, poverty, income inequities, the need for more public goods, and so on—"painlessly." If the pie continually grows bigger in absolute terms, all the claimants can theoretically have more. Even the no-growth theorists can have more resources with which to fight the consequences of growth. Growth is therefore viewed as the least bitter of all medicines for achieving bliss. Given the present rate of unemployment, it is not surprising to find almost every well-known mainstream economist (even the ecology-minded ones) calling for drastic measures to stimulate growth in the private sector. They argue that this is no time to junk the automobile industry, enforce pollution standards, or nurture more economic uncertainty: The economy is in too much of a slump already. On the contrary, we must do everything that we can to stimulate production of junk that we normally ridicule, in order to rid the economy of unemployment. External diseconomies, however important in textbook discourses, are not something to act upon now.

The growth position is articulated with more caution on the theoretical level. The phrase "in principle" (or "logically speaking") is the standard qualifier, a verbal safety device that, in the radical view, serves to obscure unpleasant truths. Robert Solow, a sophisticated advocate of the growth perspective, with a penchant for reducing issues to their essentials, has put the matter as follows: "Arguments about the desirability of economic growth often turn quickly into arguments about the 'quality' of modern life. . . . I [believe] that there is not a necessary or logical connection between your answer to the growth question and your answer to the quality-of-life question."[15] Even in the absence of growth, "there would be . . . much . . . to complain about; [and with continued growth there can be] reductions in pollution and congestion and less consumption of sliced white bread."[16] Of course, if one becomes too enthusiastic about economic growth, one is "likely to be attracted too easily [to] quantifiable and measurable things as the objects of study" at the expense of "important, intangible aspects of the standard of living."[17] This belated concession to quality-oriented addicts of whole-wheat bread and hiking is not very serious. Solow continues, "Although you can't know whether people are happier than they used to be, you can at least determine that they drink more orange juice or take more aspirin."[18] And, although in "principle" he recognizes that much of real GNP is not related to goods and services, he readily slips into the belief that numbers do not lie and comfortably asserts without qualification that the "real GNP roughly doubled between 1950 and 1970."[19]

In a more serious vein, Solow argues the "home truth" that achieving more equal distribution of income is more likely in a growing economy. Given a relatively static pie, it is unlikely that the "middle-class electorate will vote to redistribute part of its own income to the poor."[20] If the pie is growing, the chances of such generosity are assumed to increase. Of course, even if growth does not bring about greater equality in the distribution of the pie, it is still better, according to Solow, to be at the bottom of a richer society than at the bottom of a poorer one.[21]

The desirability of growth becomes even clearer when we turn from the question of distribution within a rich country like the United States to examine the distribution of wealth between the developed and underdeveloped nations. Here it is clear that, even with growth, the rich nations are unlikely to transfer sizable amounts to the poor nations of the world. "The *only* prospect of a decent life for Asia, Africa, and Latin America is more total output."[22] All hard-headed reasoning in defense of growth aside, Solow goes on in a more balanced tone:

I think that those who oppose continued growth should . . . face up to the implications of their position for distributional equity and the prospects of the world's poor. I think that those who favor continued growth on the grounds that only thus can we achieve some real equality ought to be serious about that. . . . In *principle*, we can have growth with or without equity and we can have stagnation (meaning no growth) with or without equity.[23] (emphasis added)

Posterity requires that the world continue, that we do not exhaust all the nonrenewable resources and leave millions of our descendants on the brink of total catastrophe. Posterity can best be served, growth advocates claim, not by stabilizing population, avoiding growth, or deemphasizing technological change, but by pushing forward in the opposite direction. Future growth requires that "we" find technological means of using our scarce resources more efficiently. If history is to serve as our guide, "accumulation of technological knowledge will probably make our great grandchildren better off than we are. . . . If continued economic growth is not possible, or less possible, then we probably ought to do more to promote it."[24]

Solow suggests that ultimately, behind the talk about problems of growth, what we have "is a set of attitudes" and values.[25] He likes modern life, he is an optimist, he distrusts the gloom-and-doom projections of the no-growth theorists, and he believes that what people worry about and how fast they want change are subjective issues.[26] Ideology thus emerges as the "ultimate" determinant of the way in which mainstream economists view the question of growth, a fact that certainly cannot be readily equated with general mainstream predilections for "positive" economics and its corresponding value-free nature. In view of the importance of "neutral" reasoning to a person like Solow, it is more than surprising to find how readily his "ultimate" weapons turn on such "homey" phrases as "I like modern life" and "I am an optimist."

THE RADICAL CASE

Radical economists dissent from both the notion of ecological spaceship earth and the fixation on growth characteristic of most mainstream economists. The ecologists suffer from a misconception of reality, and the mainstream economists are preoccupied with propping up the system, especially during unemployment, by policies for stimulating production of a given composition.

Radicals do not summarily dismiss the observations made by ecologists, especially those based on the natural and biological sciences. Indeed, it is important to consider the whole environment and its relation to the human species in evaluating our economic system.[27] Products and technologies that contaminate the environment, as well as the meaningless flow of trivial, and often unsafe, commodities that contribute to the living standards of Western nations and psychological distortions connected with the dehumanizing productivity needs of modern capitalist countries, are all points on which ecologists and radicals agree.[28] But, in social and political matters, radicals believe that most ecologists display great ignorance and naïveté.[29]

First, the ecologists' conception of growth is not distinct from their conception of development. They too often sound as if they are calling for a freeze of all national growth plans, regardless of the condition of the economy. From the perspective of the two-thirds of the world's population that are poor and part of structurally obsolete systems, they appear to want to freeze the existing inequities between rich and poor throughout the world. To be stabilized on top of the mountain is one matter; to be stabilized at the bottom of a cesspool of poverty, ignorance, and powerlessness is another. Calling upon the whole world to stop efforts to mechanize or industrialize when the distribution of wealth and income is so unequal appears to the poor nations of the world as an attempt to preserve the international status quo.

Second, certain aspects of the ecological argument are so unrealistic as to appear irrelevant to the modern age, even for the purpose of provoking thought. Some social scientists have called for a return to a kind of preindustrial agricultural state, without any conception of or interest in the social or political means by which such a reversal could be achieved.[30] Related to this pastoral ideal is the impression that the ecological "freaks" are mainly rich, aristocratic, mountain-climbing types who want the Green Mountains of Vermont preserved for summer retreats and hiking adventures. They protest job-creating industrial developments in depressed areas like central Maine and southern California because of their own selfish concerns.

Third, many social scientists overemphasize the imbalance between population and environment. They conclude that the world, mainly the underdeveloped world, is overpopulated and must drastically control population growth. Radicals think that this thesis obscures the important questions about the social system. This neo-Malthusian concern coincides with the way many mainstream economists view the problem of underdevelopment. They not infrequently suggest that the misery of the Third World nations can be all but resolved if birth-control practices are instituted on an extensive scale. Their reasoning, though rarely stated so bluntly, is that, with fewer people, per capita GNP would rise; this rise would stimulate savings, capital accumulation, and growth. The launching of the process is implicitly assumed to be possible without fundamentally altering the character of Third World economic and social systems. Economists thus fail to identify the real culprit, the ways in which Third World systems are related to industrial capitalist ones. How are multinational corporations and the legacy of past capitalist penetration into Third World countries responsible for current "imbalances" among the poorer nations of the world? This question is not only left unanswered; it is rarely even asked.

Finally, ecological "freaks" tend to be gimmicky or technocratic in their approach. They may conduct faddish campaigns for clearing cans off the beaches or banning bleached flour. This tendency leads to the search for a "technological fix"[31]: Let's keep our cars, but let's make certain that we make the government require auto companies to install filters on the exhaust pipes. More generally, ecologists sometimes act as if problems of pollution, environmental decay, and the like can be arrested by devices for purifying air or preventing excessive noise. Their view is something like the "clean" bomb syndrome that was pushed by the United States government when the ban-the-bomb movement was active in the 1950s.

Radicals do not oppose growth per se, but they are against a specific predisposition to growth embedded in the development of modern capitalism. Radicals ask, Growth of what and for what purposes? A very significant proportion of the GNP seems to them wasted and unrelated to national well-being. The growth syndrome and the way that mainstream economists have chosen to respond to it were presented in the form of a parable by E. J. Mishan in his book *The Costs of Economic Growth*.[32] It is worth discussing Mishan's parable at some length, for it serves to illustrate the most common radical view about American capitalism's ecological disasters and how mainstream economists choose to deal with them.

Mishan begins with an economy in which the individual consumer and producer have freedom, the former to buy firearms and the latter to manufacture them. From here he proceeds, as mainstream economists are prone to do, to make the simplifying assumption that many individuals have aggressive urges manifest in their demand for firearms. It follows "naturally" that manufacturers are motivated to produce them. It follows further, in the absence of perfect competition, that advertising can be used effectively by manufacturers to encourage consumers to expand their interest in pistols. Thus, each man is convinced to carry not only one pistol on his belt, but for reasons of status or symbolic sexual prowess, at least two. Ultimately, clever manufacturers become convinced that every young person wants more than just plain pistols and is "anxious to be seen with the latest deluxe model."[33] Consequently, holsters, special leather belts, bulletproof vests, special pants, and helmets become essential accessories.[34] Manufacturers of these accessories not only become *growth* industries; other "needs" also become apparent. Houses, except for those of the poor, must be "fitted with shatter-proof glass, while the bullet-proofing of rooms and offices in the more dangerous districts is a matter of ordinary precaution."[35] But spinoffs from the flourishing pistol business do not end here. Human capital must be accumulated in the form of knowledge and experience, for "no family is foolish enough to neglect the training of their sons, and even their daughters, in the art of the quick draw."[36] To complete the whole human-capital contribution, the investment in pistol-training teachers, pistol-training centers, and so on must be added.[37] We could, of course, continue, ad infinitum, mentioning the "need" for more life-insurance and accident-insurance companies, higher pensions for widows, money for emergency medical centers, more police to bring about "law and order,"[38] and, finally, a host of well-trained political lobbyists for and against guns, who are "needed" in a democratic, pluralistic society.

We have emphasized that all this growth has occurred under the flag of freedom to consume and freedom to produce. But, as we know, absolute freedom has its limits. Gradually, the government abandons its laissez-faire attitude and begins to become concerned about some of the more blatant excesses. This concern is picked up by mainstream economists, who are quick to recognize some social diseconomies in all those pistols and related growth enterprises; they take the form of noise from pistol shootouts, involuntary deaths (in accidents from bad shooting), and waste associated with discarded pistol junk.

Because of the government's growing concern, it seeks a more accurate assessment of the real social costs of the pistol industry. In its customary role of research godfather, it funds a number of mainstream economists to construct a high-powered statistical model involving masses of "pistological data of all kinds . . . [in order to calculate] the optimal set of taxes on the sale of pistols and ammunition in recognition of those external diseconomies."[39] Mainstream economists, being practical and realistic, come to recognize that "the economy is heavily dependent upon pistol production and all the auxiliary industries and services connected therewith. Besides, the evidence is incontrovertible: the demand for guns continues to grow year by year. It must . . . be accepted as a datum. . . ."[40] The simple idea of outlawing the whole gun industry not only seems unrealistic and absurd; it also seems a violation of the basic market freedoms to consume and produce.

What mainstream economists seek is the creation of a plan

> in which people can have both their guns and peaceful life as well. The chief features of [the] plan are based on what economists call "pistol architecture," which includes provision for no-shooting precincts fenced high with steel, the construction of circular and wavy road design to increase difficulties of gun-duelling, the erection of high shatter-proof glass screens running down the centers of roads to prevent effective crossfiring, and the setting up of heavily protected television cameras at all strategic positions in the towns in order to relay information twenty-four hours a day to a vast new centralized police force equipped with fleets of helicopters. Every progressive journalist pays tribute to the foresight and realism of . . . the plan.[41]

As the plan is costly (scarce resources breed budgetary constraints), only some fraction of it can possibly be realized. If legislative agreement on which part of the plan to implement cannot be reached, the whole plan may be shelved or another research design funded. In any event, both the government and mainstream economists recognize that there is a complex problem in this gun business that does not lend itself to easy solution. Anyone who believes the contrary is a simpleton or a utopian radical.

This parable may, of course, be a more accurate account of the way we choose to deal with crime than we care to admit. We design more sophisticated ways to detect, commit, and protect ourselves from crime. Private and public expenditures in this sphere together stimulate the growth of GNP. In any event, Mishan's parable is really intended to reflect the actual growth of the automotive industry and the ways in which we have chosen to cope with it. As the industry has grown, we have chosen to move farther from the city. The farther we have moved, the more necessary it has been to own cars and to construct roads. Once the roads have been constructed, it has become possible for more people to flee the cities. The suburbs have become crowded, and leapfrog expansion has begun again, bringing more roads, more cars, and more destruction of the rural environment, all of which have stimulated the growth of the economy. Any coordinated central plan to interrupt the process and bring people, jobs, and residential neighborhoods close together again is considered either too costly, unrealistic, or in violation of consumers' revealed preferences and their right to devote three hours a day driving private autos to and from work.

As if this unplanned and wasteful meandering were not sufficient, there is another part to the automotive story, one that is perhaps at the heart of the radical indictment of the growth mania. The automotive industry, the reader should be reminded, has often been identified as a symbol of the American capacity for great output and efficiency, the energy of the American economy, and the well-being of the American people. Radicals see it as representing the economy's addiction for waste, a symbol of our society's major sickness. Much can be and has been said about the automobile. Ralph Nader's fame followed his articulation of what was already known intuitively by millions. But there is an economic aspect of the automobile industry that we alluded to only briefly in Chapter 10: the large amounts of money spent to construct inferior cars.

A careful study was made by a prominent group of mainstream economists, who estimated the cost of resources that would have been saved had cars with lengths, weights, horsepower, transmissions, and so on of the 1949 models been produced each year up to 1960; they found that in that eleven-year period the American public had paid about $40 billion to produce cars that wore out sooner, used more gas, were less safe, and cost more to maintain.[42] Billions of dollars had been spent to make a product that was in many ways inferior to what we already had. And, as if that were not enough, all that productive waste increased GNP and was therefore identified as an improvement in our well-being! Forty billion dollars could have built 2.5 million three-bedroom homes.

The automobile industry is a dramatic illustration of what takes place on a lesser scale in the production of many other goods. It is for good reason, therefore, that most radical economists believe that any serious analysis of the American economy must recognize its need for growth for the business system but not for a decent life. To talk about the quality of American society in terms of some mysterious value system, the dangers of pushing equality in income distribution so far that it might undermine the incentives to produce goods *desperately* needed for public well-being, or the composition of GNP as if it reflected the urgently expressed wants of autonomous consumers is intellectually obscene. To radical economists, much of the growth mania is a *waste* mania, and the present composition of GNP reflects the giant corporation's increasingly unproductive role. The corporation grows as does the shell of a snail; living tissue becomes less and less in proportion to the inorganic structures. But, unlike the snail's carapace, the unproductive aspect of the business system is neither self-liquidating nor a source of calcium and other mineral deposits to refurbish the natural environment.

CONCLUSION

To grow or not to grow is, of course, *a* question, but it is not *the* question that radicals are likely to ask. To talk about "no growth" is to talk about the end of capitalism and the elimination of the privileged classes that benefit from the accumulation process inherent in growth. Ecologists and their allies tend to ignore such matters. To talk about growth because we still live in a world of scarcity, because it seems the most likely way to solve problems of poverty, is to miss the central point that much growth at this juncture involves proliferation of waste, which detracts from, rather than abetting, improvement in the human condition. Such considerations are outside the mainstream purview. In this sense, advocates of no growth and of growth pass over, each for ideological reasons, the many *critical* elements that should enter into the debate.

To radicals, growth and its prerequisite (profits) are to business as heroin is to the addict. Seeking heroin is not a choice that the addict can debate; it is not a matter of free will and the exercise of intelligence. The addict's need for heroin has been incorporated into his or her nervous system, which begins to shrivel and shake at the very thought of being deprived of a fix. The capitalist need to accumulate is very similar.

Capitalism does periodically experience zero or even negative growth. But when it does, the economy is traumatized by "deaccumulations" in the form of inventory cutbacks, unemployment, and the elimination of business "losers" who go bankrupt. In the process, the whole society is devalued. The hope, during such periods of downward readjustment, is that prices and costs can be properly related so that profitable growth and expansion can be resumed. If resumption of growth happens to depend upon manufacture of wasteful commodities, even though it is destructive to the environment, it will nevertheless seem preferable as an immediate or "practical" alternative to "no growth." For this reason, radicals think in terms of an alternative to the capitalist system. They believe that such an alternative is possible and will enable society to deal with questions like: If no growth is chosen, will it be by collective choice? If growth is chosen, what is to grow?

Before moving on to the radical alternative to capitalism, an area that we shall examine briefly in our final chapter, we must explore more facets of the capitalist mania for growth. One of them is the relation between this mania and the problem of uncontrollable inflation followed by "readjusting" recessions or depressions. Another takes us into capitalism's hinterland, its penetration beyond national boundaries. The latter development leads us to the question of imperialism. Each of these matters will be discussed in the next two chapters.

NOTES

1. See E. J. Mishan, *The Costs of Economic Growth* (New York: Praeger, 1967).

2. Ayrind V. Phatak, *Evolution of World Enterprises* (New York: American Management Association, 1971), pp. 140–241; quoted in Robert Scheer, *America After Nixon* (New York: McGraw-Hill, 1974), p. 109.

3. Scheer, *America After Nixon*, p. 111.

4. This statement should not be taken as an endorsement of the standard growth thesis over the profit-maximization thesis. Maximization of growth, it should be recalled, involves a larger volume of output (or sales) and a smaller volume of profit;

maximization of profit involves the reverse. Some Marxians, for example, Paul A. Baran and Paul M. Sweezy, gloss over this problem, arguing that long-run profit maximization and growth are not incompatible objectives. In our judgment, much of the discussion of this subject of sales maximization versus profit maximization has not sufficiently taken into consideration the possibility of changes in strategies for reacting to the business cycle. In upward phases of the business cycle, firms probably seek to maximize growth or sales at the expense of maximum obtainable profits, although it must be emphasized that both sales and profits move in the same direction. But, when the upward swing slows or the economy turns downward and costs begin to catch up with prices, business firms switch from growth objectives, given profit constraints, to profit objectives, given growth constraints. Growth targets are more rational in an expanding market, profit targets in a shrinking market. There is thus a stop-go pattern between these two goals related to the business cycle.

5. Karl Marx, *Capital*, Vol. I (New York: International Publishers), p. 592, quoted in Roger Alcaly, "The Relevance of Marxian Crisis Theory," in *The Economic Crisis Reader*, ed. David Mermelstein (New York: Vintage, 1975), p. 133.

6. Karl Marx, *Karl Marx: Selected Works*, Vol. I (New York: International Publishers, 1951), p. 208.

7. Donella H. Meadows *et al.*, *The Limits of Growth* (Washington, D.C.: Potomac, 1972).

This meeting of the Club of Rome, it should be noted, took place in 1968.

8. Many of the specifics of these ecology problems have been drawn from Hans Magnus Enzenberger, "A Critique of Political Ecology," *New Left Review* 84 (March–April 1974): 3–31.

9. E. J. Mishan, "Growth and Antigrowth: What Are the Issues?" in *The Economic Growth Controversy*, eds. Andrew Weintraub, Eli Schwartz, and J. Richard Aronson (White Plains, N.Y.: International Arts and Science Press, 1973), p. 10.

10. Enzenberger, "A Critique of Political Ecology," p. 5.

11. *Ibid.*

12. *Ibid.*

13. *Ibid.*, p. 6.

14. Robert Solow, "Is the End of the World at Hand?" in *The Economic Growth Controversy*, eds. Andrew Weintraub, Eli Schwartz, and J. Richard Anderson (White Plains, N.Y.: International Arts and Science Press, 1973), p. 48. © International Arts and Sciences Press, Inc.

15. *Ibid.*, pp. 40–41.

16. *Ibid.*, p. 42.

17. *Ibid.*

18. *Ibid.*

19. *Ibid.*, p. 50.

20. *Ibid.*, pp. 42–43.

21. *Ibid.*, pp. 32–43.

22. *Ibid.*, p. 43.

23. *Ibid.*

24. *Ibid.*, p. 46.

25. *Ibid.*, p. 206.

26. *Ibid.*, p. 207.

27. Enzenberger, "A Critique of Political Ecology," p. 27.

28. Richard J. Barnet and Ronald E. Muller, *Global Reach* (New York: Simon & Schuster, 1974), p. 336.

29. Enzenberger, "A Critique of Political Ecology," p. 27.

30. *Ibid.*, p. 25.

31. *Ibid.*, p. 26.

32. Mishan, *The Costs of Economic Growth*.

33. *Ibid.*, p. 90.

34. *Ibid.*

35. *Ibid.*, pp. 90–91.

36. *Ibid.*, p. 91.

37. *Ibid.*

38. *Ibid.*

39. *Ibid.*

40. *Ibid.*, p. 92.

41. *Ibid.*

42. Franklin M. Fisher, Zava Grilliches, and Carl Kaysen, "The Costs of Automobile Model Changes Since 1949," *The Journal of Political Economy* 70 (October 1962): 433–451.

THE STRUCTURAL
DIMENSIONS OF INFLATION

In the history of American capitalism, acute inflation has been a problem only during periods of acute shortages of goods. These periods have all been associated with war: the American Revolution of 1776, the Civil War of 1860, the major world wars of 1914 and 1941, and conflagrations like the Korean "police action" and the Vietnam entanglement. If we were to subtract the dramatic upward spurts in prices associated with these wars from the general long-term drift of prices, the profile of the nation's wholesale and consumer price indexes would be much flatter, though still displaying a cyclical character and a modest upward trend. There might still be an inflationary problem to occupy the minds of economists, though speculation suggests that it would absorb considerably less time.

That inflation has been most acute during war periods has tended to limit radicals' interest in inflation as such. As we have already suggested, radicals are more concerned with the tendency of capitalism toward stagnation in the interwar periods. For this reason, their approach to inflation has been less than systematic. Nevertheless, there are elements in the radical analysis that, when put together, provide a formidable alternative to the mainstream explanation of our present mix of inflation and unemployment.

Some of these elements have already been touched upon in Chapter 10, where we stressed monopolistic and oligopolistic pricing practices. Before proceeding farther in that direction, however, let us focus on the events that have played havoc with mainstream economists' understanding of current inflation.

THE "BIG SPLIT" IN THE MAINSTREAM

When it comes to explaining inflation, a problem that falls under the more general heading of economic stability, mainstream economists are divided into two "opposing" groups: monetarists and fiscalists. The defining characteristic of monetarists is their single-minded emphasis on changes in the stock of money as primary cause of changes in the price level and level of GNP. The fiscalists, in contrast, deny the primary role of money and tend to explain inflation by market imperfections connected with monetary and fiscal policies aimed at increasing investment and consumption. Monetarists have a fear of inflation that amounts to an *idée fixe*. Fiscalists find inflation, if not preferable, at least tolerable in view of the practical alternatives. This divergence between the two groups reflects their different estimates of the social consequences of inflation.

Because of these differences, we shall evaluate the thinking of monetarists and fiscalists separately, though we emphasize that neither believes periodic and uncontrollable inflationary spurts are endemic to the structure of capitalism. Mainstream economists in general view inflation as separate from basic questions of growth, income distribution, attitudes toward material possessions, acquisitiveness, the profit motive, and institutional arrangements that define and limit the government's functioning in relation to the ebb and flow of the private economy.

MONETARISTS—SO RIGHT AND SO WRONG

Monetarists tend to be conservative. In the context of American politics, they strongly distrust the Federal government and its spending propensities and put considerable faith in the ability of market forces to produce desirable results if only they are allowed to function without excessive outside meddling by monetary and political authorities.

Three points are repeatedly stressed by aggressive monetarists:

the unassailability of evidence on the money-price relationship, the alarming consequences of permitting inflation to continue, and the slowness or cowardice of monetary authorities in dealing with inflation.

In the history of economic thought, monetarists have traditionally been concerned about the relationship between the quantity of money and the price level. Changes in the former, all other factors remaining constant, have been assumed to lead directly to changes in the latter. Modern monetary theorists have gone somewhat farther and argued that changes in the stock of money tend to change GNP itself. They see a strong positive association between the stock of money per unit of output and price, assuming that the "public wishes to hold a stable fraction of income in the form of cash."[1] The evidence of this relationship is said to have existed for years and to be as substantial as the very best evidence used to validate any accepted economic hypothesis. Looking back into the history of Western capitalism, one well-respected monetarist observed:

> In the four centuries since the coronation of Queen Elizabeth I, there is no important episode of inflation or deflation that has been studied which contradicts the general proposition that changes in the price level stem primarily from changes in the nominal stock of money per unit of output. . . . For at least the past two centuries, inflation and deflation have occurred in many countries at approximately the same time. The empirical association across countries appears to have been even closer in more recent years. . . .[2]

It has been pointed out that "Every . . . major contraction in this country has been either produced by monetary disorder or greatly exacerbated by monetary disorder. Every major inflation has been produced by monetary expansion."[3] Even economists who are not in the monetarist camp agree that "there has never been a serious inflation . . . without an increase in the quantity of money."[4]

In our view, the answer to the monetarists does not rest on insufficiency of evidence, at least over long periods of time. But, in the short run, the assumed stability of cash holdings relative to income is questionable, a matter to which we shall return. Despite this short-run problem, the general evidence supporting the monetarists' view is still very impressive. Their critical weakness lies elsewhere.

Monetarists have also suggested that continued inflation among noncommunist nations has undermined democratic governments and their political stability, destroyed free markets, and impaired "private and public contracts, capriciously conferring windfall gains and losses."[5] Some monetarists go so far as to suggest that sustained inflation has produced decay in economic motivation, lawlessness, disorder, immorality, excessive hedonism, and wanton violence.[6]

Fears about democracy and its decay are subjective; little can be said either to confirm or to dispel them. But these fears do explain monetarists' manifest anxieties. Instead of anticipating the end of the world, as ecology-minded social scientists do, they merely anticipate the end of Western civilization.

The source of the monetarists' error is their refusal to probe deeply into the reasons why governmental and monetary authorities, whom they view as possessing power to control inflation, never learn the lessons that monetarists teach or are too cowardly to twist the monetary screws sufficiently and thus save us all from impending disaster. Milton Friedman, the nation's foremost monetarist, has argued that we simply do not possess sufficient economic knowledge to trust any authority to play with the money supply; monetary authorities should therefore be required to follow mechanically a rule that would limit the rate at which the money supply can be increased. This notion has become known as the "fixed throttle" approach to monetary policy. The rule would allow the money supply to increase annually within the range of 3–5 percent, a rate close to the "natural" growth rate of the real economy.[7] The rationale for this position is that sudden or excessive changes in the stock of money can dislodge the economy from its more or less stable growth path. The proper monetary policy requires elimination of swings in the stock of money and thus "prevents money itself from being a major source of economic disturbance."[8] The simple assumption behind the "fixed throttle" approach is that the economy—consisting of free consumers, producers, employees, and employers—is like an engine that must be well lubricated by a steady flow of monetary oil if the mechanism is to run smoothly.[9] That is, a steady change in the stock of money consistent with the historical growth rate will generate necessary confidence "that the average level of prices will behave in a known way in the future—preferably that it will be highly stable."[10]

Other, more policy-oriented monetarists, though they also

accept the predictable causal relations between changes in the stock of money and prices (or aggregate demand), stress the need to use the money supply as the primary instrument for stabilizing the economy. In this view, manipulation of the money supply alone is preferable to mixed strategies that involve fiscal meddling, because the former is assumed to be more conducive to maintenance of the private-enterprise system.

Given the statistical regularities in the claimed relationship between the stock of money and the general price level, it is not clear why the authorities do not become increasingly more sophisticated and capable of dealing with inflation. If the statistical regularities were weaker, the failure might be understandable. But the monetarists simply do not face this anomaly. Their fiscalist critics argue, of course, that in the short run velocity of money is unstable and, therefore, it can offset the consequences of changes in the money stock in perverse ways. The inflation of 1969–1971, associated with tight money, is an example.[11] Money had indeed been tightened, but its rate of turnover simply accelerated. Although monetarists have not denied this criticism, they have circumvented it by suggesting that perhaps they had underestimated the necessary time lags; rather than a six-month lag between a change in the stock of money and the resulting price change, they now suggest a lag as long as two years. Two years at the most, monetarists may argue, is not too long to wait in order to save Western civilization from the ravages of inflation.

The inability of governments and monetary authorities to "wait it out" is what goads monetarists to accuse them of cowardice. The authorities are supposedly afraid to overcome the "frictions" arising from the fact that "nominal wage rates [tend] to be rigid downward, and therefore they must [temporarily renege on their] commitment to full employment."[12] More even-handed monetarists add price rigidities resulting from the monopolistic power of corporations to their list of rigidities caused by unions. Be that as it may, the failure of the monetary and governmental authorities to do what is "right" thus seems to monetarists to reflect fear of the consequences accompanying the cure. Deflation may produce a degree of unemployment capable of threatening the stability of the social order that the monetarists and government managers want to preserve. The authorities submit to pressures to avoid unemployment and, in the monetarist view, are thus prevented, "given their inherent myopia . . . [from weighing] correctly the costs of longer-run inflationary consequences resulting from a wide range of tax, subsidy, and full-employment programs financed by or depending on the distortions of monetary creation."[13] The source of pressures favoring monetary expansion and inflation, to continue with monetarist reasoning, is hope that "monetary expansion may initially lead to . . . good results before the later bad results of higher prices. On the other hand, monetary restriction may correspondingly lead to the bad results of reduced output and employment before the good results of moderating inflation."[14]

The deep structure of monetarist reasoning, though not stated explicitly, includes the assumption of some kind of natural, or ideal, constellation of forces that can be regulated smoothly by a price system if only people will behave as machines—that is, if only workers will not organize unions, businessmen will not seek monopoly power, and governments will act sufficiently autonomously or courageously to do what natural forces require. If only trade associations that demand fair pricing did not exist, if only the poor would refuse assistance, and if only big corporations would refuse to buy politicians and legislatures in pursuit of subsidies to supplement their inefficiencies—the "if onlys" are endless, and the monetarists include all these inconvenient factors under the heading "friction," as if "friction" were a bit of rust that could be readily removed by steel wool.

The failure of monetarist thinking, in the radical view, is in its misunderstanding of society itself and of capitalism's inherent tendency to develop in manic waves of inflation that must be counteracted by depressive retreats into unemployment; these vacillations are part of the system's "breathing." Unemployment is simply functional, or restorative, to the economy's health. And manic forward thrusts are necessary if unemployment and underuse of productive capacity are to be removed.

A further misconception of monetarists, one that they share with their fiscalist colleagues, is the notion that monetary authorities are somehow outside the economic relations that define the system. Monetarists have in fact recorded their evidence accurately, but they have failed to explain it, except in the most superficial and not infrequently tautological fashion. The agencies on which they rely for solutions are actually part of the problem. And the problem is part of the sociology and economics of capitalism, which they do not understand. Monetarists' claims are statistically correct but irrelevant, which is why even conservative monetary authorities, frequently ideological "fellow travelers" of the professional monetarists, nevertheless rarely follow the recommendations of these professionals, except in limited ways. Monetarists describe the mechanics of inflation, but they fail to explain it. They do not address themselves to the reasons for the "frictions" that prevent monetary policies from working efficiently and "true" capitalist markets from functioning adequately.

FISCALISTS—LIVING WITH INFLATION

After World War II, mass unemployment was the main fear of mainstream fiscalist economists. The logic of John Maynard Keynes required the machinery of state to be used to create both budgetary deficits and monetary expansion in order to stimulate high levels of aggregate demand. As budgetary policies proved successful, the fiscalists' attitude toward inflation turned benign. At least up to the end of the period that we have called the Great American Celebration (to 1964; see Chapter 6), mild or creeping inflation (3–5 percent) was recognized as a reasonable price to pay for reasonably high levels of employment. Although monetarists perennially warned that some day creeping inflation would accelerate into a galloping or runaway variety that would bring severe economic collapse, the fiscalists tended to dismiss this possibility. In general, they argued that the costs of unemployment in terms of output losses and demoralization of workers are much greater than the costs of inflation.[15]

Because high levels of employment require high levels of aggregate demand (the single most important lesson that American economists learned from Keynes), the fiscalists argue that it is better to err in the direction of government deficits financed by substantive increases in the money supply than to take chances with smaller deficits and monetary caution. In a similar vein, most economists, at least up to 1970, associated inflation with excessive aggregate demand relative to supply.[16] Given the pervasive existence of imperfect markets, in which corporations and unions exercise monopoly power, not to mention the immobility of labor and resource bottlenecks, an economy experiencing pressure from high demand cannot achieve the simultaneous goals of full employment, uninterrupted growth in material well-being, and price stability without introducing wage-price controls. The fiscalists tend instead to sacrifice the goal of price stability.

The reasoning by which fiscalists explain inflation is eclectic and flexible. One common sequence begins with the notion that in a period of unemployment aggregate demand can be increased by means of deficit spending and expansion of the monetary base. Because corporations have monopoly power, they begin to increase prices before the achievement of full employment. Organized labor responds to price increases with demands for wage increases, which are frequently greater than rises in productivity. Eventually this process spreads from specific sectors to encompass the whole economy. In fact, the spread and its measurement are the focal point of debate among fiscalists and represent the main source of differences among them. Some fiscalists emphasize the leading role of unions in pushing up wages, which are then met by upward price adjustments. As only 25 percent of the labor force is unionized, there is the question of how wage increases in organized industries spread to those that are not organized. Other fiscalists argue that wage-price spirals associated with *expectations* about changes in wages and prices are the source of inflation. Expectations, in this view, are an independent force with its own momentum, detached from the real variables of the economy. More antimonopolistic fiscalists focus their attention on the administrative pricing strategies of giant corporations in highly concentrated industries.

The relative merits of these debates among fiscalists are not our concern. Most of them involve upward shifts in aggregate demand during one period or in some sectors, shifts that spill over into excessive cost pushes in other periods or sectors. As time passes, the original cause, it is suggested, may even become less important than this spiral momentum.[17]

What requires emphasis is the aggregate outcome: Once prices and wages begin chasing each other, for whatever reason, the bargaining groups begin to demand wages and profits in anticipation of either rising living costs or rising production costs. Rising living costs affect workers' real incomes; rising production costs determine corporations' real profits. Money claims on real product at given prices total more than 100 percent. Something must give. In order to keep the functional distribution of income between labor and capital "equitable" and the economy growing, the Federal government enters the picture with stimulating deficits, which are monetized by the monetary authorities. The result is pressure on prices even without full employment.

If supply bottlenecks are added to the market imperfections that are behind the inflation, the rate of inflation can become so high that temporary wage-price controls may seem necessary; a slowdown in the expansion of the money supply and government spending may also be in order. In any event, fiscalists are careful not to argue for excessive countermeasures because inflationary expansion tends not to achieve full employment. As they are willing to live with inflation because of the perceived alternatives, they deemphasize its dangers. Because full employment is also out of reach, they live with that also. Their hope is to keep the trade-off between inflation and unemployment within "reasonable" boundaries. What "reasonable" means not infrequently is based on the Great Depression of the 1930s: If we have a combination of monetary and fiscal policies that enables us to avoid that kind of crisis, we can consider ourselves successful. If the trade-off should become "unreasonable," however, fiscalists break out of their "fine tuning" armor and advocate "temporary" wage-price controls. More deviant fiscalists may even advocate some kind of permanent planning arrangement. But, it must be noted, to the extent that they do, they are in fact admitting that the older Keynesian game plan of indirect monetary and fiscal management is obsolete. That, of course, is precisely what is presently taking place, as a consequence of the events and realities of the period between 1965 and 1975. A brief review of some of the economic highlights of this period is in order before we launch into the radical analysis.

FROM INFLATION TO DEPRESSION:
1965–1975

Between 1965 and 1975, the observed contradictions of the late 1950s and early 1960s—moderate price increases and rising unemployment rates—became more acute. As mainstream fiscalists found it more difficult to explain inflation, given the prevalence of "chronic" excess capacity, the straight demand-pull theory lost considerable credibility. Although the government was assumed capable of preventing drastic downward swings in the economy, it became apparent that it could not readily bring about a sustained high level of employment without pushing the economy to the brink of *excessive* inflation. Economists described the new situation as one of "high-level stagnation," in which the economy was experiencing both more inflation than is healthy and more unemployment and underuse of resources than are tolerable by contemporary standards. Over the years, the definition of "full" employment has opportunistically changed to allow for unemployment of 2 percent, then 4 percent, then 5 percent; currently, some professional economists and public officials favor 6 percent unemployment as a "reasonable" full-employment target.

Many fiscalists have become disillusioned or at least uncertain about how to explain the high-level stagnation between 1965 and 1975. Although mainstream economists held many high-powered crystal balls in their hands in the form of statistical models, few anticipated the inflationary spurt between 1965 and 1972,[18] and even fewer, it must be added, anticipated the economy's dramatic deterioration after the end of the Vietnam War in 1973.

In 1965 the United States escalated its involvement in Vietnam, and as a consequence American military contracts "jumped from $27.1 billion in 1964 to $39.7 billion in 1966."[19] By 1968 defense spending had increased more than 60 percent. The total cost of the war for only the years between 1965 and 1971 was estimated at $120 billion, about $20 billion annually. This upsurge in military spending, which led to a sharp rise in the consumer price index, plunged many mainstream economists into a dither. Wanting to fight an unpopular war but unwilling to tell the public what it would eventually cost them, the government refused to raise taxes to pay for the war directly. It feared that an increase in taxes would lead to a taxpayers' revolt and strengthening of the antiwar movement. Inflation, it must be noted, is a much less recognizable form of taxation. It not only transfers purchasing power from the general population to the government; it also transfers greater amounts from those who have the least power to hedge against it, like pensioners.

As inflation at home became more and more unruly, an international monetary crisis developed; it reflected the growing competitive struggle among the capitalist nations of Europe and Japan. President Lyndon B. Johnson, in his last months in office, sought to correct some of his earlier mistakes by instituting a 10 percent income-tax surcharge, curbing American commitments and the flow of dollars abroad, and halting increases in Federal spending. Most of these measures were only mild and belated responses, too little too late.

In 1968, the first year of President Richard M. Nixon's term in office, he faced a rising consumer price index, rising more rapidly, in fact, than in any year since 1947. At the same time, the unemployment rate was slowly creeping above the 6 percent mark. His initial reaction to these inherited problems was to pursue a set of right-wing Keynesian policies. To deal with inflation, which appeared to be his main concern at that time, he tightened the money supply and trimmed the Federal budget through cutbacks in necessary nonmilitary programs. This conservative effort was also viewed as a means of coping with our growing balance-of-payment problem and the weakening position of the dollar, for a check on prices, if it succeeded, would make American commodities more competitive abroad and the dollar a more suitable currency as a standard for settling international accounts and conducting international trade.

Nixon's solution to controlling inflation was, in fact, for the government to induce a recession to stabilize prices and thus, it was hoped, to fix everything else. Nixon essentially was saying that the cost of slowing down the economy must be borne by workers through unemployment and severely limited wage increases. What went wrong, of course, was that governmentally induced unemployment did not slow the inflation. The 1968–1969 demand-pull inflation turned into the cost-push inflation of 1970–1971. With one eye on the 1972 elections and another on the international monetary crisis, the President and his conservative Keynesian advisers panicked. Within a short period of time, Nixon moved ideologically from the position of a free-market monetarist of the Milton Friedman type to that of a liberal, deficit-oriented Keynesian and then to that of a Bismarckian "socialist" wage-price controller. To fiscalists, who are prone to accept controls when "necessary," Nixon's shift proved that monetarist policies are not viable. The monetarists, of course, believe that their position remains as valid as ever; recommended monetary measures simply require more time than was granted them. In retrospect it seems that the fiscalists and monetarists were both wrong: The former underestimated the inflationary dangers, and the latter underestimated the amounts of tightening of the money supply and of unemployment that would be necessary to stabilize prices. It appears that, at least in the short run, everything in the economy was working in perverse ways.

The results of pushing the panic button took the form of a New Economic Program in August 1971.[20] The initial program consisted of a ninety-day wage and price freeze, budget cuts, a 10 percent surcharge on imports (which was rescinded in December of the same year as part of an agreement on dollar devaluation with our European allies), and the termination of the American government's willingness to convert foreign-held dollars into gold (an act that was followed by complete independence of the domestic stock of money from the supply of gold). At the end of the ninety-day wage-price freeze (phase I), a pay board was established (phase II) to supervise wages and prices, with the aim of limiting wage increases to 5.5 percent and price increases to 2.5 percent.

The immediate results of these Nixon policies between 1968 and 1972 were selective stimulation of those industries suffering most from foreign competition, deficit spending, monetary manipulation, and efforts to improve the profit position of the largest corporations. When the Penn Central Railroad went bankrupt and other giants were endangered by liquidity problems, the administration came to the rescue with emergency loans and accelerated depreciation allowances. The state intervened in order to save these large, inefficient cogs in the corporate machine.

After 1972 phases III and IV were instituted; they involved termination or modification of the measures taken in the first two phases. By 1974 almost all the formal price controls had expired, setting off some dramatic price increases in key industrial commodities like copper and steel. The common explanation of this new price spurt, even among Nixon's own economic advisers, was that his price-control "experiment" had acted only as a cork in a bottle of fizzing club soda. The cork had worked temporarily to prevent the gas from escaping, but it had not eliminated the pressure as such. When the cork was finally removed, cumulative price pressures followed their "natural" direction upward.

Both monetarists and fiscalists concluded this portion of Nixon's term with self-righteous declarations about who had been "right" and who had been "wrong." The monetarists saw wage-price controls, which the fiscalists had applauded, as a failure. If allowed time, they argued, Nixon's initial monetary policies would have worked. The fiscalists replied that wage-price controls had not been administered by believers in wage-price controls and that therefore they had not achieved the expected results. Moreover, the control system, like monetarist policies, also required more time to function properly.

Among the ebb and flow of price- and wage-control efforts other momentous events occurred between 1965 and 1975. The most critical one was the Mideast war in October 1973. The Arab oil-producing nations had pulled themselves together, had cut oil production, had announced the largest price increases in history, and had boycotted European purchasers. This worldwide crisis immediately put the American airline, trucking, and automobile industries in a state of desperation. Higher prices and Nixon's order to reduce gas deliveries to wholesalers and retailers produced unemployment, business uncertainty, and work stoppages.[21]

In August 1974, in addition to Nixon's resignation from the Presidency, an event which we shall mention only in passing, the stock market collapsed from its January 1973 peak. In October the stability of the whole banking system came under suspicion when the Franklin National Bank of New York collapsed, and large-scale layoffs were announced in the auto industry. General prices continued to rise, and in December unemployment rose to 7.1 percent. Although during most of 1973 and part of 1974 predictions of prosperity around the corner abounded, unemployment steadily increased to the official rate of 9.2 percent in 1975, the highest rate since the Great Depression in the 1930s. Popular pundits, business and banking executives, public officials, and economists increasingly began to raise the specter of another worldwide depression, a matter that we shall examine in more detail in Chapter 15.

As events between 1965 and 1975 began to register on mainstream thinking, theories of inflation, already in a state of disarray, degenerated further into ad hoc kinds of reasoning. Although mainstream economists had not anticipated the economic impact of the 1965 escalation, they now admitted that the war should have been financed, not with deficits that caused excessive demand, but with large increases in taxes. Although it was not apparent in the moderately sluggish months of late 1964, it is now claimed that the economy was then either close to full employment or suffering from many supply bottlenecks so that the 1964 tax cut perhaps came too late. The latter "fact" is considered responsible for excessively rapid wage hikes beyond productivity changes, which were quickly generalized into across-the-board wage increases. In this way, cost-push forces (in addition to demand-pull ones) have been, also in retrospect, identified as the "causes" of this inflation. What cannot be explained by the various combinations of "pulls" and "pushes" is considered to be accounted for by independent expectations.

But, because most mainstream theorists had failed to anticipate the dual nature of inflation and unemployment between 1965 and 1975, they have been forced to turn to exogenous causes, to random, unpredictable, and unique events, for an explanation. Two exogenous devaluations of the American dollar are thought to have served as fuel for preexisting inflationary fires; exogenous increases in oil prices and corresponding exogenous cutbacks in oil deliveries operated on both the demand and supply sides. Exogenous changes in the weather affected food prices. The list of exogenous events appears to be endless.

In the radical view, this reliance on exogenous variables to explain a process that has erupted at periodic intervals from the early 1950s to the present is a sign of theoretical bankruptcy. Not only is the whole debate over inflation muddled but also, and more important, much of the theorizing about it is saturated with ideological bias. As one mainstream economist has put it:

> The debate between demand pulls and cost push stems largely from the differences between the policy recommendations which the two views on the causes of inflation imply. The former leads to a recommendation of monetary restraint and fiscal orthodoxy involving a higher level of unemployment. Cost push, on the other hand, leads to such recommendations as administrative restraint on price increases and incomes policies.[22]

Policy questions are "normative" according to mainstream reasoning, and thus they are, by radical definition, in the realm of ideology.

The multiplicity of explanations, the reliance on exogenous variables, and ideological biases among social scientists who advertise their discipline as "value-free" led one mainstream economist who has studied the inflation question for years to conclude: "Contemporary understanding of the inflation issue is hardly better than it was several centuries ago, despite the sophistication of very large economic models involving great mathematical and statistical sophistication but very primitive economic understanding."[23] With this admitted chaos and confusion among mainstream economists in mind, we shall now proceed to develop the radical alternative.

PREFACE TO THE RADICAL ANALYSIS

Radicals do not have a single theory of inflation that is distinct from a single theory of capitalist development. Any phenomenon, like inflation, that occurs periodically cannot be thought about in isolated terms. That is one reason why the radical "position" on inflation is not easily identifiable; it does not receive isolated treatment. The question is a little more complex, however. Radicals have been somewhat remiss, at least until recently, in the ways that they have chosen to discuss inflation. Because of their preoccupation with stagnation, they have not extended their systematic structural analysis of capitalism to include periodic episodes of explosive inflation, which can be slowed only by means of recessions and depressions.

In one sense, nineteenth-century inflationary episodes were not manifestly different from twentieth-century ones. What has changed is some of the mechanisms, arising from shifts in the industrial structure from competition to oligopoly and monopoly. In the nineteenth century inflations resulted from the competitive anarchy implicit in the private quest for profits, from the necessity to accumulate and grow or face breakdown. The quest for profits and the need to accumulate have already been analyzed in Chapter 9. We must add Karl Marx's awareness of how the banking and credit system extended the arm of the individual capitalist. By means of the banking system, Marx wrote,

> the distribution of capital as a special business . . . is taken out of the hands of the private capitalists and usurers. But at the same time, banking and credit thus become the most important means of driving capitalist production beyond its own limits and are of the most effective vehicles of crises and swindle. . . . The credit system [is] the main lever of . . . over speculation in commerce, [and thereby] accelerates . . . violent [inflationary] eruptions [followed by] crises.[24]

Periods of unregulated growth thus breed speculative fevers, which are financed by the banking and credit systems and lead necessarily to inflation, the debasement of the currency, and overinvestments; in their turn they bring problems of profit realization. The results are crises and depressions, material and financial contractions, until the stage is set for another round of expansion.

But Marx did not probe the relation of banking and credit to the business system as systematically as he had probed the material processes of production, reproduction, and consumption. It is to the late nineteenth- and early twentieth-century radical Thorstein Veblen, however iconoclastic and difficult to categorize in terms of his socialist commitment, to whom we must turn for the first systematic analysis of the role of credit and its relations to inflation.[25] Veblen was, in the judgment of many, America's most original economist. Oddly enough, he is rarely mentioned by mainstream economists except as a maker of catchy phrases like "conspicuous consumption" or "pecuniary emulation." As our concern is with the current inflation, our treatment of Veblen will be limited to one aspect of his analysis, as developed in his clearest and, in our view, most important book, *The Theory of Business Enterprise,* published in 1904.

Veblen was concerned with the psychology of the businessman, his singularly one-dimensional preoccupation with pecuniary gain, shortening the turnover time of earnings, increasing the value of paper assets, and corresponding speculative use of the credit structure to enhance asset values. All these factors, according to Veblen's analysis, converge to produce periodic surges of inflation that cannot be supported by the market values of real output. This insupportable disparity between real profits and paper profits stimulated by credit will eventually break the inflationary bubble and bring about crisis and depression. This prediction, however, takes us beyond our immediate focus.

Veblen lived at a time when the great industrial tycoons were taking over the American industrial centers. The Vanderbilts, Goulds, Morgans, Fricks, and Rockefellers were amassing huge fortunes by buying and selling stocks and bonds through credit institutions and various shrewd manipulations. From the documents of his day, Veblen discovered the psychological principles that he believed characterize the "representative" businessman. The pursuit of pecuniary gain is said to manifest itself in such activities as seeking credit to buy and sell securities beyond earnings derived from the value of the initial assets and refunding old debts through acquisition of new debts to sustain the paper value of capital assets. The business of business, the business of banks, and the business of refunding businesses are all woven from the same cloth and are subject to competitive emulation and speculative fevers, which generate excessive spurts in the money supply (or its near substitutes) and result in inflation. As inflation, accompanied by debt, grows, the cost of retrenchment also grows; the need for more debt occurs, and inflation thus accelerates.

At the base of this credit pyramid, in Veblen's view, is the capitalization of prospective earnings, which was not consistent with the industrial foundations, the actual workshops and marketplaces where real goods and services are produced and exchanged. That is, the credit pyramid is based less on real wealth and real earnings than on such abstractions as "good will," "immaterial wealth," and "intangibles" and on the exercise of crude monopoly power and financial chicanery. The inevitable result is, as we have already suggested, crisis and depression.

What is important in Veblen's analysis, for our immediate purpose, is the argument that inflationary spurts are endemic to capitalism; inflation and its consequences grow out of the very nature of the business outlook. They are not aberrations to be examined as a special field of inquiry. They do not result merely from periodic misjudgments or failures of nerve by monetary authorities. Inflation is simply one aspect of capitalism's general *modus operandi.*

THE ENDOGENOUS NATURE OF DEFICIT SPENDING

The single most important development since the 1930s is the emergence and expansion of government spending. The specific form of this spending must be examined if we are to understand the contemporary inflationary process. Spending at the various levels (Federal, state, and municipal) of government occurs largely at the behest of and in answer to the needs of the business system. Large national and international corporations use Federal channels; smaller, regional segments of the business system rely on state and city governments. Inflation must be seen as a structural problem of capitalism; the government is part of the larger system and part of the system's problems, and it cannot therefore be relied upon as an independent corrective force.

Beginning first at the macroeconomic level, we find that inflation is caused by the way in which the government is "forced" to finance its spending and by the nature of the products, services, and projects that it must undertake in order to reproduce or protect the given stratified structure of the system. To increase employment, government turns to deficit spending. The deficits are incurred by borrowing from businesses, financial institutions, and individuals. But, because large portions of government spending are unproductive (for example, spending for military goods and similar kinds of assets), the financing of spending through deficits, in the words of Paul Baran,

> is bound to increase continuously the ratio of cash or near-cash in the hands of the public to currently produced marketable

output. . . . Under the impact of unforeseen circumstances (in particular, threats of war and concomitant scarcities) the accumulated balances of cash or near-cash may suddenly start seeking transformation into tangible goods—with speculation reducing their surplus—and cause an inflationary run on the economy. Although under the [immediate] impact of inflation profits [may] increase and the distribution of income shifts in favor of the capitalist class, the capitalist class itself is unwilling to risk the consequences of a major decline in the purchasing power of the currency. Undermining the possibility of rational calculation, depleting the liquid assets of firms and individual capitalists, inflation . . . endangers the entire credit structure . . . and constitutes a considerable threat to banks and financial institutions.[26]

As this process occurs, more liquid reserves must be pumped into the system, because a contraction would wipe out the large number of businesses and consumers who have been stimulated in the initial rise to become greater debtors. In this way,

pressures—the drive for profits and the need to protect one's already existing market—lead to a larger and larger share of relatively unsafe loans in the banks' portfolios. It should be noted that the very ease with which the larger corporations can get loans facilitates their carrying on their own business affairs beyond safe limits, as clearly seen in the steady decline in the ratio of liquid reserves relative to what the corporations own. And the harder it becomes for the corporations to repay their bank loans (because of declining liquidity), the more the banks are obliged to grant further loans to prevent borrowers from going bust and thus defaulting on the backlog of loans. As willing or unwilling collaborators in the process by which the large corporations operate closer and closer to the edge of the precipice, the banks are themselves drawn nearer to the same edge, for they can manage to lend at such a furious rate only by impairing their own liquidity.[27]

What begins as "functional finance," that is, as deficits to close the gap between actual and potential output, generates a self-perpetuating chain of inflationary debt and refinancing in the private sector among businesses and consumers; it is forged through the medium of the banks, which have a thirst for profits not unlike that of other private businesses. This fact suggests that the economy tends to become increasingly more vulnerable to cyclical dips because of fear that the debt structure will collapse and bring down the whole economy. The irony is that the very use of excessive credit to eliminate the old-fashioned business cycle has actually made the economy potentially more vulnerable to it. For this reason, the Federal Reserve Board becomes increasingly cautious about twisting the monetary screws too tightly for fear of bringing down the whole economy. And, given inflationary biases and expectations, small monetary squeezes tend to be ineffective; they are readily offset by acceleration in the velocity of income or the availability of near-money that permits expansion of purchasing power.

The mainstream view of government as an autonomous balance wheel (see Chapter 3), cautiously using its various monetary and fiscal instruments to achieve "national" objectives of full employment, growth, and price stability in the context of private enterprise and free collective bargaining, is fundamentally erroneous. What macroeconomic policy really involves is a politically engineered stop-go process designed to preserve the existing profit margins or profit shares of dominant capitalists by inducing periods of unemployment to prevent accelerated wage pushes from eating ruthlessly into profits at peak periods in the numerous "mini" business cycles of the kind that has shaped the contours of the economy in the post–World War II period.[28] But the amount of unemployment acceptable to the social order has become smaller. Income cushions like unemployment compensation are readily put into effect. They, in turn, often prevent changes in the price-wage ratio from disciplining the organized labor force and abating inflationary expectations. Even in terms of the government's narrowly defined policies of protecting profits from being squeezed and stimulating maximum profit gains, its freedom of rational action has become circumscribed as its role has become larger.

The necessity for permanent and increasing Federal deficits to ensure "tolerable" levels of output and unemployment arises from the fact that state revenues tend perennially to lag behind state expenditures. If we examine the whole post–World War II period, we find not only that deficits have become the rule but also that they tend, on the average, to grow. As Paul Sweezy has pointed out:

> In the decade 1945–1954 there were five deficit years, four surplus, and one of a balanced budget. In the next decade, 1955–1964, there were seven deficit years and three surplus. And

in the nine years 1965–1973 there were eight deficits and one surplus. Moreover, the size of the deficits has been steadily increasing: the cumulative deficit of the first four years of the 1970s was 80 percent greater than the cumulative deficit of the last four of the 1960s.[29]

The radical question, one not even raised by mainstream economists, is, *Why* must deficits be sustained and increased? The answer reflects the *modus operandi* and needs of the industrial structure, which establishes the boundaries within which the state must function. On the macroeconomic side, the radical position involves recognizing that government spending, taxation, and monetary policies are endogenous to the business system. On the microeconomic side, to which we shall presently turn, it involves analysis of the industrial structure, which also shapes the role of government. If inflationary biases and needs are indeed built into this structure, the state, as we have repeatedly suggested, is part of the problem. It cannot cope effectively with the contradiction between inflation and unemployment.

THE TRIPARTITE INDUSTRIAL STRUCTURE[30]

To understand the microeconomic side of the inflationary question, we must view the economy as consisting of three divisions: the monopolistic, competitive, and public sectors. The primary sector is the monopolistic one, which exports its tendencies to both of the other two. It thus generates needs and problems that determine the magnitude and composition of Federal and local government expenditures and revenues. Deficits, as a means of financing the gap between revenues at existing levels of output and expenditures to generate higher levels of output, arise from the tendency toward stagnation in the system (see Chapter 10) and the resistance to taxes among the population. The tendency toward stagnation stimulates the need for larger expenditures. Resistance to taxes is determined by two phenomena: the unproductive character of most goods and services produced in the public sector and the fact that large portions of these goods and services, even when they are productive, are frequently filtered through the business system before reaching the public. This filtering dilutes their apparent benefits relative to visible costs and makes them difficult to justify politically. The full dimensions of these claims and their specific relations to inflation require more detailed description of the major sectors in the economy.

THE MONOPOLY SECTOR

The monopoly sector consists of giant corporations with power to administer prices. It employs workers who belong to strong industrial unions with considerable bargaining power. Through collective bargaining, wages in this sector are highly influenced by political processes outside the market. Because of the pricing power of firms in this sector, higher wages can generally be passed on to consumers in the form of higher prices. Firms can also meet wage pressures by investing in labor-saving fixed plant and technology. This alternative has meant that over the years expansion in output in the monopolistic sector has absorbed relatively few workers. That is, profits have been preserved when wages were pushed upward through production of the same output with fewer workers. The monopoly sector is thus one important source of the system's surplus, or redundant, population, some portion of which finds it way into the low-wage, labor-intensive competitive sector. Because the monopolistic sector harnesses advanced technology, it generally tends to increase its capacity to produce faster than demand for its products increases. This tendency toward excess capacity, however, perennially threatens the full-employment growth rate, which becomes a primary concern of the state. In this way, state policies are determined by the functioning of the monopoly sector.

THE COMPETITIVE SECTOR

The second sector of the private economy consists of industries in which there are many relatively small firms that do not, as separate units, have much pricing power. The spectrum ranges from light manufacturing to service industries, from wholesale to retail ones. Profit margins in many of these industries are narrow, and the mortality rate is relatively high. These firms, like those in the monopolistic sector, are in chronic need of help—of a very different kind, however—from the state.

The relative absence of advanced technology in this sector makes it labor intensive; output therefore expands or contracts with increases or decreases in employment. Many jobs in this sector are low-paid and routine. Many full-time employees are members of the working poor, whose unsubsidized incomes are at or below the poverty level. Many other workers are transient, often minority members and women, who alternate between employment compensation and unemployment compensation. The latter is income from either the U.S. Department of Labor or local departments of welfare. In either instance, workers in this sector become part of the "burdens" placed on the public sector, which is the third component of the triad.

THE PUBLIC SECTOR

The public sector produces goods and services both directly and indirectly. In such enterprises as the postal service and education, the state owns the means of production and compensates workers directly by means of tax revenues. In its more indirect form of production, the state contracts and subcontracts to the private sector. It functions "simply" as a large buyer of goods and services from private companies. The differences between these two modes of state production are not inconsequential. It must be emphasized that, when the state indirectly generates goods and services as a large buyer, the profits are privately appropriated by the corporations, which are the direct employers of the workers; the workers are not therefore in a substantively different relation to the means of production than are other privately employed workers.

Whatever the character of the technology harnessed to produce goods and services for the state, there are reasons why they tend to be produced inefficiently, that is, why output per worker tends to be low. Direct production by the state usually involves services; it is labor intensive, and services cannot easily be expanded without increasing the number of people employed, which simultaneously increases the cost of production. Moreover, when wages in this sector increase, costs increase also, without corresponding increases in services. Indirect production by the state involves cost-plus contracts, the production of less standardized commodities like rockets, and much bureaucratic wheeling and dealing outside the market (as in Pentagon-corporate relationships). All these machinations tend to keep unit costs high relative to output. In fact, one authority has gone so far as to identify the contractual relationship between a corporation and the Pentagon as one that maximizes costs.[31]

THE MACROECONOMIC AND MICROECONOMIC DYNAMICS OF INFLATION

To understand the inflationary biases that grow from the interstices of the economy's tripartite division, we must turn, first, to the interaction between the growth of the monopoly sector and the growth of the state and, second, to the way in which wage costs spread through the whole economy more rapidly than productivity increases do. Both processes nurture big deficits, which monetary authorities are forced to monetize. In this way the money supply or near-money tends to grow at a faster rate than that of actual output at given prices. Because growth in employment lags considerably behind the monetary stimulus, monetary brakes must periodically be applied moderately, without achieving sufficient employment. Inflation and unemployment coexist with government deficits and erratic changes in the money supply. The latter two phenomena are endogenous responses, as we have repeatedly emphasized, to the exigencies of the system's industrial structure.

As the monopoly sector pursues its primary goals, profits and the accumulation of private capital, it increasingly calls upon the state to socialize (subsidize) costs by investing in research and development projects, highway construction, industrial parks, office buildings, utilities, and education. To the extent that the monopoly sector is plagued with excess capacity, it seeks to find markets well beyond the nation's political boundaries, creating and legitimizing the "need" for more state expenditures on the military. As the government generates both nonmilitary and military outlays at the behest of the monopoly sector, it grows; at the same time, it stimulates the growth of the monopoly sector. The relationship is symbiotic. However, and this point is critical, though the monopoly sector uses the state to socialize large portions of its costs, the corresponding gains are privately appropriated. The benefits associated with publicly incurred costs are not readily felt by the public. In a similar vein, it should be emphasized that about one-half to two-thirds of every dollar paid in Federal taxes goes to the production of military and related goods and services that do not enhance the well-being of the population. The private appropriation of publicly paid production and the public costs of unproductive military goods and services have produced strong negative sentiments toward financing more state activities by means of taxation, a matter to which we shall turn in a moment.

Because the monopoly sector tends to be labor saving, it generates a reserve labor pool that sooner or later finds its way into either the competitive sector, which harbors the working poor, or onto welfare rolls supported by municipal and state governments. State expenditures are thus continually being stimulated to finance unproductive workers in order to maintain the social peace. Supporting such workers by enlarging the tax base runs into more and more resistance. The middle levels of American society have come to believe that much of their hard-earned taxable income is being funneled into wasteful governmental programs—at the Federal level to maintain a government bureaucracy with apparently unlimited appetites and at the local level to help "ungrateful" blacks and "greedy" municipal workers (teachers, sanitation men, police officers), who already receive too much money for too little work. As a result, a "democratic" government like our own, in order to meet the needs of an oligarchically controlled economy, has found it increasingly difficult to meet its expenditures through tax collections; it has therefore been forced to pursue excessive deficit spending in the context of high-level stagnation. Deficit spending is a less accountable way of mobilizing resources.

Looking at the inflation question from the microeconomic side, we see that emulation among workers and other groups in the different sectors leads to wage spirals and corresponding price spirals. As strong unions demand higher wages in the monopoly sector, they stimulate public employees to demand higher wages to maintain parity. A wage spiral develops. The managers of firms in the monopoly sector respond to wage pressures in two ways: They protect their profits by increasing prices or by introducing labor-saving technology. The managers of the public sector, especially at the state and local levels, have no such options. For reasons that we have already suggested, productivity in this sector cannot readily rise to offset higher wages. As wage pushes in the monopolistic private sector set off wage pushes in the public sector, they lead to increased prices; the public wage pushes necessitate increased local taxes or a larger public debt. But, as there is no corresponding increase in the level of public services when the debt is incurred, wage pressures in the public sector are inflationary and strongly resented by nonpublic employees.[32] In any event, as wage increases begin to be generalized in these two sectors, which together encompass approximately two-thirds of the labor force, the real living standards of the working poor in the competitive sector are most adversely affected. To the extent that firms in the competitive sector are pushed to the wall by rising costs, the mortality rate spurts upward. Portions of the competitive sector and the workers connected with them become increasingly dependent upon assistance and handouts by the state. The rhythm of this process, as it ripples through the whole economy, finds empirical expression in unemployment, inflation, poverty, and the unproductive or wasteful use of resources. These results reflect the paradoxes and contradictions of modern American capitalism. They are not, moreover, due to fiscal mismanagement, repeated errors by monetary authorities, or general lack of economic knowledge, as mainstream economists monotonously contend. They are due primarily to the interrelations among the various parts of the system, which has as its prime mover the monopoly sector. The government's policies are endogenous to the system, and they take the form, moreover, of responses aimed at reproducing the system's social relations, however contradictory they may be.

THE DEBASED NATURE
OF THE CAPITALIST STATE

To bring the various details of the radical analysis together in a more general form, we must focus attention on why the state appears perennially unable to cope with the economic contradictions that we have analyzed. The economy, dominated by the monopolistic sector, generates greater government spending and activity, both to nurture its successes and to contain its failures; at the same time, the private sector resists financing a larger and more effective government. This peculiar contradiction, which is expressed ideologically and politically in many different ways among business leaders, workers, and the middle strata of the population, arises from real contradictions in the structural relations among production, the distribution of the labor force, and the composition of output. It is for this reason that the public looks to the government for assistance and solutions when the market fails, then resents the growth of the government, which, in the circumscribed context of capitalist relations, fumbles in its efforts to cope with problems that it has been mandated to resolve.

On one side of the equation, the burden of the state's unproductive role is publicly shared and resented, though it is often induced by the large corporations, whose power, though no longer invisible, is remarkably well guarded. On the other side, much of the productive activity of the state is again charged to the public in the form of taxes, though the benefits flow to the dominant corporations.

The general consequence is a debased state. This state *must* grow to keep the system in motion, but it increasingly runs into the problem of obtaining the financial mandate to grow. Both in the upward and downward phases of the business cycle—be they short- or long-lived—the powerful cogs in the business system force the agencies of the state to absorb the social costs of conducting business. The state tries to minimize private losses at the public expense in the downward swing and to maximize private gain in the upward one. The social costs of both contractions and expansions are thus shoved onto the tax-paying public, which is displaying increasing resentment. Business leaders are essentially saying, "When we fail, we want the public authorities to pay for it; when the state helps us to succeed, we want to appropriate the gains for ourselves."

A great deal of the ideological vacillation between market and nonmarket solutions, between more and fewer controls, and between more planning and less planning arises from periodic failures of the market, on the one hand, and the powerlessness of the political system to develop productive solutions outside the market, on the other. A productive solution outside the market would simply be too threatening to capitalism.

When we assign to the government so many unproductive roles, we prove to all that the government is unproductive. But that, of course, does not eliminate the need for expanding its roles. This contradiction forces the state to employ financial subterfuge, to obscure the costs and benefits of its activity. Inflation, rather than the absence of courage among monetary authorities, is one such mechanism.

The moral to be derived from this discussion of the state transcends the government's inability to cope with the problem of inflation. In both depressions and prosperous periods, there is need for more state involvement to maintain the business system. But, at the same time, this swelling leviathan must be restrained or limited in its nonwasteful problem-solving capacities. It must be ideologically debased for fear that it will offer a positive alternative to the business system itself. It is this dilemma that is at the root of our confusion about the proper role of the state or government.

What needs emphasis is that the state's inflationary role arises from the functioning of the business system. If we do not trust the state to act rationally, it should be because we do not believe that the business system that determines the state's bureaucratic biases is rational. That, of course, is what we mean when we say that the state is a "capitalist" state, not simply a neutral entity responding to pluralistic pressures. The state is the mistress of the business system; it grows with it and cannot be expected to function outside the restraints and influences emanating from the business system. If the economy has a strong propensity to inflation because the alternatives are too grim to face, the state is necessarily part of this reality.

CONCLUSION

It seems remarkably inconsistent for mainstream economists to bathe in the glory of the pluralistic system in which competing groups are encouraged to seek their own interests and at the same time to complain when the whole process of quasi-competitive emulation leads to inflationary spirals. As all the so-called diverse organized groups seek to protect their own portions of the real income pie, either at the political level (Federal and local) or at the point of production, they are only behaving in what the ideologues of the superstructure have called "the American way." When each group behaves according to "the American way" and bargains for what it has learned to expect as a matter of right (a small annual increment to its current share of income), the bundle of goods and services produced at current prices periodically becomes overclaimed. The class and group conflicts inherent in this process are "resolved" temporarily by government policies that are essentially inflationary. It is not that people suffer from illusions about money, as some mainstream economists argue. People have no choice but to struggle, to chase the tail of price movements in a system that shuns equality and commitment to the needs of society as a whole. "Public regarding," to use a term common among political scientists, is a footnote that appears *after* the ravages of private decisions.

It should not be forgotten that contradictions in the political arena and in the financial superstructure are extensions of contradictions that operate in the economy itself. As we have argued, the bargain on wages and prices that is struck in the monopolistic sector is readily transformed into a wage-tax spiral in the public sector, especially at the local level. Although price stability, or strong measures to reduce the rate of inflation, may be desirable for specific business interests, like those of American exporters whose success would improve our balance-of-payment position, these matters cannot be readily attended to without producing an international depression. Political efforts to control inflation are generally weak or short-lived, despite all the rhetoric.

Attempts to cope with inflation, we should add, run into other contradictions. Because prices begin rising long before full employment is achieved, interest rates also begin to rise prematurely, thus choking off demand for homes, commercial building, construction, and durable goods. The result, of course, is that the government becomes a participant, intentionally or otherwise, in the creation and maintenance of both unemployment and inflation. Again, the dilemma is handled by proceeding meekly and, not infrequently, ineffectively on all fronts. The outcome, to return to our more general theme, is expansion of the social expenses of the state, not only through income maintenance for unemployed workers but also through other concealed unproductive forms of spending. For example, the need for large police forces to cope with crime in our central cities results from the existence of a permanently under- and unemployed class that the economy has rejected; significant growth in our system of higher education has resulted, not so much from a desire to educate students as from a need to postpone their entry into the labor force.

There is, furthermore, an imperialistic dimension in the contradictions of a monopoly-dominated business system. As the monopoly sector tends to breed excess capacity, it is always searching for new markets. It thus becomes the vanguard of an aggressive national foreign policy, calling upon the government to protect foreign markets and strategic resources in foreign lands, as well as to finance the formation of new markets.

The multinational corporation is the newest form of business expansion abroad. Although its origin is not specifically related to the government, governmental policies have stimulated its growth. But this growth too has not occurred without numerous contradictions. Specifically, the lavish private funds available to these corporations have undermined the effectiveness of government tight-money policies to check inflation. More generally, the costs of building and maintaining an empire are incurred publicly, but the benefits are appropriated privately.

In still another vein, a considerable portion of this empire relies on a vast military machine, which in turn requires a large state bureaucracy that provides no visible benefits to the public. Because so many Federal allocations are for goods and services that generate income without corresponding real flows returning to the market, they necessarily induce inflation. Inflation is thus an adaptation to the compelling need of capitalism to grow beyond its national boundaries. The problem is compounded by the fact that so much of this growth involves unproductive expenditures. The most significant component of unproductive output has been military hardware and related goods and services, which are claimed to be essential to protect us from enemies abroad. In the radical view, this need is translated into the protection of our empire abroad, which brings us to consideration of the second major consequence of capitalism's obsessive need to grow: economic imperialism, the subject of Chapter 14.

NOTES

1. David I. Meiselman, "Worldwide Inflation: A Monetarist View," in *The Phenomenon of Worldwide Inflation*, eds. David I. Meiselman and Arthur B. Laffer (Washington, D.C.: American Enterprise Institute, 1975), pp. 73–74.

2. *Ibid.*, p. 70.

3. Milton Friedman, "The Role of Monetary Policy," *The American Economic Review* 58 (March 1968): 12.

4. Gottfried Haberler, "Inflation as a Worldwide Phenomenon—An Overview," in *The Phenomenon of Worldwide Inflation*, eds. David I. Meiselman and Arthur B. Laffer (Washington,

D.C.: American Enterprise Institute, 1975), p. 13.

5. Meiselman, "Worldwide Inflation," pp. 70–71.

6. Robert Zevin, "The Political Economy of the American Empire, December 1974," in *The Economic Reader*, ed. David Mermelstein (New York: Vintage, 1975), p. 141.

7. Friedman, "The Role of Monetary Policy," p. 16.

8. *Ibid.*, p. 12.

9. The simile is Friedman's own. *Ibid.*, p. 13.

10. *Ibid.*

11. Even over longer stretches of time, velocity may be unstable, according to some fiscalists. As

Walter W. Heller has claimed, "Income velocity of money rose roughly 28 percent during the 1960–68 period." Heller, "Is Monetary Policy Being Oversold?," in *Monetary Versus Fiscal Policy*, Milton Friedman and Walter W. Heller (New York: Norton, 1969), pp. 15–41.

12. Meiselman, "Worldwide Inflation," p. 73.

13. *Ibid.*

14. *Ibid.*

15. Although the mainstream fiscalist attitude toward inflation has changed in recent years, this description still remains generally valid. See Walter W. Heller, "Now, Now Mr. Economist, Don't Be Afraid," *The New York Times*, June 30, 1975, p. 29.

16. In the judgment of E. Mishan, they still do: "Yet, it is a fact that among professional economists, certainly among academic economists, the debates on inflation tend to cluster about the 'demand-pull' end of the spectrum." E. Mishan, "The New Inflation," *Encounter* 42 (May 1974): 12.

17. James S. Duesenberry, "Worldwide Inflation: A Fiscalist View," in *The Phenomenon of Worldwide Inflation*, eds. David I. Meiselman and Arthur B. Laffer (Washington, D.C.: American Enterprise Institute, 1975), p. 115.

18. See "The New Economics and the Contradictions of Keynesianism," a special issue of *The Review of Radical Political Economics* 4 (August 1972).

19. Victor Perlo, "Economic Aspects of Military Spending," in *The Economic Reader*, ed. David Mermelstein (New York: Vintage, 1975), p. 174.

20. For a chronological list of the major events in this period, see "The Crisis in Historical Perspective: An Economic Chronology," in *The Economic Reader*, ed. David Mermelstein (New York: Vintage, 1975), pp. 5–32.

21. On December 4–7, 1973, truckdrivers blocked highways to protest rising fuel prices.

22. R. J. Ball and Peter Doyle, "Demand and Cost Inflation," in *Inflation*, eds. R. Ball and P. Doyle (London: Penguin, 1969), p. 147.

23. Robert A. Mundell, "Inflation from an International Viewpoint," in *The Phenomenon of Worldwide Inflation*, eds. David I. Meiselman and Arthur B. Laffer (Washington, D.C.: American Enterprise Institute: 1975), p. 141.

24. Karl Marx, *Capital*, vol. 3. Quoted in Harry Magdoff and Paul Sweezy, "Banks: Skating on Thin Ice," *Monthly Review* 26 (February 1975): 1, 21. Copyright © 1975 by Monthly Review, Inc. Reprinted by permission of Monthly Review Press.

25. For the definitive biography of Veblen, see Joseph Dorfman, *Thorstein Veblen and His America* (New York: Viking, 1947).

26. Paul Baran, *The Political Economy of Growth*, quoted in Sweezy, "Baran and the Danger of Inflation," *Monthly Review* 26 (December 1974): 11–12. Copyright © 1974 by Monthly Review, Inc. Reprinted by permission of Monthly Review Press.

27. Magdoff and Sweezy, "Banks," p. 12.

28. For detailed documentation and statistical proof of this statement, see Raford Boddy and James Crotty, "Class Conflict and Macro-Policy: The Political Business Cycle," *The Review of Rad-*

ical Political Economics 7 (Spring 1975): 1–19.

29. Sweezy, "Baran and the Danger of Inflation," p. 12.

30. The major part of this analysis is drawn from James O'Connor, *The Fiscal Crisis of the State* (New York: St. Martin's, 1973).

31. See Seymour Melman, *The Permanent War Economy* (New York: Simon & Schuster, 1974), pp. 21, 51, 140.

32. Tax increases are not in this sense different from price increases. Both cut into workers' standard of living and can be used to justify further demands.

THINKING
ABOUT IMPERIALISM

The title of this chapter is intended to suggest that an attitude of caution is imperative when discussing the subject of imperialism, a subject that involves many ambiguities, many inconsistent, unclear, and loosely stated propositions. Some of these ambiguities are inherent in the subject itself, which embraces vast geographical areas and a long span of time. Without apology, our efforts will be to suggest a few ideas about contemporary imperialism and its unique relationship with capitalism. The chapter is divided into five major sections: a definition of imperialism, a summary of mainstream views, a statement of the general radical position and critique of the mainstream, a survey of the Leninist tradition, and an alternative formulation and conclusion.

IMPERIALISM DEFINED

Most radical economists claim that the United States is at present the leading imperialist nation in the world, especially in its relations with underdeveloped countries. Apart from the decade of overt war in Southeast Asia, radicals point to the

military interventions in Greece, Iran, Lebanon, the Congo, Cuba, the Dominican Republic, Colombia, Guatemala, Panama,

> Bolivia, China, Korea, and Thailand. . . . [This dominance, moreover,] points to a pattern of imperialist behavior that goes back . . . to the very beginning of the Federal Republic.[1]

In general, radicals view imperialism as an extension of capitalism, not, as mainstream thinkers suggest, as a footnote to international trade and the rational specialization of the world's labor supply or simply as an aspect of a well-intended, but sometimes misguided, foreign-aid program.

In radical circles, belief in American imperialism as an outgrowth of capitalism passes virtually unquestioned. What *is* questioned is the definition of imperialism and related problems. Such issues as the source and motivation of imperialism, its inevitability and necessity to the survival of the capitalist system, and, finally, its consequences for the development of Third World countries are analyzed and debated. Although it is impossible to examine all these aspects of the imperialist question adequately within the limits of a single chapter, it is important to consider them at least generally in order to discover their interrelations, something that is scrupulously avoided by mainstream economists.

For our purposes, we shall define American imperialism as the sustained effort to maintain Third World countries in economic positions subordinate to, dependent upon, and complementary to the United States. It is, moreover, intended to serve the needs of dominant segments of the American business system. The mechanisms used may be political (for example, subversion by the Central Intelligence Agency [CIA] of revolutionary or reform parties in Third World nations), military (for example, "police" actions to prevent Third World domestic revolutions), or economic (the use of international monetary and development agencies, as well as loans and aid programs, to thwart efforts of the Third World nations to achieve greater domestic control of their own national economies). Usually there is some combination of these three courses of action. A sort of direct or indirect "threat-submission"[2] system operates in sufficiently predictable ways to keep the subordinate countries in production routines that are compatible with American interests as ultimately defined by various segments of the corporate hierarchy. These varied kinds of intervention are viewed as imperialistic because they are not related to any reasonable definition of what constitutes American national security in geopolitical terms.[3] They violate the "accepted" or "proclaimed" international principle of national sovereignty when assertions of independence (revolutionary or otherwise) by Third World nations do not represent any threat to the United States as a national community. The full implications of this definition in the broader context of world history will be explored in the final section of this chapter. For the present, we simply emphasize, at the risk of repetition, that an internal economic mechanism drives American capitalism to dominate Third World countries, though such countries do not in fact represent any threat to the United States' security or integrity as a political community.

THE MAINSTREAM "NONVIEW"
OF IMPERIALISM

There are both technical and ideological aspects to mainstream economists' propensity to deny the existence or importance of imperialism; both need clarification. The technical aspects are usually explicit; the ideological ones are used more subtly to deny the imperialist posture of the United States or capitalism. To understand the mainstream position and its varied facets, we shall begin with a brief discussion of why the United States became entangled in Southeast Asia. This question, though we cannot answer it satisfactorily, illustrates the sense in which mainstream economists offer a "nonview" of imperialism, even though there has developed in retrospect a consensus that this particular episode in Southeast Asia was indeed an imperialist adventure.

Was our involvement in Vietnam an isolated affair, or did it reflect a propensity that has deep economic roots? Most mainstream economists answer that Vietnam was a "tragic error," an isolated affair. This precise phrase may not be the one used; the answer may emerge only indirectly. Frequently, when mainstream economists are asked specifically to address their attention to why we became involved in Vietnam, they reply that involvement resulted from "political drift," anticommunism, a gross error in judgment, or some kind of political-military miscalculation in the Pentagon, at the highest levels of government, or even by the President, who is said to have been "poorly advised." These explanations reveal no historical memory of numerous other such American involvements. We must therefore conclude that mainstream economists believe that Vietnam was a unique event, unrelated to deeply rooted forces. Moreover, most mainstream economists believe that the war had little to do with American economic interests, especially as we had few direct investments in Vietnam.

Mainstream economists thus disagree with the broader view expressed in the *Pentagon Papers* that the Vietnam War was connected with Southeast Asia's large surplus of wealth in the form of rice, rubber, ore, and tin. As Henry Cabot Lodge spelled out this point for Pentagon researchers:

> The loss of Southeast Asia would have serious economic consequences for many nations of the free world. . . . Asia, especially Malaya and Indonesia, is the principal world source of natural rubber and tin, and a producer of petroleum and other strategically important commodities. The rice exports of Burma, Indochina, and Thailand are critically important to Malaya, Ceylon and Hong Kong and are of considerable significance to Japan and India, all important areas of free Asia. Furthermore, this area has an important potential as a market for the industrialized countries of the free world.[4]

Nor do mainstream economists consider the fact that offshore oil explorations by a consortium had been continuing for a number of years with anticipation of extremely large findings.[5]

Finally, they apparently do not consider relevant the following statement by Alfred Wentworth, the vice-president of the Chase Manhattan Bank in charge of Far Eastern operations:

> In the past, foreign investors have been wary of the over-all political prospect for the region. I must say, though, that the U.S. [dramatic 1965] actions in Vietnam . . . which have demonstrated that the U.S. will continue to give effective protection to the free nations of the region—have considerably reassured both Asian and Western investors. In fact, I see some reason for hope that the same sort of economic growth may take place in the free economies of Asia that took place in Europe after the Truman Doctrine and after NATO provided a protective shield. The same thing also took place in Japan after the U.S. intervention in Korea removed investor doubts.[6]

These statements represent a sort of anomaly. On the one hand, political and business leaders of the greatest capitalist power in the world have spoken frankly about the economic motives behind our penetration into Vietnam; on the other, few mainstream economists seem willing to consider the possibility that imperialism may reflect capitalism's need to expand. The question that arises, of course, is, Why this apparent flight from the obvious? Why do mainstream economists tend to ignore the whole question? There are at least six reasons why. Together they constitute the mainstream "nonview" of imperialism.

THE NONECONOMIC CHARACTER OF IMPERIALISM

Mainstream economists tend to believe that imperialism is basically a political, military, or social process and that it is therefore a subject better left to other social scientists.

VOLUNTARY TRADE RELATIONS

Mainstream economists also believe that trade relations between Third World countries and advanced capitalist ones, however unequal, are at present more or less voluntary; by definition, voluntary relations cannot be imperialistic ones. This proposition reflects the way in which mainstream economists tend to view all capitalist relations, that is, as market relations involving voluntary exchanges. When exchange is voluntary, it is further assumed that each party makes a rational decision about its best interests without coercion of any kind. Economic imperialism exists mainly when one nation's gain from trade reflects another nation's absolute loss.[7] Imperialism exists when tribute from the conquered is exacted without choice, as in the Roman conquests; Kenneth E. Boulding has called such tributes "one-way transfers."[8] Trade involving absolute losses to one participant simply would not occur if there were freedom to avoid it. But trade that involves gain by both parties, even if pressure is applied by one party to the other, is not exploitative and imperialistic, because inherent in it is the potential for voluntary withdrawal by the party in the weaker bargaining position.

IMPERIALISM WITHOUT NECESSITY

Some mainstream economists acknowledge that American imperialism exists but deny that it exists out of necessity, arguing either that the social costs of imperialism are considerably greater than the benefits accruing to particular interests; that American investments in underdeveloped countries are a small proportion of total foreign investment and an even smaller proportion of GNP; or that capitalist nations can acquire strategic resources from underdeveloped nations through the market or can substitute other products. This argument denies that imperialism has economic roots and suggests that it results from other factors, like ideology and political or bureaucratic imperatives. Economic interests, in this view, follow the flag, rather than lead it.

POWER DIFFERENCES

It is sometimes argued that imperialism is a product of Western rationality, technological power, or simply power per se.[9] Imperialism is thus shown to be unrelated to the particular characteristics of capitalism; big power differentials (however caused) "naturally" breed arrogance in the mightier power, which does not hesitate to force its interest on weaker parties. This "power thesis" is frequently justified by reference to the "self-evident" imperialistic qualities of the Soviet Union, which clearly is not organized along capitalist lines. In this way capitalism *as a system* is absolved from its imperialist role.

ORIGINAL SIN

It is not uncommon for mainstream economists to note that the general fact of imperialistic domination of one group by another is as old as civilization itself and therefore that imperialism cannot be identified with the particular characteristics of capitalism as such. Even J. K. Galbraith, though not a mainstream economist, proceeds along traditional lines when he discusses the lesson to be learned from our Vietnam disaster. He introduces his view by looking into the past, 1075 A.D. to be exact:

> It is now just under 900 years since Trans-Alpine Europeans began extending the beneficence of their presence to the lesser races without law. Then, as still, they saw themselves as the custodians of higher civilized values and the progenitors and evangelists of these values. . . . Since 1096, Austrians, Spaniards, French, British, Dutch, Belgians, Swedes, Danes, Russians, Germans, Portuguese, and Italians have answered the call to a civilizing mission beyond their borders. The urge among non-Europeans has been shared by Arabs, Mongols, Turks, [and] Japanese.[10]

When such epochal reasoning is employed, it follows that the specifically economic roots of capitalist imperialism are dismissed. In fact, Galbraith's reasoning leads him to just such a conclusion. After suggesting the possibility (mainly to disarm his readers) that our entrance into Indochina reflected drives "for markets, for outlets for investment, for justification for military spending," he argues that history teaches us differently and that basically the war was caused by foolish and stupid men who "were themselves an historical accident."[11] Exactly how going back 900 years teaches that imperialism is an outgrowth of historical accidents Galbraith does not explain.

A more thoughtful and not uncommon way of dismissing the notion of capitalist imperialism is to interpret it as a continuation of the imperial spirit of antiquity. Imperialism goes back to "tribes, nations, races . . . [that] establish themselves as entities which define their identity in contrast or conflict with others."[12] Embodied in the present nation-state system are these primordial attachments, waiting to be unleashed. It is the nation-state itself—not the economics of capitalism—that is the root cause of imperialism. "Imperialist policies," to continue in this vein, "are nothing but exaggerated, perverted, unleashed functions of the legitimate security interests of national states; imperialism is nationalism ([tribalism, culturalism]) writ large."[13]

IMPERIALISM AS A VESTIGE OF THE PAST

Finally, mainstream economists claim that capitalist imperialism may have been necessary in the past but that the Keynesian revolution in economic knowledge has provided capitalist states with the wherewithal to counteract their tendencies toward domestic stagnation and insufficient aggregate demand without reverting to an extraterritorial search for markets or investment outlets. Imperialism, however pervasive it may actually be, is not essential to the economic survival of capitalism. For this reason, it does not warrant serious attention and cannot be motivated as alleged by radicals.

When we examine the implications of these six points, we find that the vast American economic empire is either ignored or rationalized. It is not without reason that the mainstream perspective on imperialism has been called a "nonview."

THE RADICAL COUNTERPOINT
TO MAINSTREAM'S NONVIEW

Radical economists do not fully accept the crude economic determinism implicit in the reasoning of Lodge, Pentagon researchers, and the vice-president of the Chase Manhattan Bank. Certainly, as first approximations, their statements stand as refreshing alternatives to those offered by mainstream economists. Moreover, it is not irrelevant that important officials of the government and business community have felt compelled to legitimize our heinous actions in Vietnam in 1965 as having stimulated the economic growth of this nation and the "free" world. Nevertheless, most radical economists would add to the economic drives behind our involvement the ideological motive of anticommunism. Since World War II, anticommunism has served not only to justify the construction of our entire empire but also to justify inquisitional tactics against domestic radicals. Radicals also believe that military interests, however unrelated to the real national security of the United States, have combined with defense-oriented corporations to expand sales and maintain corporate solvency. Furthermore, American involvement in Vietnam is simply a specific and extreme instance of our general neocolonial entanglement in the affairs of Third World nations, a phenomenon dating back at least to the 1890s and the protracted American war with Philippine guerrillas.

Setting aside the initial source of the imperial impulse itself, not all extended foreign entanglements are necessarily profitable to the system or the capitalist class as a whole for any length of time. As a matter of fact, American involvement in Vietnam, whatever specific advantages it may have bestowed on particular interests, may also have become inimical to general business profitability because it eroded our competitive position vis-à-vis European and Japanese capitalism. The impulse that sucked us into the Vietnamese quagmire must be analyzed independently of the momentum that caused us to overextend that involvement. The initial economic expectations may have been positive and productive, even though extended involvement turned out to be negative and unproductive. Empire building, like the behavior of neurotics, not infrequently leads to internal distortions and eventual breakdowns. In the radical view, it is not enough to say, as mainstream economists are prone to do, that the social costs of an imperial adventure like that in Vietnam exceed private gains. An intrinsic

feature of capitalism is the absence of a responsive social accounting system; such costs—like Adam Smith's invisible hand—are
invisible to the public. But costs they are; they accrue until they
distort the surface of the market structure itself, and not infrequently they have unexpected social and political consequences.

In the most general terms, it is capitalist expansion, driven by
the profit motive and concomitant desires to accumulate, that
tends to extend the nation's economic interests far beyond its
borders. Once such interests have been established, or even recognized, the superstructure acts to protect and nurture them. In
this sense, capitalism has not changed from its earliest beginnings.
Its viability requires a continuous struggle to enlarge the magnitude of privately owned capital. Dominant members of the corporate hierarchy desire the whole world as a market and wish to
control as much of it as possible. Their search for investment
opportunities and their need to protect established markets have
pushed American economic interests far beyond the nation's
geopolitical boundaries. Corporations are run by men

> who could sit at a desk in a perverted condition of sustained
> ecstasy, dream of numerical manipulations, and finally write a
> check or a cable. Driven by the lust for expansion, by a relent-
> less passion for quantity which is more general than power . . .
> or sex; without the catharsis or rhythmic relaxation or satisfy-
> ing achievement and perpetually lusting for more. . . . Blind to
> the lives distorted by his money apparatus, he command[s] the
> lives of countless men and women.[14]

Corporations, in this view, are nineteenth-century imperial tycoons transformed into elaborate institutions. The modern giant
corporation, with its specialized cost and sales departments, is a
more thorough and methodical profit calculator and capital ac-
cumulator than the rugged, colorful nineteenth-century captain
of American industry.[15]

Corporations, with their power and needs, periodically call upon
the government to protect their economic interests (however
small they may be relative to the general economy of the United
States), to control foreign territories, to manipulate weaker
ruling oligarchies, and to establish economic dependencies and
appendages in ways that have very little to do with the security
and sovereignty of the United States. Moreover, the government
not infrequently ensures their investments in these ways.

The main area of manipulative penetration, it should be noted, is the underdeveloped world, where it manifests itself primarily in economic terms. It is there that the United States poses the greatest danger; our preoccupation with overthrowing "unfriendly" governments, even mildly democratic ones, has been well documented.[16] And, though imperialism may be a more general problem, one that transcends capitalism, radicals who live in the United States recognize that it is American imperialism against which we are most capable of taking action; therefore it is American imperialism toward which they direct their attention.

Although any number of countries in Latin America could be used to illustrate the imperial game played by the American government at the behest of American corporate power, recent events in Chile have become particularly well known. In Chile there was a democratically elected government, that of Salvador Allende, a Marxist party leader. This government was unquestionably as democratic as any in Latin America. Yet American imperialist forces admittedly mobilized to "destabilize" the Allende government through a combination of withholding foreign aid, withdrawing loans, and covert CIA activities, which reportedly cost $8 million between 1970 and 1973. It is even possible that Americans joined Chilean rightists in bringing about Allende's assassination. The banal justification for this intervention was spelled out by President Gerald Ford at a news conference: "What we did was in our interests and that of the Chilean people."[17] In the press exposé of the United States' illegal intervention, little has been said about how our interests were defined, although there was some mention of the arrogance in the assumption that we know what is good for the Chilean people. What seemed most to disturb honest pundits of the press and others was that perjury may have been committed by the head of the CIA and by other governmental officials as well.[18] Let us suppose that the government had not lied; would that make our empire builders' reactions to indigenous reform efforts less culpable?

From the radical perspective, the question of whether the government speaks frankly or camouflages its policies with omissions, half-truths, and lies is less important than a more profound truth—that our counterrevolutionary activities in Chile were not isolated political ones or simply the result of "dishonest" or "misguided" political leaders' perceptions of our national interests. Our meddling in Chile's internal affairs cannot be understood without examining Anaconda and Kennecott copper interests, as well as the grand counterrevolutionary plan submitted by International

Telephone and Telegraph (ITT) to the White House for consideration. It was no accident that Chilean Admiral Ismael Huerta announced within one week after the coup against Allende that the "door was open for resumption of negotiations on compensation for United States copper holdings nationalized by President Allende."[19]

Business views on Latin America (to turn to a more general argument), as well as those of government authorities, are not based on abstract considerations of democracy, elections, freedom, or the need to exercise power simply because it is there; they are based on corporate earnings, which, in Latin America, tend to exceed investments by approximately $1 billion annually.[20] In more concrete dollars-and-cents terms, for each dollar invested in Latin America between 1946 and the present, between $2.50 and $4.00 have come back.[21]

From this general framework, including some of the specific events and facts noted, the radical reply to the mainstream "nonview" of imperialism has been formulated. It parallels the six arguments developed in the preceding section.

IGNORING THE ECONOMIC FACTOR

To avoid thinking about imperialism as an important and permanent aspect of the capitalist process is to avoid dealing with a significant *economic* reality of modern capitalist development, especially as it determines our relations with Third World nations. It is for this reason, according to radicals, that the United States' periodic acts of "political" intervention in the domestic affairs of underdeveloped countries come as surprises to mainstream economists and are viewed as the isolated acts of "bad" or "misguided" politicians—as if our imperial decisions were made by self-aggrandizing Pentagon bureaucrats who just happen to have appeared for no economic reasons. In any event, such imperial acts are viewed by mainstream economists as insignificantly related to underlying economic forces and interests. This conclusion is a natural consequence of the mainstream habit of thinking about the political system as independent of the economic one. Because this habit rests on an erroneous foundation, there is much about the relations between capitalist and underdeveloped nations that falls completely outside the range of mainstream thinking.

INVOLUNTARY TRADE RELATIONS

The unequal distribution of power between underdeveloped and developed nations has led to trade bargains that greatly favor the latter. In this way, wealth is transferred from the poor to the rich nations. To mainstream economists, these adverse trade patterns seem based on voluntary relations and owing simply to the low productivity of poor countries. For this reason, the trade differences seem to them predictable and rational, reflecting underlying economic realities. Mainstream theory does not argue that both parties to trade must benefit equally; it argues simply that both parties must benefit, even though the benefits may be grossly unequal in distribution. To radicals the use of the word "voluntary" to describe trade relations between the types of countries under discussion represents a perversion of the English language. The "voluntary" quality of trade relations between capitalist and Third World nations is equivalent to the "voluntary" choice of surrendering one's wallet in exchange for protection against "enemies," rather than being shot in the head. Mainstream economists ignore the imperial threat that has operated in the past and continues to operate in the present.

Although radicals admit that the low productivity of underdeveloped countries can exacerbate adverse terms of trade with rich capitalist nations, they insist that the dominant-subordinate relations established between rulers of capitalist countries and oligarchs of underdeveloped ones are parasitic and coercive in ways that prevent poor nations from overcoming the barriers to higher productivity. Radicals simply deny, on the basis of historical evidence, that it is legitimate to describe the link between Third World and capitalist nations as "voluntary."

As to the question of whether Third World countries benefit from trading with capitalist countries even when the terms are highly unequal, radicals approach the question in the spirit articulated by Karl Marx: "If the free traders cannot understand how one nation can grow rich at the expense of another, we need not wonder, since these same gentlemen also refuse to understand how within one country one class can enrich itself at the expense of another."[22] Furthermore, radicals argue that the poverty and misery prevailing in the Third World can be attributed to both past and present capitalist exploitation and control. Frequently, exploitation can be traced back at least to English, French,

Spanish, and Portuguese colonial structures established in the fifteenth century. These structures broke up the indigenous non-white societies and launched them on the path of dependence and overspecialization, thus ensuring their future as permanent objects of exploitation. Although these specific colonial structures have crumbled, radicals argue that new forms and mechanisms have emerged to accomplish substantially similar results,[23] for modern capitalist countries are still transferring wealth to themselves. The historical and present consequences of capitalist penetration are of three kinds.

First, when the consequences are evaluated historically, from the forcible entry of capitalist adventurers in the colonial period to the present, evidence of absolute impoverishment and misery among a significant portion of the colonial and former colonial populations can be established. Not only have millions of lives been lost as a result of the long capitalist march into Third World territories, but also capitalism has brought diseases, soil exhaustion, poverty, and social dislocations. Even in the present phase of "enlightened capitalism," there are millions of Third World non-whites who have not experienced the material blessings of capitalist development.

Second is the growth of relative deprivation, both within the underdeveloped nations themselves and between the underdeveloped areas and the advanced capitalist ones. As capitalism has incompletely thrust its tentacles into the poorer nations of the world, it has generated greater inequalities between small clusters of relatively rich people in the metropolitan centers of Third World nations and much larger numbers of the poor existing in the hinterlands at or close to subsistence levels. It has also promoted a persistent and sometimes growing gap in wealth and income between the Third World and advanced capitalist countries. In this way, normal capitalist development produces *under-development*.[24] That is, this dual tendency is part of a single phenomenon: the uneven development and exploitative production and trade relations of capitalism.

Third, quantitative considerations aside, one general effect of capitalist imperial penetration of underdeveloped economies, especially from the colonial point of view, has been the permanent dislodging of the older "virtues" of Third World societies without substituting viable alternative values. This matter was put in rather benign terms by one respected economist:

Capitalism, simply because it is a current embodiment of scientific revolution, is an enormously expansive and aggressive force which often presents an almost insuperable challenge to precapitalist traditional societies, and which may disorganize them more than it benefits them. . . . Traditional societies and traditional identities . . . have been unable to generate an indigenous adaptation to the knowledge and pressures of the modern world.[25]

The point has been stated somewhat differently by the Marxist Paul A. Baran:

[Imperialism] effectively disrupted whatever was left of the "feudal" coherence of the backward societies. It substituted market contracts for such paternalistic relationships as still survived from century to century. . . . It linked their economic fate with the vagaries of the world market and connected it with the fever curve of international price movements. . . . All that happened was that the age-old exploitation of the population of underdeveloped countries by their domestic overlords, was freed of the mitigating constraints inherited from the feudal tradition. This superimposition of business *mores* over ancient oppression by landed gentries resulted in compounded exploitation, more outrageous corruption, and more glaring injustice. . . . The bonanza that was capitalism, the fullness of things that was modern industrial civilization, were crowding the display windows—they were protected by barbed wire from the anxious grip of the starving and desperate man in the street.[26]

Western capitalist penetration of Third World economies appears to have plunged them into perennial purgatory. It has neither stimulated the development of a strong, indigenous capitalism nor completely broken up the old order. In a sense, it has produced a combination of underdeveloped capitalism with crippled and decadent precapitalist institutions, because of its incomplete penetration of market elements. The existing market elements have not coalesced into viable, expanding capitalist systems capable of liberating the general population from the precapitalist past. The result is weak Third World societies, prey to manipulation, corruption, bribery, and domination by outside capitalist governments and businesses. These characteristics, moreover, reflect the central tendency of such societies.

CORPORATE HIERARCHY
AND THE IMPERIAL IMPULSE

In response to claims that the social costs of imperialism are greater than particular benefits to vested interests and that American investments in the Third World are a very small proportion of GNP and total foreign investment, radicals argue that imperialist policies are not determined according to aggregate interests. On the contrary, they are determined by the few who dominate the business hierarchy. Hierarchy functions in a social structure as weighting functions in an index whose elements are unequal in sensitivity. It is thus a critical component of the radical perception of the problem of imperialism. Decisions about relations with the Third World are determined by people in a stratified economic structure. At the apex of this structure (composed of the 200 or so largest corporations) the benefits of imperialism are significant, however "marginal" or costly they may be to the economy as a whole. This top echelon, moreover, has disproportionate power to bend the political system in an imperialist direction and to ensure that the costs of empire are "democratically" shared among the total population in the "national interest." In reality the matter is often much simpler, for most chieftains of the dominant political parties view the national interest as synonymous with the interests and well-being of the major corporations. As representatives of the state, office holders seek to reproduce capitalist relations and to provide circumstances for their expansion. In this sense, there really is no meaningful "war" between the politicians, who presumably represent the "people," and the dominant corporations, which epitomize the business system.

THE ROLE OF POWER

Mainstream economists have a tendency to obscure the relationship between capitalist expansion and its domination of underdeveloped nations. They argue that it is power differentials per se that breed imperialism or that it is Western rationality, leading to differences in technological capability between advanced and less advanced nations, that breeds imperialism.[27] For whatever reasons that power differentials emerge, the "power" argument rapidly degenerates into reasoning of this kind: The Soviet Union is imperialistic; the Soviet Union is not a capitalist nation; the Soviet Union is a big power; therefore it is big power per se and not capitalism that breeds imperialism. Regarding imperialism as a function of the internal structure of capitalism is considered erroneous.

If the Soviet Union had lived up to its pristine socialist principles, if the image of socialism had not been so completely tarnished by the internal brutality of Stalinism and the Soviet Union's postwar policy toward eastern Europe, American radicals might have been in a better position to argue, with fewer convoluted qualifications, that modern imperialism is primarily a function of capitalism. Yet, even if the Soviet Union had evolved differently and even if American radicals had been in a more secure intellectual position to defend "socialism" in its "homeland," it is unlikely that the relationship of the United States with the Third World would have been much different from what it is today. The United States would, of course, have been forced to rationalize its interventionist policies differently; that is, rather than defending the world against brutal communism, which itself has a vast empire threatening the "free" world, we would have found it in our "national interest" to save the world only from the anarchy, disorder, and violence brewing in Third World countries. Mainstream economists would probably have argued, as they did before the bogey of Russia and communism arose, that Third World peoples have to be "ready" to handle their own political and economic destinies before we can terminate imperial policies, which, however unfortunate, are necessary to ensure broader world stability.

In the radical view, the Soviet Union's "expansion" has been for the most part "border-oriented." It is, in other words, "perimeter imperialism," that is, based, perhaps to a pathological degree, on considerations of border security, but not involving dominating entanglements *far* beyond its frontiers.[28] More important, perhaps, is the fact that mainstream economists, in the radical view, use the Soviet Union as an ideological gimmick to avoid examining the nature of American imperialism and its relation to the internal structure of capitalism.

THE UNIQUENESS OF CAPITALIST IMPERIALISM

Connected with the observation that imperialism has always been with us, that it is as old as civilization itself, is the notion that imperialism cannot be viewed as a function of capitalism. Although the term "imperialism" is relatively modern, having come into use for the first time in the 1880s, there can be no doubt that the Assyrian, Persian, Athenian, and Roman empires were founded on exploitation and tribute. Although many ancient empires had capitalistic elements embedded in their social structures, it is clear that what drove these empires into action was related to forces other than purely commercial ones; ancient empires were simply not built around capitalist institutions. Nevertheless, we believe that it is illegitimate to dismiss capitalist imperialism simply because other kinds of imperialism once existed. There is a normative problem here that should be explored. Ancient imperialist manifestations did not violate established codes of national or ethnic sovereignty. As the well-known historian of antiquity M. I. Finley has put it, "The ancient world was one of unceasing warfare, and the accepted rule was that the victor had absolute rights over the persons and property of his captives."[29] Analogously, no mainstream economist would argue that chattel slavery in the modern world is legitimate or tolerable simply because slavery has existed almost from the beginning of civilization and is therefore a normal state of affairs. All would find it necessary to invoke a normative qualification: Slavery in the modern world is intolerable because it violates all modern canons of human dignity.

STAGNATION AND IMPERIALISM

As for the claim that imperialism is necessary to protect capitalism from its tendency toward stagnation, the question that generally arises is whether the modern capitalist state, armed with Keynesian wisdom, can find in domestic expenditures a substitute for the stimulus of empire building. There has been too much dogmatism on this point among both radical and mainstream economists. As we have pointed out elsewhere, on the one hand, mainstream economists argue as if it were axiomatic that imperialism is unnecessary, given the small advantages associated with imperialist undertakings. On the other, Harry Magdoff, writing in the Marxist tradition, has implied that terminating imperialism is tantamount to terminating capitalism. Mainstream economists point to the experience of Japan, the Scandinavian countries, and western Europe after World War II to prove that imperialism and the militarism that accompanies it are not necessary to capitalist prosperity. Paul Sweezy, a Marxist, has argued that capitalism is an international system; Japan and western Europe need not adopt their own military brand of Keynesianism because the

United States, the dominant and most powerful member of the international capitalist club, has assumed the role of military guardian for all its members. Where would Japan or western Europe be if the United States should enter into a serious depression?[30] For Sweezy, the answer is self-evident, and, moreover, it is increasingly being verified by the facts of the recent inflationary recession and the common view among European statesmen and business leaders that Europe's recovery is completely dependent upon what happens to the American economy.

In our own judgment, the matter is more complex than has so far been indicated. It is an understatement to say that there may even be some unknowns in the equation. We believe that both radical and mainstream economists are probably incorrect in their speculations on this point. The loss of Russia, China, Cuba, eastern Europe, North Korea, and North Vietnam did not destroy the capitalist system, at least as it is defined by radicals. These losses were not without consequence; they did produce some perverted reaction formations, which mainstream economists gloss over. Perhaps more to the point is the fact that the United States never recovered from the Great Depression of 1930 until it was necessary to mobilize its resources for war. Yet the international picture is murkier. Germany and the Scandinavian countries did recover rather early in the 1930s. Although we should be careful about using Germany as an example during this period, it does appear that Keynesian solutions work whether administered by fascists or militant laborists who have acquired solid political support. What appears not to work in crises is bland Keynesianism of the kind to which American policy makers are accustomed. It is certain, in our view, that the end of the capitalist imperialist system will have many unintended consequences that will surprise everyone. Radicals, however, whatever their differences among themselves, prefer to cope with these unpredictable consequences of the demise of imperialism than to cope with the known consequences of its continuation.

Twist and turn as mainstream economists are prone to do to avoid examining the economic roots of American imperialism, imperialism does not vanish. Although ostriches may survive storms by putting their heads in the sand, they certainly do not prevent the storms. Such storms, moreover, do considerable damage, if not to clever ostriches, to other living creatures. The imperial storm, as we have shown, is not easily analyzed. In the final section of this chapter, we shall therefore try to suggest an alternative analytical approach. Before embarking upon this task, we must turn to Nikolai Lenin's view of the subject, for his influence on the radical tradition has been pervasive.

THE LENINIST LEGACY

Believing that modern imperialism is pervasive is one matter; identifying its root causes and explaining its changing patterns are other matters. Although many who write about imperialism from a specifically Leninist point of view would not necessarily disagree with the overview of the subject that we have presented in the previous pages as the general radical position, true Leninists would find it theoretically deficient. Our description of the impulse to grow and accumulate profits in the context of competition and private ownership of means of production would seem too general. They believe that the history of imperialist forms is related to specific stages of capitalism. So far three such stages have been described.

Stage 1 lasted from approximately 1790 to the end of the nineteenth century, a period in which pure competitive capitalism came to an end. In that period, industrialists played leading roles; their imperialism was motivated mainly by the need for cheap food and raw materials, and it was relatively benign. Great Britain, the leading capitalist nation of the time, used "free trade" aggressively as the rationale, or justification, for its imperial role.

As competition gave way to monopoly, as capitalist enterprises consolidated into larger units, stage 2 emerged; banks and financial institutions rose to positions of influence and control. The imperial vanguard of the capitalist system came to consist of financial oligarchs, rather than industrial ones. The term "finance capital" appropriately characterizes the substantive nature of this second stage. "Since the bankers deal in capital rather than commodities, their primary interest in the underdeveloped countries is in exporting capital . . . at highest possible rates of profit."[31] Stage 2 provided the basis for Lenin's famous pamphlet, "Imperialism, the Highest Stage of Capitalism." He argued that, with the decline of competition, the rise of financial capitalism, and the export of capital, the pressure to redivide the world among existing capitalist countries, which had already established their spheres of influence in the colonial period, had become the decisive motivation of imperialism. Because monopolization of the economy tended to generate both excess industrial capacity and excess profits, exporting capital to the less developed countries, where capital was scarce, would temporarily "solve" the capitalist problem of stagnation. But, because the underdeveloped world was already divided into "spheres of influence," redivision under the pressure of monopolistic drives led to an imperial scramble among capitalist nations that bred rampant nationalism, chauvinism, and racism, which finally culminated in World War I. The alternatives were civil war within capitalist nations themselves or expansion outward, a choice that was clear to some imperial spokesmen of the time. In the words of Cecil Rhodes in 1895:

> I was in the East End of London [a working class quarter] yesterday and attended a meeting of the unemployed. I listened to the wild speeches, which were just a cry for "bread! bread!" and on my way home I pondered over the scene and I became more than ever convinced of the importance of imperialism. . . . My cherished idea is a solution for the social problem, that is, in order to save the 40,000,000 inhabitants of the United Kingdom from a bloody civil war, we colonial statesmen must acquire new lands to settle the surplus population, to provide new markets for the goods produced in the factory and mines. The Empire . . . is a bread and butter question. If you want to avoid civil war, you must become imperialists.[32]

Because the average scale of enterprises had grown dramatically, a growth that was itself both a cause and an effect of the development of the monopolistic stage, industries in stage 2 had acquired an avaricious appetite for raw materials,

> not only in the already discovered sources . . . but also in potential sources. . . . And land which is useless today may be improved tomorrow if new methods are devised (to this end a big bank can equip a special expedition of engineers, agricultural experts, etc.), and if large amounts of capital are invested.[33]

The search for raw materials in the Third World was thus intensified.

The dialectic of Lenin's export-capital thesis, it should be noted, was supposed to be the development of the underdeveloped areas. As financial institutions mobilized capital for Third World areas, it was assumed that they would create the technical and class basis for industrialization and the emergence of bourgeois societies, which would in turn sooner or later become competitive with the more advanced capitalist societies that had created them. The culmination of this process would eventually plunge the whole international capitalist edifice into crisis. As this expected consequence never quite occurred, the logic underlying it was dropped or radically modified. Lenin's "highest" stage was to be succeeded by yet another.

Stage 3, beginning with World War I and lasting to the present, has been dominated by multinational corporations that are similar neither to the small commodity-oriented industrial enterprises of the nineteenth century nor to the big financial complexes that dominated Lenin's thinking about imperialism. "In size, complexity, or structure and multiplicity of interests these [multinational] corporate giants of today differ markedly from the industrialists or bankers of an earlier period."[34] A more graphic picture of the multinational corporation and the extent of its global spread has been furnished by David Horowitz:

> Standard Oil of New Jersey has a budget [in 1969] exceeding $15 billion, or double the GNP of Cuba. More powerful than many sovereign states, it has 150,000 agents, organizers and hired hands operating 250 suborganizations in more than 50 countries. It is part of an international syndicate which controls the economic lifeblood of half a dozen strategic countries in the underdeveloped world. In itself it is a major political force in the key electoral states of New York, Pennsylvania, New Jersey, and Texas, and it has close links with other syndicate members that are major political forces in California, Ohio, Louisiana, Indiana and elsewhere. Its agents and their associates occupied the cabinet post of Secretary of State in the Administrations of Eisenhower, Kennedy, and Johnson, and at the same time had influence in the CIA and other foreign-policy-making organizations of government at the highest level. It has its own intelligence and paramilitary networks, and a fleet of ships larger than the Greek Navy. It is not a secret organization but it is run by a self-perpetuating oligarchy whose decisions and operations are secret. And these affect directly, and significantly, the level of activity of the whole U.S. economy.[35]

This multinational imperialist phase represents a serious departure from phase in both economic and political terms, and it has therefore led to theoretical problems that Leninists have not yet faced squarely.[36] Be that as it may, the multinationals have incomes larger than many countries. They are distributed all over the globe, and they have subsidiaries and internal structures that enable them to play with costs, prices, and resources in order to escape national controls. By increasing, for example, the prices of raw-material imports produced by a subsidiary in an under-developed country to be processed in an advanced capitalist one, multinationals can generate higher phantom costs. This move reduces taxable income in the country where the final product is sold.[37] In general, multinationals have varied and flexible mechanisms of control, all of which are aimed at maximizing the long-run total profits of the corporations themselves.

The goal of each multinational corporation is to maximize its profits and to ensure the expansion of its wealth, which means that any particular part of each must be subordinate to the whole.[38] To realize such ends, multinationals require governments "to protect the 'free world' and to extend its boundaries wherever and whenever possible. . . . All the major struggles going on in the world today can be traced to this hunger of the multinational corporations for maximum *Lebensraum*."[39] To facilitate the activities of these multinational corporations requires "maintenance of a tremendous global military machine."[40]

Because the United States is the national base of the major multinational corporations, as well as the political leader among capitalist nations throughout the world, it has inherited the responsibility for maintaining an international military juggernaut that can protect the international business system's network of interests. A critical requirement of these interests is a steady flow of raw materials from the Third World on terms favorable to the industrial corporations. Without such primary products, the capitalist nations will falter. Moreover, the production of military hardware "coincidentally" serves the internal function of sustaining a high level of aggregate demand, thus arresting the potential for stagnation that is always present in mature capitalist nations. Imperialism in such capitalist societies thus functions to preserve international capitalist relations, on one hand, and to absorb surplus capital and labor, on the other. The latter function helps to prevent capitalism from achieving its "natural" state of "unemployed equilibrium." The multinational corporation, the newly evolved unit that propels the imperialism, reflects a monopoly stage of capitalism in which the commodity and banking functions of earlier stages are integrated with production and distribution; that is, intracorporate production and sales functions involving foreign-based assembly subsidiaries and mass advertising have become international in scope and have dramatically altered in scale.[41]

In summarizing current views of imperialism that are allegedly derived from the Leninist tradition, we find four major points.

First, imperialism is still considered in relation to evolutionary stages of capitalism. Although monopoly capitalism and imperialism are related, the monopoly stage is recognized as possessing two phases; the stage theory is thus more complex than was originally suggested by Lenin. Nevertheless, it has not been discarded.

Second, imperialism is *necessary* to capitalism. In fact, it is impossible to conceive of capitalism without it. Magdoff has argued that imperialism is not a matter of choice for a capitalist society; it *is* the capitalist way of life.[42] The implication is that terminating imperialism would be tantamount to ending capitalism, not simply forcing capitalism to undertake more intensive Keynesian efforts to develop internal policies for avoiding stagnation.

Third, although the relative magnitude of investments in the underdeveloped portions of the world is declining, the dependence of American capitalism upon them is as great as or greater than in past decades. Strategic raw materials are absolutely necessary to the survival of American capitalism and therefore to the survival of European capitalism as well.

Finally, Third World countries are not being readily developed as a result of their contact with capitalist ones. Contemporary capitalism drains these countries of capital (because terms of trade tend to be unfavorable to Third World regions) or builds up overspecialized dependence on raw materials that do not spill over into the underdeveloped country's hinterland. Even when Third World nations have achieved nominal political independence, their economies remain even more dependent than in the past. This dependence has enabled multinational corporations and capitalist governments, in particular that of the United States, to develop a whole battery of indirect mechanisms for controlling and exploiting Third World nations.

AN ALTERNATIVE FORMULATION AND CONCLUSION

Imperialism does not lend itself to precision or neat conclusions. Because it encompasses such a vast geographical and temporal domain, we believe that a reasoned general statement is preferable to a more detailed statement necessitating numerous qualifications.

In approaching the question of how to think about modern imperialism, we cannot avoid the use of a normative criterion appropriate to a single historical epoch. The relevant epoch for our purposes is that of the nation-state system organized around the principle of national sovereignty. It is the principle of national sovereignty that legitimizes certain kinds of security preoccupations and condemns others; for example, "helping" a smaller nation to ensure domestic tranquillity is legitimate, but taking sides in another nation's civil war is not. When a nation's imperial activities consistently go beyond the range of reasonable national-security requirements, when mechanisms for controlling other regions are unrelated to any reasonable threat from those regions, then evidence of imperialism exists in its purest form. It is here that radicals can make the best case against capitalism. The nation-state dominated by a capitalist economic engine has displayed an inner need to expand and to establish economic interests far beyond its boundaries. It is for this reason that Vietnam and American entanglements in Latin America are strong examples of imperialism and the Soviet Union's political domination of eastern Europe is a weak one. Vietnam and Latin America represent virtually no threat to American national sovereignty or security. In fact, successful revolutionary governments in many countries would be only too willing to deal with us on more equitable terms. In contrast, the history of the relations between eastern Europe and the West, on one hand, and its use against the Soviet Union on the other, has provided the Soviet Union with a rationale that falls within the way nation-states normally act to protect themselves.

Joseph Schumpeter viewed capitalism as benign and its rationality as opposed to anything that can be identified as imperialistic. To him imperialism was "objectless expansion" associated with atavisms derived from precapitalist societies.[43] Ironically, his definition of imperialism (as objectless expansion) probably applies more to capitalism than to other kinds of systems for the very reason that mainstream economists so often note: The social costs of imperialism are greater than the sum of its benefits to particular interests. It is precisely because the social costs of empire are greater than the gains to particular interests that it is "objectless," without rational social objective. If the country as a whole gained from it, imperialism, however inhumane, might make some sense in terms of a national or social accounting system.

For this reason, radical economists' common argument pegging imperialism to the control of strategic resources is weak. It may very well be that the capitalist penchant for wanton expansion and specialization has unique dimensions requiring particular kinds of highly specialized natural resources more rapidly and in greater volume than would be so under an alternative and more rational system. It may be, as we believe, that bauxite and magnesium are critical to the functioning of the American economy and therefore that business interests bend the political system to ensure a steady supply of these resources from underdeveloped countries. The problem is that the argument is not related to the particular characteristics of capitalism as a system. Logically, any system might be driven to adopt imperial mechanisms if it experienced a dire scarcity of resources threatening its functioning.

What is unique about capitalist imperialism is that *it does not require justification of its penetration and domination other than the normal profit motive that also keeps capitalism operating in the domestic sphere.* When radicals argue that imperialism arises from the logic of capitalism, they mean that imperialism is a natural extension of the inner workings of capitalism. The same is not true of other kinds of systems. The elites that govern socialist systems may, given insecurities about their own positions, be driven down the imperial road. But this process represents a breakdown or degeneration of the routines and cohesion that sustain the system; it is not an extension of the system's natural mode of functioning. Nor is it due to the perceived need for profit that determines the behavior of the giant corporations that dominate American capitalism.

NOTES

1. Thomas Weisskopf, "Theories of American Imperialism: A Critical Evaluation," *The Review of Radical Political Economics* 6 (Fall 1974): 41.

2. See Kenneth E. Boulding, "Introduction," in *Economic Imperialism*, eds. Kenneth E. Boulding and Tapan Mukerjee (Ann Arbor: University of Michigan Press, 1972), p. x.

3. The perception and meaning of national security may vary considerably, a problem that cannot be adequately dealt with here. Moreover, rhetoric supporting decisions in this sphere is generally cast in defensive or even paranoid terms. Whether such rhetoric is truly believed or is deliberately used to manipulate national support for imperialist policies cannot easily be determined. Particular instances must be analyzed in detail to uncover common pretenses or rationalizations.

4. Henry Cabot Lodge, in *The Defense Department History of United States Decision Making on Vietnam*. The Senator Gravel Edition, I (Boston: Beacon), p. 436. Quoted in Paul Joseph, "The Making of United States Policy in Vietnam," *Socialist Revolution* 3 (1973): 119.

5. See Seymour Melman, *The Permanent War Economy* (New York: Simon & Schuster, 1974), fn. 3, p. 325.

6. Quoted in Harry Magdoff, *The Age of Imperialism* (New York: Monthly Review Press, 1969), p. 176.

7. This argument was put forth by Abba Lerner in a seminar at Queens College, May 1973.

8. Boulding, "Introduction," p. xi.

9. *Ibid.*, p. xviii.

10. J. K. Galbraith, "On History, Foolishness and Vietnam," *The New York Times*, July 12, 1975, p. 25.

11. *Ibid.*

12. Henry Pachter, "The Problem of Imperialism," *Dissent*, September–October 1970, p. 487.

13. *Ibid.*

14. L. L. Whyte, *The Next Development in Man* (New York: Mentor, 1950), p. 116.

15. See Paul A. Baran and Paul M. Sweezy, *Monopoly Capital* (New York: Monthly Review Press, 1966), Chapter 2.

16. See Andreas Papandreou, *Paternalistic Capitalism* (Minneapolis: University of Minnesota Press, 1972).

17. "President Publicly Backs Clandestine CIA Activity," *The New York Times*, September 17, 1974, p. 1.

18. See Tom Wicker, "Perjury on Chile?" *The New York Times*, July 25, 1975, p. 31.

19. *The New York Times*, September 30, 1973, p. 14; cited by Maurice Zeitlin, "Corporate Ownership and Control: The Large Corporation and the Capitalist Class," *The American Journal of Sociology* 79 (March 1974), fn. 12, p. 1093.

20. See Thomas E. Weisskopf, "Capitalism, Underdevelopment and the Future of Poor Countries," *The Review of Radical Political Economics* 4 (Winter 1972): 1–35; see also two special

issues of *The Review of Radical Political Economics* devoted to the question of imperialism: "Case Studies in Imperialism and Underdevelopment," 3 (Spring 1971); and "Capitalism and World Economic Integration: Perspectives in Modern Imperialism," 5 (Spring 1973); see, finally, Harry Magdoff, *The Age of Imperialism.*

21. Theotonio Dos Santos, "The Structure of Dependence," *American Economic Review* 60 (May 1970): p. 234, reprinted in *The Political Economy of Development and Underdevelopment*, ed. Charles K. Wilber (New York: Random House, 1973), p. 114.

22. Karl Marx, "Address on the Question of Free Trade, 1848," *The Poverty of Philosophy* (New York, 1963), p. 223; quoted in Arghiri Emmanuel, *Unequal Exchange: A Study of the Imperialism of Trade* (New York: Monthly Review Press, 1972), p. vii.

23. Santos, "The Structure of Dependence," pp. 232–234.

24. This general theme, which has influenced many radicals, was first systematically developed by Andre Gunder Frank, "The Development of Underdevelopment," in *Imperialism and Underdevelopment*, ed. Robert I. Rhodes (New York: Monthly Review Press, 1970), p. 19.

25. Boulding, "Introduction," p. xvii.

26. Paul A. Baran, "On the Political Economy of Backwardness," in *The Economics of Underdevelopment*, eds. A. N. Agerwala and S. P. Singh (London: Oxford University Press, 1958), pp. 76–77.

27. Boulding, "Introduction," p. xv.

28. Except for the period after World War II, when the Soviet Union looted East Germany, it is very difficult to demonstrate Soviet economic imperialism corresponding to our own economic relations with underdeveloped countries. In many respects the countries with which the Soviet Union has systematic ties (in eastern Europe and Cuba) probably exploit the Soviet Union, rather than the other way around. Why the Soviet Union should allow itself to be economically exploited by smaller and weaker nations is an important question to which good answers are probably not available. Our own view is that the Soviet Union is pathologically anxious about the security of its borders in eastern Europe and is therefore willing to "pay tribute" to maintain political hegemony. There may also be some fear on the part of Soviet bureaucrats that a liberal or politically free eastern Europe would set off demands for similar freedom within the Soviet Union itself, thus threatening the privileges of the administrative elite. So far, in any event, the Soviet Union has not sought to develop dominant-subordinant relations in areas far beyond any reasonable claim to geopolitical security rights.

In thinking about the Soviet Union and Soviet foreign policy, we believe that there is much confusion about the nation's suffocating internal structure, which Western academics find intolerable; it is assumed that bad internal arrangements breed bad external ones and that the Soviet internal structure must therefore breed an aggressive foreign policy. Some anti-Soviet radicals suffer the same kind of confusion for different reasons.

We can illustrate this point with an analogy from ancient history. There can be little doubt that commercially minded Athens had built an aggressive empire unrelated to its geopolitical security; nevertheless, by ancient standards it remained a relatively "free" nation. Sparta, on the other hand, however regimented and intolerable its society seems from a modern individualistic perspective, was significantly more conservative, cautious, and unaggressive in its foreign relations. The connections among a nation's foreign policy, the degree of its tolerance of internal dissent, and the nature of its economy are considerably more complex than is generally acknowledged.

29. M. I. Finley, *Aspects of Antiquity* (New York: Viking, 1960), p. 167.

30. Paul Sweezy, "Capitalism, for Worse," in *Capitalism: The Moving Target*, ed. Leonard Silk (New York: New York Times, 1974), pp. 125–126.

31. Paul Baran and Paul Sweezy, "Notes on the Theory of Imperialism," *Monthly Review* 17 (March 1966): p. 17.

32. Quoted by V. I. Lenin, "Imperialism, the Highest Stage of Capitalism," in *Lenin on Politics and Revolution*, ed. James E. Connor (New York: Pegasus, 1968), p. 137.

33. *Ibid.*

34. Baran and Sweezy, "Notes on the Theory of Imperialism," p. 18.

35. David Horowitz, "Social Science or Ideology?" *Social Policy*, September–October 1970, p. 30. Copyright © 1970 by Social Policy Corp.

36. See Pierre Jalée, *The Pillage of the Third World* (New York: Monthly Review Press, 1968); see also Santos, "The Structure of Dependence," pp. 231–236.

Jalée's thinking epitomizes, in our judgment, the contradictions of those who seek to pay homage to Lenin's theory without adhering to it or its implications. He claims that imperialism is as rampant as ever and that Lenin's legacy lives on, then proceeds to develop a model quite different from Lenin's own. Jalée deals with the actual dependent relations that have been established between capitalist and Third World countries, but he argues that the Third World has become quantitatively less important to the advanced capitalist nations. Although he notes that imperialism still appears to be necessary to capitalism, he then suggests that perhaps capitalism has found a way to maintain reasonably high levels of domestic prosperity through government spending projects short of war and imperialism.

37. See Ronald Müller and Richard D. Morgenstern, "Multinational Corporations and Balance of Payments Impacts in LDCs: An Econometric Analysis of Export Pricing Behavior," *Kyklos* 27 (1974): 304–321.

38. Baran and Sweezy, "Notes on the Theory of Imperialism," p. 26.

39. *Ibid.*, pp. 30–31.

40. *Ibid.* p. 31.

41. See Richard J. Barnet and Ronald Müller, *Global Reach* (New York: Simon & Schuster, 1974).

42. Harry Magdoff, "The Logic of Imperialism," *Social Policy*, September–October 1970, p. 29.

43. See Joseph Schumpeter, *Imperialism and Social Classes*, trans. by Heinz Norden, ed. by Paul M. Sweezy (London, 1951).

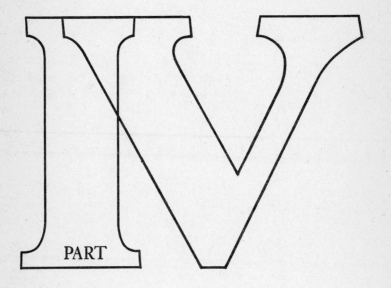

PART IV

HISTORICAL DYNAMICS
AND THE DECADE AHEAD

Concluding chapters not infrequently suggest beginnings to other books. The choice here is either to summarize succinctly our arguments in the previous chapters or to try to introduce some new considerations. Although we have chosen the latter course, we shall nevertheless try to relate our speculations about the decade ahead to aspects of what we have argued so far.

The analytical framework used here is derived from the work of Joseph Schumpeter and Karl Marx. To be more specific, we seek to explain the sources of some of the fundamental political and social changes that we expect to occur in the decade ahead. Our explanation arises from a study of junctures in American history that were similar to the present one in that they launched changes in the superstructure that distinctly altered the character of social and economic life in the ensuing periods.

Our method is to look at relations among the processes by which innovations in technological and economic organization generate waves of investment and intervals of capital accumulation; the ebb and flow of these waves cause changes in the form of class conflict; and changing forms of class conflict lead to changes in the political and social order, or, in the broadest sense, the superstructure. It is our hope that a broad ranging interpretive effort of this kind will suggest some directions for further inquiry.

ANOTHER GREAT DEPRESSION?

Is there going to be another great depression comparable to that of the 1930s? Such a question would not have been taken seriously five years ago. Today it arouses anxiety in a great many people. The reasons why it is currently being taken seriously are perhaps as important as the answer to it, especially in view of the aggressive confidence, both in the stability of capitalism and in the means and knowledge available to government, business leaders, and economists for quickly correcting any signs of a breakdown, that mainstream economists have displayed over the past twenty-five years. Nevertheless, doubts have escalated; the editors of *Time* have stated some of them:

> [Not too long ago]—at least in the U.S., Canada, Western Europe and Japan—this modern capitalism seemed to be on the verge of producing the permanently affluent society. Keynesian policies had kept recessions brief, mild and infrequent; the end of World War II opened the largest period of sustained growth ever. American economist George Stigler announced that "economics is finally at the threshold of its Golden Age—nay, we already have one foot through the door." Today few would express such euphoria. . . .[1]

Business Week quoted Sir Siegmund Warburg, a leading English financier: "This crisis will be of much longer duration than the one that started in 1929."[2] Milton Friedman's pessimism took on new dimensions when he suggested that in the long sweep of history, capitalist freedom will turn out to be "an accident" and that humanity will sink back into a state of "tyranny and misery."[3] Finally, a number of superstar liberal economists, including Gunnar Myrdal, Kenneth Arrow, and Wassily Leontief, have been arguing for an alternative to capitalism that would involve comprehensive social planning.

In a journal published for a scholarly audience, it was observed, "The doomsayers among us see the current world economic slowdown not as an ordinary recession of the familiar postwar variety but as the onset of something closer to what happened in the early 1930s."[4] Although the authors of this comment denied the reality behind this gloom and argued that it reflects "free-floating anxiety" derived from other sources,[5] we believe the reverse: Fears of deep depression are justified and are probably causing generalized anxiety. Some mainstream economists allude to possible "structural shifts" that may be preventing "automatic forces [from bringing] demand back to pre-recession trends."[6] Be that as it may, the consensus appears to be that depression fears abound among mainstream economists and that even an upturn in the near future will not bring the mix of unemployment and inflation to tolerable levels. We believe that these sentiments are well founded but that mainstream economists are ill equipped to grasp why.

Mainstream economists are experiencing the collapse of the Keynesian framework, which has served them for the past twenty-five years. This framework is too narrow, and therefore whole classes of economic and related phenomena have been inadequately explored. Economists sense that "something" is stirring "out there beyond those hills," like the peasant rumbling in Anton Chekhov's *The Cherry Orchard*, but the present mainstream theoretical map does not include it. So far they have tended to explain current contradictory economic trends by referring to "exogenous" events like the oil crisis, food shortages, and unexpected devaluations of the dollar.

The immediate problem is that the instruments of the welfare-liberal capitalist state are not only failing to support the various parts of the market, but also may even be partly obstructing recovery. Note, for example, what two respected Keynesian economists have observed about the "automatic stabilizer" that now appears to be functioning as a destabilizer:

Between the fourth quarter of 1973 and the third quarter of 1974, real GNP declined at an annual rate of 3.6 percent. However, prices, as measured by the deflator for GNP, rose at a rate of 11.1 percent. The consequence of this was that nominal GNP increased at a rate of 7.2 percent. Along with this came a rise in nominal personal income at a rate of 8.4 percent. Because the income tax system is geared to nominal income, and because it is progressive, this rise in nominal personal income caused personal income taxes to rise at a rate of 12.9 percent. The consequence was that the ratio of taxes to personal income rose from 14.5 percent to 15.0 percent in the space of only three quarters, and at a time when real GNP was falling. . . . This meant that real disposable income fell even faster than real *GNP, even though an automatic stabilizer is supposed to ensure the opposite.*[7] (emphasis added)

In theoretical and ideological terms, the Keynesian economic and social synthesis (see Chapter 6) has crumbled. Much current theorizing, if we can call it that, has degenerated into hypotheses that cannot be integrated into a larger theoretical system. The Keynesian vision has vanished, and no new one has appeared on the horizon. The adherents of any school of thought, however flexible, are bound to be shaken when such a breakdown occurs. To understand why it has come about, we must shift gears and analyze the present crisis from a fundamentally different perspective.

THE RETURN OF THE LONG WAVE

In Chapter 10, we argued that mature American capitalism, left alone, manifests tendencies toward stagnation that have been checked or arrested only by important innovations. The exploration of the effects of such innovations was launched by Schumpeter.[8] Borrowing from the work of the Russian-born economist Nikolai D. Kondratieff,[9] Schumpeter argued that the historic contours of American capitalism can be defined as a series of sustained waves of upward movement, alternating with waves of downward movement. Each complete cycle supposedly lasts forty to sixty years. The historical rhythm of these movements is indicated in Figure 15.1.

The "valley" of each long wave has culminated in a severe depression; in retrospect, it is clear that these depressions have marked new stages in the development of American capitalism. Cycles of shorter duration (twenty years), reflecting retarded growth rates in output, have been suggested by Moses Abramovitz, who has observed, like Schumpeter, that "the culminating event of each period of retarded growth has been a business depression of unusual severity and almost always of unusually long duration."[10]

The details of wholesale-price movements and other indexes compiled to demonstrate long-run rhythms are not our concern. Our own view is that these rhythms, though present, cannot be readily demonstrated in statistically satisfactory ways. Despite

Figure 15.1 • The Long Waves

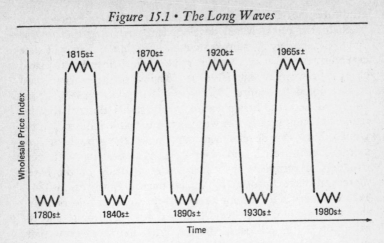

this problem, there has been a revival of interest in long waves.[11] Individuals representing a wide range of political views have suggested that economic sluggishness, which many expect to follow the current recession, may be connected to a longer secular trend that helps to shape the shorter fluctuations. This thinking may, of course, explain the apparent overreaction of the mainstream to the 1973–1975 recession.

Underlying these long-run price movements are basic shifts in economic forces. Upsurges in secular economic activity result from fundamental technological and organizational innovations that appear in embryonic forms during periods of profound depression. These innovations eventually come to displace previous means and forms of production. Investment opportunities multiply as innovations prove increasingly profitable, and they decline as innovations are absorbed and disseminated throughout the economy. As Schumpeter put it, "the more an innovation becomes established, the more it loses the character of an innovation and the more it begins to follow impulses instead of giving them."[12] Secular upswings are thus followed by secular declines.

We may now have arrived at the end of an elaborate investment boom launched in the late 1930s. This upward movement was concentrated in the automobile, trucking, aircraft, petroleum, plastic, synthetic-fiber, and electronic-communications industries, as well as in suburban housing, highways, and airports.[13] Critical to this whole configuration has been the growth of state expenditures, heavily invested in the infrastructure and subsidizing much of the research and development generating the upward boom. Before delving more systematically into the matter of state expenditures, we note that the wave of investment and related changes between 1940 and 1965 is analagous to the other upward sweeps noted in Figure 15.1. The upswing of 1788–1815 was associated with the first phase of the English Industrial Revolution, embracing mainly ironworks and the textile industry. In the United States this development encouraged the growth of agricultural, commercial, and shipping activities, along with construction of turnpikes and canals. A good many of the latter, moreover, were financed by public money. The period 1840–1870 was marked by the appearance of the steam engine, booming ship construction, extensive wheat and cotton farming, and the expansion of the railroads. Manufacturing industries grew more numerous, competitive, and mechanized. Mechanization in particular was encouraged by the growth of a machine-tool industry. The first twenty years of the twentieth century witnessed the electrification of the country, the emergence of retail marketing chains, the rise of the nation's first major boom in durable consumer goods, and, of course, the coming of the automobile.

Each of these upward swings began, as we have indicated, in the trough of a long wave; in each instance basic innovations served as the launching pad for a general upward climb. In Schumpeter's view, the earlier phases of innovation are financed through increases in bank credit, which sooner or later causes prices to increase more rapidly than output.[14] Conceivably, wages also lag somewhat, for such upward swings begin in surplus-labor markets. A combination of factors—like an increase in the money supply, lagging wages, rising prices, and new investment outlets arising from innovations—generates a sustained long-run upswing in the rate of investment and related economic indexes. At some point in this process, a speculative mood develops, generating price spurts, conceivably accentuated by wars that encourage inflationary trends.

In each rising wave new forms of production encourage upward mobility in the population, especially in the middle ranges of the class structure. This process breeds a narrow and acquisitive social definition of well-being and social and political change. Each upward swing culminates in a major crisis, which is perceived as a serious threat to the status of the newly risen middle stratum, which not infrequently contributes radical or reform leadership in the ensuing downward swing and depression. The "crisis at the peak" is more serious than the hesitations of the decades of upswing, for it occurs after a long inflationary trend and many speculative investment adventures of questionable wisdom. In any event, the initial recession is followed by a trend toward more frequent inventory cutbacks, growth in excess capacity, longer and more serious intervals of short-term unemployment, price deflation, and falling rates of profit. Each downward swing culminates in an unusually severe depression, as in the 1840s, 1890, and the 1930s (see Figure 15.1).

The specific economic explanation of the downswing varies with each complete cycle. Schumpeter has suggested that output from bank-financed expansion eventually becomes excessive relative to demand, and thereby leads to a "downward pull on the price level exactly as it should according to the *modus operandi* of our mechanism of innovation."[15] The trend in real output thus may still be expanding in the downward phase, but it is overshadowed by periodic gluts in the market, unemployment, and falling prices, which give to the downward swing a different social meaning from what might be reflected in aggregate figures over the decades; that is, the downward periods breed a depression social climate.

Consistent with Schumpeter's view is the possibility that a cost-price squeeze may produce sustained need for liquidation related to overproduction. One economic historian has explained the severe crises of 1870 and 1890 by suggesting that the "farmer risked being squeezed between low prices and high fixed cost, and the businessman encountered the real overproduction and an income-price squeeze similar to that faced by the farmer."[16]

Our schematic presentation does not reflect automatic progressions; the waves do not proceed in accordance with any "natural law." On the contrary, each of these cycles has been characterized by unique features, as well as by metacyclical disturbances (like wars), that make it difficult to generalize from them, except perhaps very broadly. Innovations have different gestation periods, which define the nature of the downswings. Nevertheless, these long rhythms do suggest, however tentatively, an explanation of some qualitative changes in the social and political order that have occurred at particular points in American history. Our task in the following pages is to speculate on what can happen in the decade or so ahead; in the process, we hope to cast some light on the current theoretical quandary and consequent pessimism prevailing among establishment economists and leaders.

"ECONOMISM" VERSUS "STRUCTURALISM"

In the history of American capitalism, class conflict has tended to alternate between narrow preoccupation with established organizational avenues (economism) and broader struggles involving new organizational routes to change the social and political fabric (structuralism). Economistic struggles tend toward incremental gains (though not necessarily by nonviolent means), toward immediate or partial objectives (not infrequently pecuniary) closely tied to the interests of particular groups in the population. They require little conscious consideration of broad class matters, and their goals are not defined by society as a whole. They do not involve forging new organizational channels through which issues or conflicts can be defined, and they do not challenge the basic social and political parameters of the system or existing organization of the various strata of the population.

Structuralist struggles, on the other hand, have broad class characteristics and frequently manifest themselves in the creation of new organizations meant to be generalized to whole classes or even the whole society. The very parameters of the system become concrete targets of opposition in the public arena.

The upward swings that we have discussed are conducive to "economistic" struggles. Growth means more general social mobility; people are more likely to accept the social order and to aspire to climb within it and less likely to think about changing the structure. Incrementalism and group-oriented struggles are the dominant means of improving status within the structure. Actual or anticipated upward mobility takes the edge off broader class struggles. Status conflicts within class divisions are, on the other hand, more sharply defined; "resolutions" of such conflicts are achieved in narrow quantitative terms within the established social framework. Moreover, sustained upward swings and eventual dramatic rises in the mobility of the middle stratum nurture periodic speculative fever. The most affluent portions of the rising middle stratum often reach the top through speculative successes or because they have shared in the original innovations that have initiated the upward swings. Clusters of innovation, creation of excessive credit, and a speculative climate frequently combine, along with such external stimuli as wars, to bring about dramatic inflationary spurts.

When the process ends in crisis and in the beginnings of a long secular decline, the opposite kind of social climate asserts itself. In the atmosphere associated with the downward phase of the long cycle, class conflict shifts from economistic forms to structuralist ones. New efforts are made to modify the basic status relations among classes. Structuralist conflicts center on a "bundle" of interrelated issues, which, at the extreme end of the spectrum, involve revolutionary struggle against the whole superstructure—that is, against political, legal, and social rules aimed at maintaining and reproducing the class structure of society (see Chapter 9). They focus on the distribution and redistribution of income and wealth as determined outside the narrow boundaries of market relations. This focus, of course, brings the conflict into the political sphere, for the questions raised frequently revolve around the differences in status of broadly defined classes. The troughs of the long waves, which usually overlap severe depressions, breed the conditions in which structuralist innovations occur. Initially small in scale, they are usually extended during the next long upward phase.

Before proceeding farther, we must emphasize that we are not suggesting that economistic conflicts disappear during the shift to structuralist ones or that structuralist conflicts reflect unconcern about immediate issues and marginal improvements in material welfare. What we are talking about are questions of degree, frequency, and tendency.[17] We are suggesting only that the class struggle changes form, and that such changes can be understood in terms of the long upward and downward swings in the economy that we have already described. In the long downward swings, when recessions are more frequent, deeper, and of longer duration—and when long-run profit rates tend to fall—class conflict necessarily shifts from the "economistic" form to the "structuralist" one because economistic struggles become less effective, both defensively and offensively. The given social relations at the point of production cannot deliver as readily because the capitalists are in a cost-price squeeze that causes deterioration of their profit horizons. At least up to the 1930s, trade unions often had problems of survival during depressions because of loss of membership and the crippling of the bargaining position. When they faltered, workers more frequently turned to politics. This shift, as we have argued, meant that the superstructure became the arena for class conflict. It should be noted that in such periods the dominant economic classes also begin to think along structuralist lines and become amenable to "changes from above," which are often considered necessary to "stabilize" the social order and thus to preserve the existing distribution of power, wealth, and prestige within the system.

In the downward swing that occurred approximately from 1815 to the mid-1840s, for example, the kind of social and political struggles that we are calling "structuralist" included a working-class struggle for a public school system; the emergence of the Democratic party; development of Jacksonian egalitarian democracy along with the Jacksonian spoils system, which gave more political fluidity to the class structure; the introduction of national nominating conventions; more liberal interpretations of state constitutions; the elimination of property qualifications for holding office; the demand from western farmers for a greater voice in the political affairs of the nation; and the development of new banking arrangements and facilities to deal with economic reality in more "hard-nosed" terms. Whatever we call this period, the gradual aggregation of structuralist conflicts that culminated in the severe depression of 1838–1845 had spawned a new social and political configuration. The period also marked the beginnings of the American Industrial Revolution, which sharply altered the previous commercial and artisanal nature of the American economy.

In the same vein, during the downward slide from the mid-1870s to 1900 the structuralist conflicts included the rise of socialist parties in eastern urban centers, the spread of populism and muckraking, the beginnings of the civil service, the establishment of the Interstate Commerce Commission, development of new organizational efforts aimed at stabilizing the union movement, and the "trustification" of the economy. All these shifts represent a major shift of power within the propertied classes. The direction of the economy during much of this period led "groups . . . to restructure economic institutions, both private and public, to provide a more stable framework for economic growth."[18]

From 1920 to 1940 structuralist considerations led to the New Deal, which we have touched upon in Chapter 5. Because the New Deal is so pertinent to the explanation of the faltering welfare-liberal capitalist state, we shall examine more closely some of the structural innovations that occurred in this period.

THE RISE OF THE WELFARE-LIBERAL CAPITALIST STATE

Most economists think of the innovations discussed by Schumpeter as being primarily material or technical and concentrated in the private sector. This view is limited, however. In Schumpeter's argument, organizational changes affecting the nature of economic life are also relevant.[19] In our view, the New Deal, especially because of its launching of the "fiscal state," was such an organizational, or structural, innovation, one that eventually became the catalyst for a sustained upswing. On the left end of the political spectrum, class conflict led to such developments as unemployment legislation, the Works Project Administration (WPA), the Social Security Act of 1935, the undistributed corporate tax act, and the Wagner Act, which not only gave workers the right to organize but also set up enforcement machinery in the form of the National Labor Relations Board (NLRB).

At the other end of the spectrum, the struggle brought all kinds of financial subventions funneled through the Reconstruction Finance Corporation (RFC), the strengthening of the Federal Reserve system to assist and save the banks, establishment of the Securities and Exchange Commission to protect small investors from fraud, laws to help maintain retail prices and to keep competitive retail establishments from devouring themselves, and especially direct subsidies to the private business sector for producing more—or less. Most of the government's interventions to help the business community were aimed at shoring up the market system, rather than replacing it.

When the dust finally settled, when the numerous structural innovations could be examined in hindsight, it became clear that the New Deal had been the catalyst for the permanent enlargement of a national administrative infrastructure, with bureaus, agencies, and boards exercising more *national* economic functions. The New Deal established for the Federal government a fiscal role where previously none had existed. In the process, a new, highly visible national bureaucracy was born; it replaced elements of the previous governmental superstructure, which had tended to act more reflexively in favor of more narrowly defined business interests. It may be said that the capitalist class ceased planning for the government and, because of the turbulence of the time, reluctantly allowed the government to plan for it. The emergence of a more fully national government with a larger, more permanent staff of full-time civil service functionaries meant that the government could no longer be readily manipulated as if it were a mere "committee of the ruling class." Segments of the newly established bureaucracy acquired and nurtured their own constituencies to justify their own growth and power. At the minimum, capitalists now had to work harder and devote more resources to insure their economic interests politically. In general, of course, the organizational biases of the state still favored nurturing and protecting private ownership of the means of production. Nevertheless, the growing scale and complexity of governmental activities made it less easy for business to ignore the government when it chose or simply to purchase political patronage. The correlation between business interests and governmental policies became more complex.

In sum, the basic structural innovation in the 1930s took the form of a more administratively viable national government, which was necessary to facilitate, stabilize, regulate, and stimulate the capitalistic economic engine on a more systematic basis. The pragmatic humanity of the New Deal in some domains, however important its effects, was incidental to its more permanent creations for underwriting costs and stabilizing demand. A combination of organizational changes and subsidies associated with World War II launched another long upward trend that lasted approximately from 1940 to 1965. We have called this period the Great American Celebration (see Chapter 6).

Distortions of the Vietnam War aside, the economy seems once again to have turned a corner and to be in the midst of a secular slowdown similar to those experienced in the historical periods just described. If this analysis is correct, the next ten years or so can be expected to produce ups and downs centered around a trend toward creeping stagnation. There are several likely consequences. First, not only will the current inflation slow down significantly; it will also eventually culminate in a great depression comparable to those of the 1840s, 1890s, and 1930s. Second, class conflict during this interval will not only broaden; it will also shift to the political arena. Third, domestic reform and structural change, involving creation of planning agencies for job development and elimination of inequities in the distribution of income and wealth, will become the dominant preoccupations of the nation. Fourth, a new crop of reform and radical leaders will emerge from the downward mobility process presently underway in the middle stratum of the population that has prospered over the past twenty-five years. Finally, as our concern for internal reform grows, our preoccupation with foreign issues and questions will recede into the background, at least, in comparison with the period between 1940 and 1965.

A fundamental cause of the general reversal that we are forecasting is the nature of state expenditures. One of the sources of the upward sweep that we have outlined has become a critical factor in the predicted decline. Our reasoning, though speculative, rests on a fuller analysis of state expenditures.

FUNCTIONS OF STATE EXPENDITURES

State expenditures—both Federal and local—have two primary functions: to facilitate growth and to maintain harmony, that is, to prevent alienation from turning into a serious revolt against the social order.[20] These alternatives are shown schematically in Figure 15.2. The first function produces two kinds of expenditures: social investment to nurture the growth of private capital and social consumption to socialize the costs of reproducing the laboring class. Of these two, social-investment expenditures have predominated since the beginning of American capitalism. Laissez-faire mythology to the contrary, the history of American capitalism is replete with government subsidies, tariffs, giveaway programs, land-grant deals, loans, and development projects (for canals, highways, industrial parks, and so on) aimed at stimulating private accumulation of capital. The 1930s witnessed the acceleration of this process. Harold Faulkner, the well-known American economic historian, is correct when he argues that the New Deal was not new; it was "an extension and continuation of an older method and older philosophy. Roosevelt asserted that he was trying to save the capitalist system rather than destroy it, and the legislation affecting finance, industry, and agriculture is indisputable proof."[21]

Education, health, and insurance expenditures are major examples of social-consumption expenditures. They have increased considerably since the 1930s and reflect a departure from the practices of the nineteenth century. Although they are directly beneficial to the workers who receive them and their families, they are also useful in lowering the costs of producing and reproducing the manpower necessary to the business system. As such costs have grown relative to the capacity of an individual household or

Figure 15.2 • Functions of State Expenditures

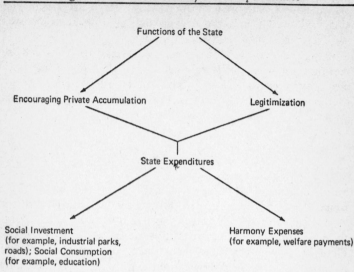

the individual corporation, they have become a systematic responsibility of the state.

The second kind of state expenditures is aimed at maintaining the legitimacy of the system in the minds of those who are periodically rejected by it; we call them "harmony expenditures." Welfare payments, food stamps, and support of a good deal of local police activity fall into this category. Such expenditures also represent a sharp departure from nineteenth-century practice; moreover, they have distinctly unproductive dimensions, at least, in direct relation to the profitability of the business system. Essentially they serve to maintain consumption without corresponding production. They periodically cause conflict among the various strata of the population, for they give rise to the question, Who is to pay for the "loafers"? When the numbers of "loafers" are relatively small, the problem is manageable. And, when the economy is growing rapidly, transfer costs (legalized charity) can be masked by the growth "dividend." But, when the private sector enters a downswing or a period of slow growth, when the numbers of alienated poor constitute a consequential minority, inter- and intraclass conflict over state expenditures takes on a different dimension, a point to which we shall return shortly.

In viewing the New Deal as a departure from earlier episodic structural changes in the American social order, it is well to remember that it involved a rise in state expenditures (and the corresponding state bureaucracy to administer them) aimed at reproducing the working class and legitimizing the social order, especially among its most alienated members. To the extent that large numbers of recipients of harmony aid come from minority ethnic and racial groups, intraclass differences among workers become a serious problem (see Chapter 11).

Harmony expenditures, primarily because they were launched in a period of deep depression and were *not* closely linked to changes in productive capacity, have been considered necessary and potentially stimulating, capable of affecting aggregate demand without serious price repercussions. They were expected to abet absorption of the surplus (the output that unemployed labor could in fact produce). Because very large numbers, representing a cross section of the entire working class, as well as members of the middle stratum of the population, were the initial beneficiaries of the new state expenditures, the question of who would pay for the welfare-liberal capitalist state was not seriously debated among mainstream economists. Their abstract theorizing about functional finance served simply to justify the support of pump-priming schemes involving larger deficits. The microeconomic class conflicts inherent in such schemes were left out of account.

As long as the growth launched in the late 1930s and dramatically accelerated by the war was sustained by a combination of private and public expenditures, mainstream economists could afford to ignore the class conflicts inherent in the new state functions. But that is no longer possible. The slowing of the economy and the widespread belief that the state itself is responsible for excessive unemployment and inflation have put an end to standard Keynesian remedies, which are increasingly being recognized as a bane, rather than as a boon. They have built into the economy all kinds of cost rigidities and income floors that are now causing market prices and costs to behave in perverse ways. Wages cannot decrease; income-maintenance schemes and various kinds of subsidies, combined with monopolistic power to administer prices, itself viewed as governmentally induced, stimulate price increases before unemployment can bring down prices in the factor markets. The burden of paying for unproductive consumption is affecting the state's ability to finance productive activities. To the extent that the public sector is nurturing cost rigidities in the private sector, as well as draining demand from it, it has become the source of a profit squeeze. To the extent that the state is being forced to retrench, especially at local levels, unemployment is rising. Behind much of the inconsistency and vacillation in state expenditure patterns is the simple fact that the state still moves to the rhythms of the private sector, a fact that undermines the allegedly functional finance schemes of traditional deficit-oriented Keynesian economists.

At the heart of radical analysis of governmental fiscal and monetary policies is the assumption that the state itself is involved in the numerous contradictions of the capitalist industrial structure. Because of their initial conception of the way politics and economics are interwoven, radicals do not compartmentalize these issues or suggest that market solutions would be adequate "if only" the government or monetary authorities would make correct independent decisions. There are no exogenous positions of power in the real economy. The assumed independent power of the state to avoid or correct contemporary capitalism's basic contradictions is one of the most fundamental illusions of the mainstream.

The unproductive maintenance of capital (especially at the Federal level, where war contracts are awarded to large national and international corporations) not only obstructs the flow of capital to more productive enterprises; it also prevents business failures. Yet periods in which inefficient production units are weeded out are essential preconditions for the revival of upward movement in the private spheres of the system. As William Simon, President Ford's Secretary of Treasury, told the Senate Committee in a moment of candor: The free enterprise system has two sides, "success and failure . . . if you remove the failure from it, we have destroyed our system."[22] Moreover, the Federal tax burden becomes more acute when public expenditures are used to maintain unproductive enterprises and output.

At the local level, the tax structure is used to maintain unproductive consumption and enterprises like health programs and schools whose contribution to economic productivity is indirect and slow. Again the tax burden is increasingly felt during a slowdown. Metropolitan economies are much larger than the political administrative units that raise taxes. To the extent that the central cities have lost their economic bases, they have been forced to increase their harmony expenditures from deficient tax bases. They have thus become a dead weight on the productive spheres.

When we examine the consequences of expenditures by both Federal and local governments, all subtleties aside, we find that a good part of Federal expenditures consists of subsidies to unproductive capitalist producers and that a good part of local governmental subsidies goes to unproductive working-class consumers. The result is that a significant portion of the middle stratum, which rose to status positions between 1950 and 1965, is being squeezed by high taxes and waning economic opportunities.

The exact occupational composition of this middle stratum is not well defined. Although its biggest earners tend to be white-collar workers—managers, administrators, professionals, and technical, sales, and skilled workers—many blue-collar workers like plumbers, truck drivers, and mechanics have incomes sufficiently above the subsistence threshold to permit discretionary spending.[23]

The income boundaries of this group can be more precisely defined. The minimum family income is about $12,000 a year and the maximum about $35,000 a year. According to *Business Week*, "this income group now accounts for roughly 53 percent of the country's 55 million families."[24]

We are less concerned with the exact composition and measurement of this stratum than with what the editors of *Business Week* call the great "middle-class" squeeze of inflation and taxes:

> Within the last two years [1973–1974], it has seen the purchasing power of its dollar shrink nearly 20 percent, the value of household savings and other wealth or assets decline 11.5 percent, and the size of household debts rise 18.6 percent.
>
> Compared with the rich and the poor, the middle class also tends to be hit harder on taxes—the fastest-rising item in family budgets, increasing nearly 65 percent in six years. According to the Joint Economic Committee of Congress, a family with an intermediate income of $14,466 last year [1974] paid 26.5 percent more in personal taxes than in 1973 and 21.6 percent more in Social Security payments. That compared with 14.3 percent increase for transportation, 13.5 percent for housing, and 11 percent for food.
>
> Over-all last year's tax bite took 19.5 percent of the "intermediate" family budget—[not much] less than the 22.2 percent bite on the average high-income family and more than the 16.2 percent paid by the low-income family. The misery of the middle class cannot begin to compare with that of the poor—even if the poor spend a smaller part of their budget on taxes.

Yet critics of the tax system note that the poor have their subsidies, while the rich have their tax loopholes.

The middle class, on the other hand, receives few tax breaks.[25]

What makes this middle stratum so readily taxable, of course, is that its income is in the form of wages and salaries. Most of these people live in suburbs, though some remain inside the city boundaries. They are big consumers of services and durable goods; the former have experienced very rapid increases in prices, and the latter have been subject to high interest rates. Moreover, many in this middle stratum are learning, for the first time in their adult careers, the meaning of unemployment. They are losing their assumptions about steady, incremental improvements in material well-being. As a result, in the view of the editors of *Business Week*, their "expectations are [being] shattered, and the middle class is on its way to becoming another 'lost generation' like the one that disappeared in the 1929 crash."[26]

DIMENSIONS OF THE COMING CRISIS

The crisis of American capitalism has three interrelated dimensions: an economic crisis, involving a slowdown in the American economy, which we expect to culminate in a severe worldwide depression by the early 1980s; a crisis of the state, reflecting inefficient division of authority between the Federal and local levels and a corresponding pattern of unproductive expenditures that accentuate the contradictions inherent in the structure of the private market; and a class crisis, involving a squeeze on the middle stratum that emerged between 1950 and 1965 and on a working class divided along racial lines. We shall discuss each of these dimensions briefly.

THE ECONOMIC DIMENSION

The slowdown in the American economy, as we have argued, does not reflect simply another inventory readjustment characteristic of previous post-World War II recessions. It arises from the link between the innovations clustered in the private sector and the rise of state expenditures, which appear to have reached an effective limit in the present political and administrative context. Many of these expenditures are presently affecting the capitalist sector in counterproductive ways, which has eroded, if not destroyed, the popular commitment to many aspects of the welfare state. E. J. Mishan, the well-known British economist, has summed up this disillusionment:

> We may plausibly conclude that there are turbulent times ahead for the West. For we seem to have reached a stage where we have to make a political choice between price stability and maintaining traditional freedoms—to the extent, at least, of leaving intact the existing power of trade unions and shop stewards. Certainly, price-stability, the welfare state, and free collective bargaining, are no longer mutually compatible.[27]

We must add the growth of cynicism about the political behavior of the modern corporation. The two important mainsprings of the welfare-liberal capitalist system—the state as countervailing force and the alleged enlightened long-run self-interest of the modern corporation—have thus collapsed. It is not without reason that large numbers of people have developed a profound distrust of both governmental and corporate remedies for our numerous social and economic difficulties. Mainstream economists and important corporate leaders are also beginning to find themselves in a dilemma over how to cope with the slowdown.

Because they are beginning to sense that many entrenched welfare mechanisms and business subsidies are working perversely, mainstream economists are now attacking the present system from two apparently different directions. The conservative wing is pushing for less regulation, some tax relief for the middle stratum, and less government spending. What "deregulation" appears to mean in principle is the fostering of more competition in the private sector by removal of government controls and supports of various kinds. In reality it means something else. Conservative ideology often embodies an attack on the welfare aspects of the liberal capitalist state, an attack that feeds the prejudices of the middle stratum of American society. The economic consequences of conservative deregulation policies would probably include further weakening of the smaller and more fragile portions of the enterprise system, like the independent oil producers and small businesses presently protected by retail-maintenance laws. The conservative wing, in short, is seeking a planned process of deaccumulation that will ultimately work in favor of the more powerful corporate giants.

The more liberal segment of the establishment favors more comprehensive planning.[28] Specific schemes vary from systematic refinancing in order to bail out weak corporations to social-engineering blueprints for guiding politicians in planning state expenditures and goading corporations toward specified production goals. Whatever the details, the basic assumption is that the government must develop mechanisms beyond the present Keynesian ones; it must proceed to play a more productive (capital-accumulating) role if the private sector is to be reorganized and full employment achieved. The "enlightened" members of the establishment are saying, at least implicitly, that current government mechanisms are unproductive and therefore useless in achieving long-run recovery.

What is interesting about the apparent division between conservatives and liberals, ideology aside, is that their rhetorical framework has shifted from the short run to the long run. Both suggest that the kinds of changes needed to put the economy back on a sound footing are "structural." This change in the time horizon, even though the politics of the moment may prevent it from becoming operational, reflects a judgment that there are no fast Keynesian "solutions" to the current cluster of economic problems and that the economy is unlikely to experience a satisfactory short-run recovery. Yet no one seems to have an explanation for why the slowdown following the 1975 "recovery" is being projected onto the long run. Our belief, however difficult to prove, is that we are in the downward phase of a long cycle. Although this cycle is not well understood, partly because of its time span and partly because it is periodically interrupted by short-term upturns, its recognition may explain the "structural" preoccupations that have emerged rather suddenly among those whose optimism a few years ago was, if not blind, at least short-sighted.

THE POLITICAL DIMENSION

The political crisis reflects the fact that the two main levels of government, Federal and local, are instruments of different segments of the private economy. The Federal executive branch is an instrument of the monopolistic national and international corporations, and the local governments are instruments of smaller, more competitive industries. The problem is compounded by the institutional and legal separation of these two levels, which means that neither can cope with the economy as a whole. This inefficient separation, moreover, has bred two separate systems of political patronage, in which large numbers of politicians have deep vested interests.

As the means of production have expanded, the economy has become an almost seamless interdependent web. But interdependence has not automatically brought into being an appropriate ideological, social, and political superstructure. This observation was made in somewhat different terms by George Cabot Lodge of the Harvard Business School, a former Republican candidate for the U.S. Senate and Assistant Secretary of Labor in the Eisenhower administration. He has argued that, as a nation, we are still thinking in terms of John Locke's emphasis on individualism, property rights, competition, minimum government, and specialization—at a time when the economy calls for community, recognition of rights to minimum income and health, communal control of the economy, a planning state, and a holistic view of society.[29]

However we describe the discordant relation between the superstructure and the general economy, it is most visible at the local level, where small political units are struggling painfully to cope with metropolitan and regional economies shaped by national and even international forces. The Federal government is unlikely to attempt to override these many political divisions until public desperation forces it to do so. Underlying the inefficient distribution of political power between the national and local levels of government are vested economic interests that depend upon this very inefficiency. Significant portions of the competitive sector depend upon the patronage (contracts, regulating biases, and so on) of local governments. The political machines that run such governments are in turn sustained by support from the more competitive and locally based portions of the business system.

The Federal government, as we have suggested, is the focal point of the big corporations with national and international needs. The White House is the main channel of patronage and quick action for this segment of the business system.[30] Congress seems to be caught somewhere in the middle. General congressional incoherence on many basic economic issues is not without cause: Congress's constituencies are local, but its pretensions are national. Individual members are frequently forced into horse-trading on bills and legislative back scratching that makes little sense in terms of the requirements of a national economic program. Congress as a whole thus magnifies contradictions. It is a weak instrument for achieving economic innovation, and there are few signs that it will change appropriately in time. To the extent that the heterogenous nature of the American two-party structure reflects the kinds of political divisions that we have noted, both the Republicans and Democrats are incapable of bringing ideological coherence to counteract the growing "structural" malaise that has emerged in the public arena.

THE CLASS DIMENSION

Finally, the class crisis involves, on one hand, an ideologically crippled working class, which thinks, as most Americans do, in purely "me too" terms and, on the other, a "scared" middle stratum, which we have already discussed. As a matter of historical record, in crises the middle stratum sometimes veers to the left and sometimes to the right. No doubt it is from this stratum that leaders of structuralist reform will emerge. It is a complex stratum, and, in a country like the United States, it cannot be ignored as a political force or assumed to be reactionary. In our judgment, its educational qualificataions will enable it to play a critical role in determining the nature and direction of the class conflict in the decade ahead.

There are also profound intraclass dimensions to the forthcoming conflict. As workers in various sectors of the economy lose their power of collective bargaining, because of the existence of a permanent reserve of unemployed workers or because of new governmental controls on labor-management relations, the ethnic and racial divisions that always lurk in the crevices of the American society may drive politicians toward demagoguery. At the moment, moreover, it seems that much of this projected chaos may occur in the absence of a viable leftist movement capable of tapping and cultivating the most humane qualities of the American temperament. A great deal of angry energy is likely to be released as the economy slides in the years to come. If our structuralist thesis is correct, this energy is likely to find a political outlet and to be aimed at structural changes. More and more mainstream thinkers are sensing a kind of polarization, though its exact dimensions of implications are still unspecified. Of course, radical economists tend to argue, as Douglas Dowd has done, that

> In today's setting, tension, conflict, and controversy grow and spread, whether in economic and social analysis or in society itself, leading to polarization. For reasons arising out of the

deep nature of the present crisis the main efforts of social scientists appear likely to move in two contrary directions, and to comport with the accompanying major political movements of the foreseeable future: rationalizations of a rightward political shift, justifying increasingly centralized, "planned," and coercive capitalism, or analysis showing the necessity and the desirability of socialism.[31]

Exactly how the predicted crisis will resolve itself is far beyond our present scope. One conclusion seems certain: Much of what we have argued in this final chapter makes little sense in the framework of mainstream economics. The reasons are methodological and reflect the whole radical economic perspective developed in this book.

"PERFECT" MARKETS AND THEIR "IMPERFECTIONS"

Mainstream economics is not defined so that it incorporates a relationship between history and current data, with logic serving as an organizing device. The radical economist sees the facts of the present and the future as part of a historical continuum. Economic facts do not simply interact on a timeless plane in which stimuli initiate behavioral responses that can be predicted or defined by an abstract model, itself a product of pure deductive reasoning. Whereas the primary mainstream metaphor for the economy is the machine involving mechanistic adjustments, the radical metaphor is mostly derived from the notion of the organism, which emphasizes birth, growth, maturity, and decay. Radical economics is concerned with the ways in which the human species, technology, and the environment are connected in an economic system that evolves in time. It is concerned with economic determination of noneconomic structures and noneconomic feedback affecting the economic system. Both these processes are ignored or treated casually by mainstream economists. Lest this judgment be considered harsh, we note the words of a prominent mainstream economist, James Tobin:

> Most contemporary economists feel ill at ease with respect to big topics—national economic organization, interpretation of economic history, relations of economic and political power, origins and functions of economic institutions. The terrain is

unsuitable for our tools. We find it hard even to frame meaningful questions much less answer them.[32]

There is a fundamental disparity between what mainstream economists identify as the economic problem—scarce means and unlimited wants—and what they identify as problems of the real world. That is, real problems seem unrelated to their definition of economics; they fall under the heading of "imperfections" that prevent markets from working properly. These "imperfections" include "wrong" decisions by government and monetary authorities. As we have dealt with this reasoning in earlier chapters, we shall concentrate here on other reasons why markets do not work.

The explanations are many, but none is related to the foundation upon which mainstream economists construct the economic problem. Markets are said not to work because workers have organized unions, which create "frictions" or "excessive" group expectations in collective bargaining; because businesspeople organize oligopolies or monopolies and cause "stickiness" in the pricing mechanism, enabling them to hedge against inflation; because people, being "attached" to their communities or friends, do not respond quickly to price and income variables (which means that money income is different from psychic income); or, finally, because information is unavailable or too costly, which means "hesitancy" or "uncertainty" in responding to the call of the market. "Frictions," "stickiness," "attachments," "hesitations" are the "imperfections" that mainstream economists view as obstacles to proper functioning of the market. Yet such obstacles are the quintessence of reality. It is for this reason that much of mainstream theory appears to obscure substantive economic issues and questions.

What is the real nature of these alleged imperfections? To mainstream economists they are a kind of rust that can be eliminated by correct "lubrication" policies. To radicals, they represent organizations that people have built because they find "pure" market relations impersonal and intolerable. "Pure" market relations generally do strike people as completely devoid of humanity. The market system is a complex impersonal machine that mainstream economists hold in theoretical awe, despite the fact that many of them hold positions of tenure that very much interfere with the perfection of the academic marketplace. This remark is not meant to be snide. It simply suggests that everyone believes strongly in the competitive market for other people, and everyone seeks organizational means to evade the rigors of the market for his or her own survival and security. The market system nurtures a peculiar perversion of the Kantian imperative: "What is necessary for others [competition], I should seek to avoid." Because this imperative operates in a context of unequal distribution of wealth and power, a responsive government finds its capacity to enforce and maintain competitive situations "equally for all" constantly eroded. More likely, government officials also find it in their interests to, or are pressured to, further permit the growth of noncompetitive status for some but not others.

Mainstream economists simply do not understand how the social interests and psychological attitudes secreted from "pure" or "impure" market relations lead to the building of nonmarket organizations—some defensive, some aggressive—and that these organizations are *endemic* to human society. The "imperfections" that they wish to eliminate from the economic machine thus turn out to be either essential to human needs or necessary to survival in the market.

Be that as it may, historically, capitalism has not moved in the direction of perfect markets; as radicals see it, the welfare-liberal capitalist state exists somewhere between nineteenth-century capitalism and a more completely planned socialist society. This halfway solution depends upon indirect aggregate "planning" and various kinds of income-maintenance programs that enable individuals to survive outside the market that has rejected them. Private ownership of the means of production has remained. In the decade ahead, structural questions of the magnitude of those raised in the 1930s will emerge, and they will take us far beyond the welfare-liberal halfway development. Radicals believe that these structural questions will revolve around planning: its form and content. Shall we have a more integrated kind of state-capitalist planning from above without fundamental redistribution of income and wealth? Or shall we move toward a democratic planning arrangement and an egalitarian division of the pie? That is what the next decade of class conflict will be about. The drama will be enacted, moreover, not in the marketplace, but in the political arena. The issue will be: Who will dominate the state and determine its expenditures?

NOTES

1. "Can Capitalism Survive?" *Time*, July 14, 1975, p. 56. Reprinted by permission from *Time*, The Weekly Newsmagazine; Copyright Time Inc., 1975.

2. *Business Week*, November 23, 1974, p. 43; quoted in Douglas F. Dowd, "Accumulation and Crisis," *Socialist Revolution*, 5 (June 1975): 40.

3. Quoted in "Can Capitalism Survive?" p. 56.

4. Harold Van B. Cleveland and W. H. Bruce Brittain, "A World Depression?" *Foreign Affairs* 57 (January 1975): 223.

5. *Ibid.*, p. 241.

6. Thomas F. Dernburg and Arnold Packer, *Long Range Fiscal Strategy: Revenue Options*, prepared for U.S., Congress, Senate, Committee on the Budget, 94th Cong., 1st sess., 9 October 1975, p. 1.

7. *Ibid.*, p. 5.

8. Joseph Schumpter, *Business Cycles: A Theoretical, Historical, and Statistical Analysis of the Capitalist Process* (New York: McGraw-Hill, 1939).

9. Nikolai D. Kondratieff, "The Long Waves in Economic Life," *The Review of Economic Statistics* 17 (November 1935): 105–115.

10. Moses Abramovitz, in *Employment, Growth, and Price Levels*, U.S., Congress, Joint Economic Committee, 86th Cong., 2nd sess., 10 December 1960, p. 412.

11. See Eric Hobsbawm, "The Crisis of Capitalism in Historical Perspective," *Marxism Today*, October 1975, pp. 300–307; Robert Zevin, "The Political Economy of the American Empire," in *The Economic Crisis Reader*, ed. David Mermelstein (New York: Vintage, 1975), pp. 133–151; Robert L. Heilbroner, "Global Depression," *The Economic Problem Newsletter*, Fall 1974, p. 1; James B. Shunan and David Rosenau, *The Kondratieff Wave* (New York: Delta, 1972); and W. W. Rostow, "Kondratieff, Schumpeter, and Kuznets: Trend Periods Revisited," *Journal of Economic History* 25 (December 1975): 719–753.

12. Schumpeter, *Business Cycles*, abr. ed. (New York: McGraw-Hill, 1964), p. 229.

13. Zevin, "The Political Economy of the American Empire," pp. 142–143.

14. Schumpeter, *Business Cycles*, abr. ed., p. 197.

15. *Ibid.*

16. W. Elliot Brownlee, *Dynamics of Ascent: A History of the American Economy* (New York: Knopf, 1974), p. 192.

17. It should be noted that we are also not seeking to explain broader ideological currents like social Darwinism and the Protestant ethic.

18. Brownlee, *Dynamics of Ascent*, p. 192.

19. Schumpeter, *Business Cycles*, 1939, Vol. 1, p. 84.

20. The classification of state expenditures in this section is derived from James O'Connor, *The Fiscal Crisis of the State* (New York: St. Martin's, 1973).

21. Harold Underwood Faulkner, *American Economic History*, 8th ed. (New York: Harper, 1960) pp. 682–683.

22. "New York City Fiscal Crisis." Hearing Before the Committee on Banking, Housing, and Urban Affairs. U.S., Senate, U.S. Government Printing Office, Washington, D.C., 1975, p. 74.

23. "The Squeeze on the Middle Class," *Business Week*, March 10, 1975, p. 54.

24. *Ibid.*

25. *Ibid.*, p. 52.

26. *Ibid.*

27. E. J. Mishan, "The New Inflation," *Encounter* 42 (May 1974): 24.

28. Jacob K. Javits, "The Need for National Planning," *The Wall Street Journal*, July 8, 1975, p. 14; Jacob K. Javits and Hubert H. Humphrey, "The Balanced Growth and Economic Planning Act of 1975," quoted in Herbert Stein, *Economic Planning and Improvement of Economic Policy* (Washington, D.C.: American Enterprise Institute), p. 1.

29. George Cabot Lodge, *The New American Ideology* (New York: Knopf, 1975); see also a review by Leonard Silk, "Ideology vs Economics," *The New York Times*, October 22, 1975, pp. 22, 72.

30. For examples of the kinds of deals that are made between the White House and big business, see Robert Scheer, *America After Nixon* (New York: McGraw-Hill, 1974).

31. Douglas F. Dowd, "Accumulation and Crisis," *Socialist Revolution 5* (June 1975): 10.

32. James Tobin, "The Political Economy of the New Left," *Journal of Economic Literature* 10 (December 1972): 1216.

INDEX

About the Author

Raymond S. Franklin is Professor of Economics at Queens College of the City University of New York and is on the editorial board of the *Journal of Economic Issues*. He received his Ph.D. from the University of California at Berkeley. Professor Franklin is co-author, with Solomon Resnik, of *The Political Economy of Racism*.